THE 365

MOST IMPORTANT

BIBLE PASSAGES

FOR YOU

THE 365

MOST IMPORTANT

BIBLE PASSAGES

FOR YOU

*Daily Readings and Meditations
on Experiencing
God's Richest Blessings in Your Life*

FaithWords
Hachette Book Group
237 Park Avenue
New York, NY 10017

Visit our website at www.faithwords.com.

Printed in the United States of America

First Edition: April 2011

10 9 8 7 6 5 4 3 2 1

FaithWords is a division of Hachette Book Group, Inc.
The FaithWords name and logo are trademarks of Hachette Book Group, Inc.

Library of Congress Cataloging-in-Publication Data

ISBN 978-0-446-57499-0

Editor: Lila Empson Wavering

Manuscript: Jonathan Rogers; Dwight Clough and Beth Lueders, writers of the Snapdragon Group

Design: Whisner Design Group

As in Paradise, God walks in
the Holy Scriptures,
seeking man.

—Elisabeth Kübler-Ross

All Scripture is inspired by God and is

PROPHITABLE ~~useful~~ to teach us what is true and to

make us realize what is wrong in our

lives. It corrects us when we are wrong

and teaches us to do what is right.

—2 Timothy 3:16 NLT

VS 16 ALL SCRIPTURE IS GIVEN BY INSPIRATION
OF GOD AND IS PROFITABLE FOR DOCTRINE,
FOR REPROOF (CORRECTION), FOR INSTRUCTION
IN RIGHTEOUSNESS,
VS 17 THAT THE *MAN OF GOD MAY BE COMPLETE,
THOROUGHLY EQUIPPED FOR EVERY GOOD WORK.

II TIM 3.16 NKJ

Contents

Introduction 19

A Beginning

In the Beginning 22
In the Image of God 23
Made for Relationship... 24
A New—but Skewed—Perspective................................ 25
The Dawn of Hard Labor... 26
The First Murder 27
The Wrath of "Have It Your Way" 28
A Sign of Mercy 29
The Scattering.. 30
An Astonishing Capacity for Belief............................... 31
A Choice: Faith or Self-Sufficiency 32
The Graciousness of Faith.. 33
A Mysterious Figure 34
A Sky Full of Blessings... 35
Letting God Be God.. 36
The Cutting of the Covenant 37
Sarai's Fresh Start.. 38
A Ridiculous Prediction.. 39
A Rescue—and a Backward Look 40
A Boy Named Laughter 41
Hope for the Rejected 42
The Hard Faith of a Father... 43
A Faithful Matchmaker.. 44
Rebekah Pursues Her Calling.. 45
Kingdoms at War.. 46
A Nation for a Bowl of Soup 47
A Scoundrel's Blessing 48
God's Love for the Unlovely 49
The Man Who Held On... 50
A New Man, a New Brotherhood 51
New Consequences for Old Habits................................ 52
Character and Circumstance 53
A Blessing to the Nations 54
God's Overruling Mercy.. 55

A Journey

The Pharaoh Who Forgot—and the God Who Didn't 58

Surprising Deliverance 59

God's Work, God's Way 60

A Surprising Assignment... 61

Who Am I, Lord? Who Are You?.. 62

A Showdown in Pharaoh's Court 63

Liberation Got Ugly 64

Israel's Emancipation Proclamation... 65

An Avoidable Tragedy... 66

Fear Not, Stand Firm... 67

Hope at the Bottom of the Sea... 68

Moses' Song of Joy 69

Daily Bread, Radical Trust 70

Raised Hands of Support 71

Remembrance, Hope, and the Law.. 72

The First Table of the Law 73

Thunder and Grace 74

Seat of Mercy... 75

Worship at the Feet of an Idol... 76

In the Cleft of the Rock 77

A Face That Shines 78

The Work of Skilled Hands.. 79

Bringing Your Best to God... 80

The Wages of Sin.. 81

God Remembers.. 82

Cloud by Day, Pillar by Night... 83

Two Ways of Complaining to God.. 84

Moses' Zeal for Glory.. 85

Outrageous Abundance 86

Another Kind of Vision 87

The Logical End of Grumbling 88

Second Thoughts 89

Look Up and Live 90

Hear, O Israel 91

Remember—and Fear.. 92

God's Blessing on the Stubborn.. 93

A Choice... 94

Seeing from a Distance 95

Courage beyond Our Comfort Zone.. 96

Why We Carry Stones 97
Remember Rahab.. 98
Intentional Courage 99
Clear-Eyed Faith 100
A Vicious Cycle 101
God's Special Forces 102
The Strong Made Weak 103
Never Too Late 104
The Will to Follow 105
The Fruits of a Good Reputation.. 106
Blessed with Joy... 107

A Kingdom

The Heart's Deepest Cry 110
Answered Prayers 111
Falling Down before the Almighty 112
Give Us a King! 113
Chosen.. 114
A New Direction for Prayer 115
Waiting on God.. 116
The Lord Gives Us Victory... 117
The Stuff Kings Are Made Of 118
Reckless Faith? 119
Without a Sword... 120
People Love a Winner... 121
The Better Man... 122
Crazy, Dishonest, or Loyal? 123
Ends and Means... 124
A Ghost Story.. 125
Finding Strength 126
Whom Do We Believe? 127
The Forever King.. 128
When Good Intentions Are Not Enough 129
Who's in Charge?.. 130
Something Bigger... 131
Power Doesn't Always Corrupt.. 132
Wrong Place, Wrong Time, Wrong Actions....................... 133
Sin and Self-Preservation.. 134
The Moral of the Story.. 135
A Nasty Spiral 136

Contents, continued

Faking It 137
A Near Miss, a Forced Retirement 138
Joy over Dignity 139
David's Plan—and God's 140
A Royal Mess 141
A Father's Blessing 142
A Great Choice 143
A Gruesome Test 144
A Builder's Prayer 145
What Do You Give Someone Who Has Everything? 146
Wisdom in All of Life 147
The Center and Focus of Our Worship 148
A House of Prayer for All Nations 149
Dangerous Liaisons 150

Dissolution

Who Is in Control? 152
Remembering the Giver of the Gift 153
God Provides in Hard Times 154
What Have I Done to You? 155
Hearts on Fire 156
What We Need between Battles 157
Suitable Replacements 158
God's Endless Provision 159
Miracles for the Status-Conscious 160
The Eyes of Faith 161
Any Other God 162
A Fresh Start for Judah 163
Ruling by the Book 164
Knowing Our Place 165
Interchangeable Gods 166
Sins of the Fathers 167
Righteous Preparations 168
The God of History 169
Keeping Our Focus 170
Three Kings 171
For Better or Worse 172
Israel's Second Chance 173
First I Prayed 174
The Law of God and the Lives of His People 175

CONTENTS, CONTINUED

An Unlikely Deliverance? 176
Knowing What's Good for Us 177
Let's Talk about It 178
Answering the Call 179
God with Us 180
The Lion, the Lamb, and the Little Child 181
Prepare for Comfort 182
Learning to Fly . . . and Wait 183
Mission Accomplished 184
Come Back! 185
Suffering for Obedience 186
Life Goes On 187
The Widowed City 188
A Weeping Prophet, a Message of Hope 189
A Terrifying, Welcome Vision 190
New Hearts for Old 191
Whom Do You Trust? 192
The Good Shepherd 193
Dry Bones 194
Eating Right 195
Consider the Source 196
Doing the Right Thing 197
The Writing on the Wall 198
Who's in Charge? 199
Cheating Hearts 200
The Hateful Prophet 201
A Change from the Inside—of a Fish 202
An Astonishing Turnaround 203
The Man Who Just Didn't Get It 204
Robbing God 205
Healing Judgment 206

Interlude

The Challenge 208
Big Enough 209
Starting Fresh 210
Dig Deep 211
Real Help 212
Telling God Everything 213
Seeing Your Worth 214

Contents, continued

Watching and Waiting 215
Be God's Guest.. 216
Breaking Out in Song.. 217
Timely Support 218
Dumped by God?.. 219
Your Personal Shepherd 220
A Clean Celebration 221
Above All Else... 222
God, Hear Me 223
Forgiveness Brings Joy.. 224
Test God's Goodness... 225
Worth the Wait... 226
Divine Thirst... 227
Always Strong, Always There...................................... 228
Clean Heart, Clean Start 229
Longing for God.. 230
SOS from the Pit 231
Protective Presence... 232
Worthy of Praise 233
Count Your Blessings... 234
Endless Mercy... 235
True Devotion 236
God Taking Sides... 237
Exercising the Heart.. 238
Watchful Protector 239
Peace Be with You.. 240
Seeking God's Favor 241
Proper Credit.. 242
Expectant Waiting... 243
Praiseworthy Name... 244
Unforgettable Love Song.. 245
When the Music Fades.. 246
Contagious Gratitude.. 247
The Ultimate Know-It-All 248
Giving God Attaboys 249
Voice Lessons 250
Smart Move... 251
Idle Character 252
Nothing to Envy.. 253
Putting Out Fires... 254

Captivatingly Beautiful... 255

Success or Significance?... 256

Savoring Each Moment 257

Seeing with New Eyes 258

Racing to Be with You.. 259

The Promised One

God Will Find a Way.. 262

Seeing beyond the Present... 263

Beneath the Radar... 264

Good News of Great Joy.. 265

Wanting the Very Best 266

What the Wise Men Saw 267

Seeing with Our Hearts 268

Uncharted Territory... 269

The Reason behind the Miracle 270

He Knows Us 271

How Things Really Work 272

A Different Mind-Set... 273

Escaping the Trap of Worry... 274

Good Gifts 275

Each Little Decision You Make 276

Hidden Things.. 277

Teachable Moments... 278

Stepping Out of the Boat 279

The One Question We All Must Answer 280

Only God Understands 281

Open Hands... 282

Come Out of Hiding 283

An Invitation for Everyone 284

Lessons from the Garden 285

Lessons from the Storm 286

The Cure for Hidden Hurts 287

Closer Than We Think 288

One Thing 289

Catching More Than Fish 290

Inner Wealth 291

Deceived by Appearances... 292

The Moment before the Miracle 293

Simply by Stopping 294

Contents, continued

Finding Our Way Home 295
The Back of the Line 296
Safe 297
Vindicated 298
At Your House 299
Whole and Lasting Life 300
Thirst Quencher 301
No More "I Can't" 302
On the Fringe 303
The Test of Perfection 304
True Freedom 305
He's Got Your Back 306
A Greater Good 307
Adoring Fans 308
Cleaning House 309
Giving Back 310
A Matter of Priorities 311
Staying Watchful 312
The Face of Jesus 313
Memorable Meal 314
Top Dog 315
Cheerful Humility 316
Reservations Guaranteed 317
More Fruit 318
Parting Is Sweet Sorrow 319
What Matters Most 320
"Whenever" Acceptance 321
Assisting Arrest 322
Hanging in the Shadows 323
Prisoner Exchange 324
Selfless Serving 325
Remember Me 326
The Weight of the World 327
All in the Details 328
Sweet-Smelling Spices 329
Eyes of Expectancy 330
Alive and Well 331
Follow the Leader 332
Believing Is Seeing 333
In Jesus' Name 334

Multiplication

Promise of Power 336
Constant Companion 337
Connected on Purpose 338
True Freedom 339
Free Speech 340
Purity vs. Pretense 341
Stopping at Nothing 342
Who Are You? 343
Words of Forgiveness 344
Giving Someone a Break 345
When God Rocks Our World 346
Bigger Plans 347
When Good People Differ 348
The Power of the Gospel 349
Helping People See 350
Learning from Opposition 351
Two Paths 352
What Jesus Offers 353
Horribly Wrong 354
Freedom 355
More Than Worth It 356
Eternal Purposes 357
A Measure of Faith 358
Hidden from the Arrogant 359
The Cure for Everything 360
Our Eternal Identity 361
The Power to Persevere 362
The "Magic" of Giving 363
Fool's Gold 364
Performance vs. Faith 365
Backed into a Corner 366
Competing or Embracing? 367
The Secret of Fruit 368
Two Foundational Questions 369
God's Good Work 370
No Longer Enemies 371
Your New Identity 372
The Real Enemy 373
Our Anchor 374

Contents, continued

An Opportunity to Make a Difference 375
The Gateway to Greatness 376
Knowing Christ 377
The Presence of Peace 378
The Name of Jesus 379
The Secret of Contentment 380
Paying Your Dues 381
Lessons from the Airplane 382
The Power We Have Been Given 383
What God Sees 384
The Door to Heaven Opened 385
The Secret of Faith 386
Strength to Endure 387
Evidence 388
Good Words 389
No Halfway 390
Just Like Him 391
Love—a Way of Life 392
Fully Alive and in Charge 393
Everything New 394
Your Invitation 395

If you have knowledge,
let others light their candles by it.

—Thomas Fuller

INTRODUCTION

The Bible is a series of little stories that add up to one big story. It is the story of God and his people. He made them for himself. He made them to enjoy him. But his people chose otherwise. The rest of the story tells of God's pursuit of his people—his willingness not only to rescue the people who had rejected him, but also to give his life in order to do it.

The story gets ugly at times. There is real danger, real hurt, real sorrow. But in the end, God succeeds in getting his people back.

As Frederick Buechner said, "The story of any one of us is in some measure the story of us all." Each of us has rebelled. And each of us is being pursued by a God who is relentless in his love. The grand epic that we call the Bible is your story too.

No more will anyone call you Rejected, and your country will no more be called Ruined. You'll be called Hephzibah (My Delight), and your land Beulah (Married), because God delights in you and your land will be like a wedding celebration.

Isaiah 62:4 MSG

A Beginning

The story begins in a garden. God. A man. A woman. Everything unfolded from there. A fall. A promise. A hope for better things. The book of Genesis is full of strange, mysterious stories that sometimes feel as if they came from another planet. But still, in their humanness they resonate with the humanity of the reader.

> In the beginning God created the heavens and the earth. The earth was formless and void, and darkness was over the surface of the deep, and the Spirit of God was moving over the surface of the waters. Then God said, "Let there be light"; and there was light. God saw that the light was good.
>
> Genesis 1:1–4 NASB

In the Beginning

In the beginning God created the heavens and the earth. Now the earth was formless and empty, darkness was over the surface of the deep, and the Spirit of God was hovering over the waters.

And God said, "Let there be light," and there was light. God saw that the light was good, and He separated the light from the darkness. God called the light "day," and the darkness he called "night."

Genesis 1:1–5 NIV

In the beginning was the Word, and the Word was with God, and the Word was God. He was with God in the beginning.

Through him all things were made; without him nothing was made that has been made. In him was life, and that life was the light of men. The light shines in the darkness, but the darkness has not understood it.

John 1:1–5 NIV

There was only darkness, chaos, and emptiness. There was only nothing. And then there was everything, spoken into existence by the voice of God: "Let there be . . ." With those words, light shone out of the darkness, order arose out of chaos, and the emptiness was filled with good things, beautiful things—things that gave God pleasure.

It was good, God said. It wouldn't be long before the perfection of the natural order would be wrecked, but this first chapter of Genesis reminds us of something we all feel in our hearts already: the way things are is not the way things were supposed to be. The Creation story tells us that everything in this universe—every single thing—is of supernatural origin. Every event is an echo, however distorted, of God's voice speaking, "Let there be . . ."

It was the Word that set things in motion, and that Word still speaks. For the Word is Christ. He was with God before the beginning; indeed, he *was* God, shining in the darkness. The Word still speaks. The Light still shines.

In the Image of God

God spoke: "Let us make human beings in our image, make them reflecting our nature so they can be responsible for the fish in the sea, the birds in the air, the cattle, and, yes, Earth itself, and every animal that moves on the face of Earth."

God created human beings; he created them godlike, reflecting God's nature. He created them male and female.

God blessed them: "Prosper! Reproduce! Fill Earth! Take charge! Be responsible for fish in the sea and birds in the air, for every living thing that moves on the face of Earth." . . .

God looked over everything he had made; it was so good, so very good!

Genesis 1:26–28, 31 MSG

To err is human," according to the old saying. Maybe so. But there's a lot more to being human than error-proneness. We have all been made in the image of God. That urge to create, to bring order out of chaos, to make our mark on the world; the anger we feel in the face of injustice, the pleasure we feel in the face of beauty, the hope we feel for a better future—all of that is the image of God finding expression in us, human beings.

It is true that the image of God we express is distorted, even fractured. But there it is nevertheless, glimmering in this interaction, shining in that choice, bursting forth in our longings. God's image in us forever calls us back to the One who is its original.

That realization changes the way we look at ourselves. It also changes the way we look at others. "There are no ordinary people," C. S. Lewis wrote. "You have never met a mere mortal." Once you start seeing the image of God in yourself and others, the world never looks the same again.

MADE FOR RELATIONSHIP

The LORD God said, "It is not good for the man to be alone. I will make a helper who is just right for him." So the LORD God formed from the ground all the wild animals and all the birds of the sky. . . . But still there was no helper just right for him. So the LORD God caused the man to fall into a deep sleep. While the man slept, the LORD God took out one of the man's ribs and closed up the open- ing. Then the LORD God made a woman from the rib, and he brought her to the man.

"At last!" the man ex- claimed.

"This one is bone from my bone, and flesh from my flesh! She will be called 'woman,' because she was taken from 'man.'"

Genesis 2:18–23 NLT

Throughout the Creation story, a phrase repeats like a refrain: "God saw that it was good." The day was good. The night was good. The seas were good. The dry land was good. The trees, the plants, the mountains, the rivers, the birds, the creeping things, the beasts of the field, Adam, Eve—God saw all of it and saw that it was good.

So it is a little jarring when God declares that something is not good. "It is not good for the man to be alone," God says. He cor- rected Adam's aloneness by creating a companion out of his very flesh and bone.

"At last!" Adam said. That little exclamation is telling. The world was freshly made. This was before the Fall, remember. Adam had the delights of the Garden spread out before him. He even had the full presence of God. And yet in the absence of another human being with whom to enjoy it all, Adam couldn't truly enjoy it. Time dragged on.

We were made for relationship, not for self-sufficiency. It isn't good for any of us to be alone.

A New — but Skewed — Perspective

[The serpent] spoke to the Woman: "Do I understand that God told you not to eat from any tree in the garden?"

The Woman said to the serpent, "Not at all. We can eat from the trees in the garden. It's only about the tree in the middle of the garden that God said, 'Don't eat from it; don't even touch it or you'll die.'"

The serpent told the Woman, "You won't die. God knows that the moment you eat from that tree, you'll see what's really going on. You'll be just like God, knowing everything, ranging all the way from good to evil."

When the Woman saw that the tree looked like good eating and realized what she would get out of it—she'd know everything!—she took and ate the fruit and then gave some to her husband, and he ate.

Genesis 3:1–6 MSG

The serpent promised Eve new eyes to see what God sees. Adam and Eve got a new perspective, all right, but it wasn't God's perspective. The serpent taught them to doubt God's goodness, to see convoluted hidden agendas beneath the straightforward commands God gave for their happiness. The serpent taught them, in short, to find misery where God had intended only good for them.

No longer comfortable in their own skin, Adam and Eve hid from God. They believed that the shame they were experiencing must reflect God's *true* view of them. The serpent, after all, had told them that eating the forbidden fruit would open their eyes. The terrible irony is that before they ate the fruit, Adam and Eve already had a godlike view of the world they inhabited. The serpent took away the very thing he promised to give.

Since that day in the Garden, our perspective has been skewed. We find it very hard to believe what may be the simplest, most fundamental truth of all: God loves us, and he wants what is best for us.

The Dawn of Hard Labor

The LORD said to the woman, "You will suffer terribly when you give birth. But you will still desire your husband, and he will rule over you."

The LORD said to the man, "You listened to your wife and ate fruit from that tree. And so, the ground will be under a curse because of what you did. As long as you live, you will have to struggle to grow enough food. Your food will be plants, but the ground will produce thorns and thistles. You will have to sweat to earn a living; you were made out of soil, and you will once again turn into soil."

Genesis 3:16–19 CEV

Before Adam and Eve sinned, the earth offered up its good things willingly. It even watered itself. Everything changed, however, after that first sin. Now cursed, the ground produces thorns and thistles more readily than fruits and vegetables. Since the Fall, work has been a struggle—a push back against a hostile world.

Work is not the result of the Fall. Even before they had sinned, Adam and Eve had the job of tending the Garden. From our post-Fall perspective, it's hard to imagine what such work might have entailed if there were no weeding, no spading, no pulling rocks out of the ground. But whatever that work entailed, we can be confident that it was a work of cooperation with the earth, free from the frustration and futility of the work we experience where the weeds always grow back, no matter how many times we pull them.

Because of sin, everything is harder than it has to be. Work is harder. Childbirth is harder. Relationships are harder. And yet this is still our Father's world, and he still calls us to push through the hardships to gain such rewards as this world yields.

The First Murder

In the process of time it came to pass that Cain brought an offering of the fruit of the ground to the LORD. Abel also brought of the firstborn of his flock and of their fat. And the LORD respected Abel and his offering, but He did not respect Cain and his offering. And Cain was very angry, and his countenance fell.

So the LORD said to Cain, "Why are you angry? And why has your countenance fallen? If you do well, will you not be accepted? And if you do not do well, sin lies at the door. And its desire is for you, but you should rule over it."

Now Cain talked with Abel his brother; and it came to pass, when they were in the field, that Cain rose up against Abel his brother and killed him.

Genesis 4:3–8 NKJV

The brokenness of the post-Fall world reached a new level in the relationship between Cain and Abel, the first brothers. They both brought their offerings to God. Abel, a herdsman, brought an animal; Cain brought fruits or vegetables.

God accepted Abel's sacrifice and rejected Cain's. Cain was furious—whether furious at God or at Abel, the Bible doesn't say. Nor does the Bible spell out why God rejected Cain's sacrifice, but it seems likely that it was the state of Cain's heart—and not the technicalities of produce offerings versus animal sacrifice—that stood between Cain and God. "If you do well," God admonished Cain, "will you not be accepted?" God followed the question with a stern warning: "If you do not do well, sin lies at the door. And its desire is for you, but you should rule over it."

Even as he looked into Cain's dark heart, God gave the first murderer a choice. But Cain chose to enslave himself rather than master his sin. His egregious act was a manifestation of a deeper sin inside. Each of us has the same choice: what we do with it is up to us.

THE WRATH OF "HAVE IT YOUR WAY"

The earth was corrupt in God's sight, and the earth was filled with violence. God saw how corrupt the earth was, for all flesh had corrupted its way on the earth. Then God said to Noah, "I have decided to put an end to all flesh, for the earth is filled with violence because of them; therefore I am going to destroy them along with the earth.

"Make yourself an ark of gofer wood. Make rooms in the ark, and cover it with pitch inside and outside. . . .

"Understand that I am bringing a deluge—floodwaters on the earth to destroy all flesh under heaven with the breath of life in it. Everything on earth will die. But I will establish My covenant with you, and you will enter the ark with your sons, your wife, and your sons' wives."

Genesis 6:11–14, 17–18 HCSB

We tend to treat Noah's flood as a children's story. The ark floats jauntily atop the rising waters, a smiling giraffe poking its head through the upper porthole. But the story of the Flood is a story of God's wrath.

God's wrath is not an easy or pleasant thing to contemplate. But it expresses itself throughout the Bible, in the New Testament as well as the Old. God's wrath is the flip side of his love. If you love anyone, you already know how your anger burns against anything that would harm that person. God's wrath is reserved for that which seeks to destroy the people he loves. Sin destroys lives, relationships, happiness. The anger of God is the anger of surgeons who cut away cancers rather than see them consume their victims.

God pours out his wrath by finally giving people what they want. The people of Noah's time wanted to live beyond God's restraint. So God finally lifted his restraining hand—the hand that restrained the floodwaters. In the end, the people got exactly what they wanted, and it was the end of them.

A SIGN OF MERCY

God said, "This is the sign of the covenant which I am making between Me and you and every living creature that is with you, for all successive generations; I set My bow in the cloud, and it shall be for a sign of a covenant between Me and the earth.

"It shall come about, when I bring a cloud over the earth, that the bow will be seen in the cloud, and I will remember My covenant, which is between Me and you and every living creature of all flesh; and never again shall the water become a flood to destroy all flesh.

"When the bow is in the cloud, then I will look upon it, to remember the everlasting covenant between God and every living creature of all flesh that is on the earth."

Genesis 9:12–16 NASB

In the Old Testament no less than the New, God's anger is always answered by his grace. The worldwide destruction of the Flood was followed immediately by the promise of hope. Never again, God promised, would he send the kind of flood that Noah and his family had just lived through. And the sign of that promise was a bow in the sky—a rainbow.

It is worth noticing that the bow is aimed to shoot its arrows up toward heaven, not down toward earth. The bow is not a threat against humankind that says, "Straighten up, people, or the arrows of God's wrath are going to rain down on you again." No, this bow is poised to shoot at the heart of God. It is as if God is saying, "Cross my heart and hope to die." In this agreement, God puts himself on the hook.

There are some two-sided covenants in the Bible, in which God's people agree to hold up their end of the bargain. But this covenant is all God.

THE SCATTERING

[Men] said, "Come, let us build ourselves a city, with a tower that reaches to the heavens, so that we may make a name for ourselves and not be scattered over the face of the whole earth." . . . The LORD said, "If as one people speaking the same language they have begun to do this, then nothing they plan to do will be impossible for them. Come, let us go down and confuse their language so they will not understand each other."

So the LORD scattered them from there over all the earth, and they stopped building the city. That is why it was called Babel—because there the LORD confused the language of the whole world. From there the LORD scattered them over the face of the whole earth.

Genesis 11:4, 6–9 NIV

God's first command to humanity was "Be fruitful and multiply, and fill the earth" (Gen. 1:28 NASB). In other words, spread out across the earth. When people spread out, it isn't long before they start speaking different languages and creating different cultures. That seems to have been God's plan all along—to have not a monoculture but a full panoply of tribes and nations, each praising God in its own way. The Bible has much to say about "every tribe and nation" coming to God.

But in the generations after the Flood, the people had other plans. They didn't want to fill the earth. They wanted to stay right where they were and become great—maybe even as great as God. So they began building a great tower that would reach to the heavens—challenging God's authority and creating a rallying point for their culture.

God had other plans for them. He confused their language and scattered them to the four winds. It was a punishment, certainly. But it was also a mercy, for it forced the people out of their delusion of self-sufficiency and into something richer and more adventurous.

An Astonishing Capacity for Belief

The LORD said to Abram: Go out from your land, your relatives, and your father's house to the land that I will show you. I will make you into a great nation, I will bless you, I will make your name great, and you will be a blessing. I will bless those who bless you, I will curse those who treat you with contempt, and all the peoples on earth will be blessed through you.

So Abram went, as the LORD had told him, and Lot went with him. Abram was 75 years old when he left Haran. He took his wife Sarai, his nephew Lot, all the possessions they had accumulated . . . in Haran, and they set out for the land of Canaan.

Genesis 12:1–5 HCSB

Abram hailed from somewhere in modern-day Iraq, most likely from a tribe of moon-worshippers. Nothing in the Bible indicates that there was any excellence on Abram's part—either moral or otherwise—that attracted God's attention among so many pagans. Subsequent events suggest, in fact, that Abram was average at best in the character and integrity department.

But God called Abram anyway. Abram, this childless seventy-five-year-old, would be a great nation someday, and through him God would bless all the nations. All Abram had to do was leave everything he had ever known and follow this mysterious voice to a new country. The voice doesn't mention, by the way, where this new country is, or how long it will take to get there.

Amazingly, Abram followed. Whatever his shortcomings, the man had an astonishing capacity for belief. He staked his whole life on the conviction that God's promises were true. Again and again, Abram made a mess of things. But he always returned to this first conviction: God's promises are true. That capacity for belief is what made Abram the father of our faith.

A Choice: Faith or Self-Sufficiency

Abram went down to Egypt to live there for a while because the famine in the land was severe. When he was about to enter Egypt, he said to his wife Sarai, "Look, I know what a beautiful woman you are. When the Egyptians see you, they will say, 'This is his wife.' They will kill me but let you live. Please say you're my sister so it will go well for me because of you, and my life will be spared on your account."

When Abram entered Egypt, the Egyptians saw that the woman was very beautiful. Pharaoh's officials saw her and praised her to Pharaoh, so the woman was taken to Pharaoh's house. He treated Abram well because of her, and Abram acquired flocks and herds, male and female donkeys, male and female slaves, and camels.

Genesis 12:10–16 HCSB

The journey God called Abram to undertake wasn't safe. Abram had to pass through the lands of many unfriendly kings. As Abram's danger grew, his fear grew—especially in the land of the mighty pharaoh. Pharaoh was the sort of man who took whatever he wanted. Abram was afraid Pharaoh would want his wife, Sarai, and kill her husband to have her.

Abram had a choice: he could renew his trust in the God who promised to see him through, or he could attempt to solve the problem in his own strength and wisdom. He chose the latter. It was a perfectly understandable reaction; when things feel out of control, our first instinct is to attempt to take control. But in relying on his own shrewdness, Abram made a royal mess of things. He forsook his wife, prostituting her to save his own skin.

When we trust in our own resources, we draw a very strict limit around the solutions that are available to us. Many of those solutions are worse than the original problem. When we rely on God, we open ourselves to a whole universe of solutions.

THE GRACIOUSNESS OF FAITH

Lot, who was moving about with Abram, also had flocks and herds and tents. But the land could not support them while they stayed together, for their possessions were so great that they were not able to stay together. And quarreling arose. . . .

So Abram said to Lot, "Let's not have any quarreling between you and me, or between your herdsmen and mine, for we are brothers. Is not the whole land before you? Let's part company. If you go to the left, I'll go to the right; if you go to the right, I'll go to the left."

Lot looked up and saw that the whole plain of the Jordan was well watered, like the garden of the LORD. . . . So Lot chose for himself the whole plain of the Jordan.

Genesis 13:5–11 NIV

When there was trouble between Abram's servants and Lot's, Abram extended a graciousness that mirrored the grace he had received from God. The two households would have to go their separate ways. As the elder relative, Abram had every right to dictate to his nephew the terms of the separation. But he didn't; he let Lot choose which land to take.

Why was Abram willing to leave that monumental decision to another? Perhaps he understood that neither he nor Lot was really making the decision. God was at work, and God was the One who would be giving Abram the land he wanted Abram to have.

As it turned out, Lot's choice to settle in the lush, well-watered plains of the Jordan didn't make him a great patriarch. Life among the wicked cities of the plains—including Sodom and Gomorrah—wrecked Lot's family completely. God rewarded Abram's act of faith, on the other hand, with a renewal of his promise: "All the land that you see I will give to you and your offspring forever" (Gen. 13:15 NIV). That land, by the way, included the Jordan Valley, which Abram had just given to Lot!

A MYSTERIOUS FIGURE

After [Abram's] return from the defeat of Chedorlaomer . . . Melchizedek king of Salem brought out bread and wine; now he was a priest of God Most High.

He blessed him and said, "Blessed be Abram of God Most High, possessor of heaven and earth; and blessed be God Most High, who has delivered your enemies into your hand."

He gave him a tenth of all.

The king of Sodom said to Abram, "Give the people to me and take the goods for yourself."

Abram said to the king of Sodom, "I have sworn to the LORD God Most High, possessor of heaven and earth, that I will not take a thread or a sandal thong or anything that is yours, for fear you would say, 'I have made Abram rich.'"

Genesis 14:17–23 NASB

Melchizedek is one of the most mysterious figures in the Bible. In the midst of a pagan land, this priest of the true God appears out of nowhere to speak a blessing on Abram, and then he disappears just as suddenly as he came. He would probably be mostly forgotten—like one of the names in the middle of the genealogies—except for the fact that the book of Hebrews refers to Jesus as "a priest forever according to the order of Melchizedek" (5:6 NASB).

That phrase itself is mysterious, but it seems to be related to the fact that Melchizedek was both a priest and a king. Throughout the Bible, the roles of priest and king are kept very separate (King Saul, for one, got in serious trouble for mixing the two roles). The two exceptions are Melchizedek and Jesus. Jesus rules over his people as King and God, but he also mediates between God and his people as a priest. Which is yet another mystery. Perhaps it is appropriate that one of the first foreshadowings of Christ be such a mysterious figure as Melchizedek.

A Sky Full of Blessings

The word of the LORD came to Abram in a vision: "Fear not, Abram, I am your shield; your reward shall be very great."

But Abram said, "O Lord GOD, what will you give me, for I continue childless, and the heir of my house is Eliezer of Damascus?" And Abram said, "Behold, you have given me no offspring, and a member of my household will be my heir."

And behold, the word of the LORD came to him: "This man shall not be your heir; your very own son shall be your heir." And he brought him outside and said, "Look toward heaven, and number the stars, if you are able to number them." Then he said to him, "So shall your offspring be."

And he believed the LORD, and he counted it to him as righteousness.

Genesis 15:1–6 ESV

Abram was an old man. His wife, Sarai, was old too—decades beyond childbearing age. So when God came to him in a vision and repeated the promise once more, it's not hard to understand Abram's incredulity. "I continue childless," he said, "and the heir of my house is Eliezer of Damascus." It was a painful thing for Abram to think about: it wasn't even a distant relative, but a servant who would inherit everything he had worked for.

But that wasn't what God had in mind when he promised to make a great nation of Abram. He wasn't talking about any foreign servant inheriting his estate for lack of any other heir. No, as unlikely as it sounded, God was going to give Abram his very own son.

God took him outside the tent and told him to look up to the heavens. "Number the stars," God said, "if you are able to number them. So shall your offspring be."

Abram lifted his head, and he took in the vast and shimmering sky—each star a son, a daughter, each one a blessing to the rest of the world. And somehow, Abram believed again.

LETTING GOD BE GOD

Sarai, Abram's wife, had borne him no children. But she had an Egyptian maidservant named Hagar; so she said to Abram, "The LORD has kept me from having children. Go, sleep with my maidservant; perhaps I can build a family through her."

Abram agreed to what Sarai said. So after Abram had been living in Canaan ten years, Sarai his wife took her Egyptian maidservant Hagar and gave her to her husband to be his wife. He slept with Hagar, and she conceived.

When she knew she was pregnant, she began to despise her mistress. Then Sarai said to Abram, "You are responsible for the wrong I am suffering. I put my servant in your arms, and now that she knows she is pregnant, she despises me. May the LORD judge between you and me."

Genesis 16:1–5 NIV

Abram's life of faith was as full of peaks and valleys as any roller coaster. In Genesis 15 we saw Abram believing God's impossible promise to make him a great nation. In the very next chapter we see him taking matters into his own hands again.

Knowing she couldn't possibly bear children at her age, Sarai invited Abram to sleep with her maidservant Hagar in hopes that she would bear a child who would be the beginning of Abram's great nation. The promise, after all, said that Abram would father a great nation; it didn't specify that the children he fathered had to be legitimate.

So Abram slept with the servant woman, and she got pregnant. Soon Sarai began to realize what a mistake she had made. Hagar succeeded where Sarai had failed for so many decades, and Sarai could no longer stand the sight of her. In her eagerness to help God keep his promise and in her unwillingness to wait any longer, Sarai had traded in her dignity, and Abram had let her. It was a full-blown tragedy before it was over—all because Abram and Sarai couldn't let God be God.

THE CUTTING OF THE COVENANT

GOD said, "Bring me a heifer, a goat, and a ram, each three years old, and a dove and a young pigeon."

[Abram] brought all these animals to him, split them down the middle, and laid the halves opposite each other. But he didn't split the birds. Vultures swooped down on the carcasses, but Abram scared them off. As the sun went down a deep sleep overcame Abram and then a sense of dread, dark and heavy. . . .

When the sun was down and it was dark, a smoking firepot and a flaming torch moved between the split carcasses. That's when GOD made a covenant with Abram: "I'm giving this land to your children, from the Nile River in Egypt to the River Euphrates in Assyria—the country of the Kenites, Kenizzites, Kadmonites, Hittites, Perizzites, Rephaim, Amorites, Canaanites, Girgashites, and Jebusites."

Genesis 15:10–12, 17–22 MSG

It was a terrible, bloody business. Abram killed three large animals, sawed each in half through bone and muscle, and laid the pieces out. He had to fight off the vultures that were attracted by the smell of blood and death.

Abram probably recognized the making of a familiar ritual—the "cutting of a covenant." When two kings made a treaty, they sometimes cut an animal in half and walked between the pieces as a way of saying, "If I don't keep this agreement, may I be like this animal." Sometimes both parties walked between the pieces, sometimes it was only the weaker of the two kings.

In the darkness of night, Abram woke to a vision of God—in the form of a smoking firepot—passing between the pieces of the animals. It was not the weaker of the two parties putting himself on the line for the sake of the covenant, but the stronger. God was saying, "If I don't give this land to your offspring as I have promised, may I be broken like these broken animals."

37

SARAI'S FRESH START

God said to Abraham, "As for Sarai your wife, you shall not call her name Sarai, but Sarah shall be her name.

"I will bless her, and indeed I will give you a son by her. Then I will bless her, and she shall be a mother of nations; kings of peoples will come from her."

Then Abraham fell on his face and laughed, and said in his heart, "Will a child be born to a man one hundred years old? And will Sarah, who is ninety years old, bear a child?"

And Abraham said to God, "Oh that Ishmael might live before You!"

But God said, "No, but Sarah your wife will bear you a son, and you shall call his name Isaac; and I will establish My covenant with him for an everlasting covenant for his descendants after him."

Genesis 17:15–19 NASB

Sarai was ninety years old when God gave her a fresh start. No longer would she be known by the old Babylonian name she had been born with. Henceforth she would be called Sarah—Princess—and she would be the mother of nations.

Abram had been called upon to believe some wild things over the previous three decades. But the thought of his ninety-year-old wife giving birth was too much. He couldn't get his head around it. So he gave God another suggestion. Why couldn't Ishmael, Abram's son with the servant woman Hagar, be the son of the promise? Perhaps Abram felt bad for the boy Ishmael. Illegitimate or not, he was still Abram's flesh and blood.

More to the point, Ishmael was already there. It took enough imagination to see God making a great nation out of Ishmael. But an as-yet-unborn son of a ninety-year-old woman? That was impossible to picture.

God had his own plans. "No," he insisted. "Sarah your wife will bear you a son." God was doing something utterly new, and Abram's ability or inability to picture it was immaterial.

A Ridiculous Prediction

One of them said, "I'm coming back about this time next year. When I arrive, your wife Sarah will have a son." Sarah was listening at the tent opening, just behind the man.

Abraham and Sarah were old by this time, very old. Sarah was far past the age for having babies. Sarah laughed within herself, "An old woman like me? Get pregnant? With this old man of a husband?"

God said to Abraham, "Why did Sarah laugh saying, 'Me? Have a baby? An old woman like me?' Is anything too hard for God? I'll be back about this time next year and Sarah will have a baby."

Sarah lied. She said, "I didn't laugh," because she was afraid.

But he said, "Yes you did; you laughed."

Genesis 18:10–15 MSG

Three strangers showed up at the tent of Abraham and Sarah beneath the oaks of Mamre. Abraham must have recognized them as angels—the manifestation of God—for he ran out to meet them and bowed down before them. He insisted that they stop awhile and rest in the spreading shade of the oak trees and wash their feet. He called for Sarah to prepare bread for the visitors while he selected a calf to slaughter and cook for them.

When they had eaten, the visitors made an astonishing announcement: within a year, Sarah would give birth to Abraham's son. And from the other side of the tent flap came a short laugh of surprise. It was an old woman's laugh—Sarah's. Perhaps there was a touch of mockery in it.

"Why did you laugh?" the visitor asked. But surely he understood why she laughed. The thought of a ninety-year-old woman giving birth was ridiculous. But God uses the foolish things of the world to shame the wise. Sarah would soon see that nothing is too hard—or too ridiculous—for God.

A Rescue—and a Backward Look

Lot reached the village just as the sun was rising over the horizon. Then the Lord rained down fire and burning sulfur from the sky on Sodom and Gomorrah. He utterly destroyed them, along with the other cities and villages of the plain, wiping out all the people and every bit of vegetation. But Lot's wife looked back as she was following behind him, and she turned into a pillar of salt.

Abraham got up early that morning and hurried out to the place where he had stood in the Lord's presence. He looked out across the plain toward Sodom and Gomorrah and watched as columns of smoke rose from the cities like smoke from a furnace.

But God had listened to Abraham's request and kept Lot safe, removing him from the disaster that engulfed the cities on the plain.

Genesis 19:23–29 NLT

Lot's sojourn in the cities of the plain ended in a hail of fire and brimstone—God's judgment for the outrageous violence and perversity of the cities' residents. God spared Lot and his family, allowing them to flee across the plain as the fires destroyed Sodom and Gomorrah. But the refugees were under strict orders: they were not to look back. God was giving them a fresh start, a new future.

As they left, however, Lot's wife couldn't help herself. Perhaps she began thinking of the roots the family had put down in Sodom. In their hurry to escape, they must have left most of their possessions behind. There was wickedness aplenty in Sodom, but at least she had known what to expect there. Before them yawned an uncertainty as vast as the plain they walked across. So she turned for one last look at the life they were leaving.

That one last look *was* her last look. In her reluctance to leave behind the dead but familiar life of Sodom, Lot's wife forfeited her opportunity to embrace the future God had for her.

A Boy Named Laughter

The LORD visited Sarah as he had said, and the LORD did to Sarah as he had promised. And Sarah conceived and bore Abraham a son in his old age at the time of which God had spoken to him. Abraham called the name of his son who was born to him, whom Sarah bore him, Isaac. And Abraham circumcised his son Isaac when he was eight days old, as God had commanded him. Abraham was a hundred years old when his son Isaac was born to him.

And Sarah said, "God has made laughter for me; everyone who hears will laugh over me." And she said, "Who would have said to Abraham that Sarah would nurse children? Yet I have borne him a son in his old age." And the child grew and was weaned. And Abraham made a great feast on the day that Isaac was weaned.

Genesis 21:1–8 ESV

A year after Sarah laughed in derision at the angel's announcement that she would give birth to a son, the oaks of Mamre echoed again with Sarah's laughter. It wasn't a mocking laugh this time, though. It was the pure laughter of joy. Sarah had given birth to a son. She named him Isaac, which means "laughter."

At long last, Sarah and Abraham could see that God was fulfilling that most unlikely promise to produce a great nation out of the dried-up bodies of a hundred-year-old man and a ninety-year-old woman. How many times had Sarah lost heart? How many nights had she cried in sorrow at not having a child? How many times in the last thirty years had she remembered God's promise and thought of it not as a source of hope, but as a bitter taunt?

But now she had so much to laugh about. The sadness and frustration melted away like a dream. Tears of sorrow became tears of joy as Sarah held in her arms a little boy named Laughter.

HOPE FOR THE REJECTED

Early the next morning Abraham took some food and a leather bag full of water. He gave them to Hagar and sent her away. Carrying these things and her son, Hagar went and wandered in the desert of Beersheba.

Later, when all the water was gone from the bag, Hagar put her son under a bush. Then she went away a short distance and sat down. She thought, "My son will die, and I cannot watch this happen." She sat there and began to cry.

God heard the boy crying, and God's angel called to Hagar from heaven. He said, "What is wrong, Hagar? Don't be afraid! God has heard the boy crying there. Help him up and take him by the hand. I will make his descendants into a great nation."

Genesis 21:14–18 NCV

Great news for Sarah was terrible news for the servant Hagar and her son Ishmael. Now that she had produced a legitimate heir, Sarah wanted both the boy and his mother out of her household. "The son of this maid shall not be an heir with my son Isaac," she said (Gen. 21:10 NASB). Abraham was caught in the middle. He felt a certain loyalty to Ishmael, who was, after all, his son.

God reminded Abraham that Isaac, not Ishmael, was the son of the promise. Isaac represented God's plan. Ishmael was Sarah and Abraham's plan, their effort to overrule the God whose timing they did not understand. So God told Abraham to listen to his wife, to send the boy Ishmael away. That doesn't mean, however, that God abandoned Ishmael or his mother.

When Hagar gave up hope in the wilderness, God had mercy on her and on her son, rescuing them when their food and water ran out. Beyond that, he made a great nation out of Ishmael. Ishmael fathered twelve princes, who spread throughout the Middle East.

The Hard Faith of a Father

The LORD said, "Go get Isaac, your only son. . . . I will show you a mountain where you must sacrifice him." . . .

So Abraham got up early the next morning and chopped wood for the fire. He put a saddle on his donkey and left with Isaac and two servants for the place where God had told him to go.

Three days later Abraham looked off in the distance and saw the place. He told his servants, "Stay here with the donkey, while my son and I go over there to worship. We will come back."

Abraham put the wood on Isaac's shoulder, but he carried the hot coals and the knife. As the two of them walked along, Isaac said, "Father, we have the coals and the wood, but where is the lamb for the sacrifice?"

"My son," Abraham answered, "God will provide the lamb."

Genesis 22:2–8 CEV

What was going through Abraham's mind as he heard those terrible words? "Go get Isaac, your only son. . . . I will show you a mountain where you must sacrifice him." Yet Abraham obeyed.

Abraham had seen God make good on his promises. He knew that God was trustworthy, even when his ways seemed mysterious, or even absurd. Because—face it—it is absurd for God to require a man to kill the son that God himself had given after so many years.

"God will provide the lamb." Abraham was sure of it. He was convinced that God had something up his sleeve—some other plan that he hadn't yet revealed. But even in that picture of a father leading his only son to die on a hill, he was beginning to reveal the plan by which he would provide the Lamb who would take away the sins of the world. It was too absurd for God to ask Abraham to go through with the sacrifice of his only son, but thousands of years later, God would do that very thing, for our sake.

A FAITHFUL MATCHMAKER

How Abraham's servant chose the right woman for Isaac:

[Abraham's servant prayed,] "Let the young woman to whom I shall say, 'Please let down your jar that I may drink,' and who shall say, 'Drink, and I will water your camels'—let her be the one whom you have appointed for your servant Isaac." . . .

Before he had finished speaking, behold, Rebekah . . . came out with her water jar on her shoulder. The young woman was very attractive in appearance, a maiden whom no man had known. She went down to the spring and filled her jar and came up. Then the servant ran to meet her and said, "Please give me a little water to drink from your jar."

She said, "Drink, my lord." And she quickly let down her jar upon her hand and gave him a drink.

Genesis 24:14–18 ESV

Picture Abraham's oldest, most trusted servant, standing with his camels beside the well outside a foreign city, watching the young women come and go. His master, unwilling to let his son marry a Canaanite, had given his servant the task of finding a wife for Isaac among his kinspeople in Mesopotamia. But the servant didn't know a soul in the city of Nahor. There were many young women to choose from, and yet he knew nothing about them.

Rather than trusting outside appearances, the old man prayed for a sign that would reveal the heart of the woman who was right for Isaac. He would ask a young woman for a drink of water. If the young woman was the right one, she would not only give him a drink, but she would also offer to water his camels.

Before the servant had even finished his prayer, beautiful Rebekah came to the well. She gladly gave him a drink. Then she offered to draw water for his camels, just as the old man had prayed. Rebekah was the one; hers was the servant's heart that would keep alive the line of Abraham.

REBEKAH PURSUES HER CALLING

The betrothal of Rebekah and Isaac:

[Rebekah's relatives] said, "We will call the young woman and ask her personally." Then they called Rebekah and said to her, "Will you go with this man?"

And she said, "I will go."

So they sent away Rebekah their sister and her nurse, and Abraham's servant and his men. And they blessed Rebekah and said to her: "Our sister, may you become the mother of thousands of ten thousands; and may your descendants possess the gates of those who hate them."

Then Rebekah and her maids arose, and they rode on the camels and followed the man. So the servant took Rebekah and departed. . . . Then Isaac brought her into his mother Sarah's tent; and he took Rebekah and she became his wife, and he loved her.

Genesis 24:57–61, 67 NKJV

Rebekah's betrothal is a beautiful story of a young woman pursuing her calling. It was an unusual situation, this old servant showing up and asking the young woman if she wanted to make the long journey home with him to marry a man she had never met. Arranged marriages were common, and there was a close family connection (Isaac and Rebekah were first cousins), so this wasn't totally unorthodox, but still it must have seemed sudden.

Rebekah's family was sensitive to her desires: "Will you go with this man?" they asked. When she said she would, the family spoke beautiful words of blessing over her: "Our sister, may you become the mother of thousands of ten thousands"—words that proved true.

With that, the young woman left behind the tents of her old family and was brought into Sarah's tent. Rebekah, like her in-laws before her, took a huge leap of faith, and completely new vistas opened before her. Isaac and Rebekah would have their ups and downs, but the story of how they came together is one of the great love stories of the Bible.

KINGDOMS AT WAR

Isaac's wife could not have children, so Isaac prayed to the LORD for her. The LORD heard Isaac's prayer, and Rebekah became pregnant.

While she was pregnant, the babies struggled inside her. She asked, "Why is this happening to me?" . . .

The LORD said to her, "Two nations are in your body, and two groups of people will be taken from you. One group will be stronger than the other, and the older will serve the younger."

When the time came, Rebekah gave birth to twins. The first baby was born red. Since his skin was like a hairy robe, he was named Esau. When the second baby was born, he was holding on to Esau's heel, so that baby was named Jacob.

Genesis 25:21–26 NCV

The stories of Genesis remind us that the universal, even the cosmic, dwells in the most mundane facts of our earthly existence. Rebekah was carrying twins—active twins who kicked in her belly. It couldn't have been comfortable. So she asked a question that thousands of women carrying twins have no doubt asked: "Why is this happening to me?"

Perhaps it was a rhetorical question. She must have been shocked by the answer: "Two nations are in your body." There was more than the discomfort of pregnancy happening. It was a power struggle that would continue to play out in the lives of the twins, ultimately playing out in the geopolitical struggles of the Israelites, Jacob's descendants, and the Edomites, Esau's descendants.

We're all in the midst of a huge, cosmic drama. It pulses just below the surface of the mundane that consumes so much of our attention. We feel the turmoil within and ask, like Rebekah, "Why is this happening to me?" The kingdom of God and the kingdoms of the world are at war.

A Nation for a Bowl of Soup

One day Jacob was boiling a pot of vegetable soup. Esau came in from hunting in the fields, weak from hunger. So Esau said to Jacob, "Let me eat some of that red soup, because I am weak with hunger." . . .

But Jacob said, "You must sell me your rights as the first-born son."

Esau said, "I am almost dead from hunger. If I die, all of my father's wealth will not help me."

But Jacob said, "First, promise me that you will give it to me." So Esau made a promise to Jacob and sold his part of their father's wealth to Jacob. Then Jacob gave Esau bread and vegetable soup, and he ate and drank, and then left. So Esau showed how little he cared about his rights as the firstborn son.

Genesis 25:29–34 NCV

Esau had a vision problem. He could see only that which was directly in front of him. Faint with hunger after a long day's hunt, the sight and smell of a pot of stew kept him from seeing what was truly valuable.

Jacob cut a deal with Esau. Sure, he could have some stew. He just had to trade away his birthright—the right as firstborn to be the father's main heir. Esau looked around him. His family heritage must not have been much to look at. Some herds. Some scrubby pasture-land. No doubt they had heard the promises God had made to their grandfather Abraham, to make a great nation of the family. But there was no great nation in sight—just a father, a mother, and a couple of brothers who didn't get along.

But the bowl of stew was real, and it would meet Esau's immediate need. The way Esau saw it, you can't head a great nation if you've died of hunger. Call it a lack of imagination or a lack of faith; Esau gave up his birthright for a bowl of stew.

A SCOUNDREL'S BLESSING

[Jacob] had a dream, and behold, a ladder was set on the earth with its top reaching to heaven; and behold, the angels of God were ascending and descending on it.

And behold, the LORD stood above it and said, "I am the LORD, the God of your father Abraham and the God of Isaac; the land on which you lie, I will give it to you and to your descendants.

"Your descendants will also be like the dust of the earth . . . and in you and in your descendants shall all the families of the earth be blessed.

"Behold, I am with you and will keep you wherever you go, and will bring you back to this land; for I will not leave you until I have done what I have promised you."

Genesis 28:12–15 NASB

Ever the deceiver, Jacob played one dodge too many. Having already tricked Esau out of his birthright, he posed as Esau to cheat his blind father, Isaac, into bestowing on him the blessing meant for the elder brother. Not surprisingly, Esau went into a rage that sent Jacob running for his life.

As Jacob fled, God came to him in a vision. This is where you might expect God to give Jacob a good scolding. But he didn't. Instead, God made a promise: Jacob's descendants would be like the dust of the earth and would inhabit the very land where Jacob lay.

Why did God bless Jacob rather than Esau? It's a hard question to answer; perhaps it had something to do with the fact that Jacob, for all his issues, was better at believing God than Esau was. But one thing is obvious. The blessing God extended to Jacob was not a reward for good behavior. God blessed Jacob—and, by extension, the rest of us—for his own reasons. Grace is a mystery. Sometimes grace is even a scandal.

GOD'S LOVE FOR THE UNLOVELY

When GOD realized that Leah was unloved, he opened her womb. But Rachel was barren. Leah became pregnant and had a son. She named him Reuben (Look-It's-a-Boy!).

"This is a sign," she said, "that GOD has seen my misery; and a sign that now my husband will love me."

She became pregnant again and had another son. "GOD heard," she said, "that I was unloved and so he gave me this son also." She named this one Simeon (GOD-Heard). She became pregnant yet again—another son. She said, "Now maybe my husband will connect with me—I've given him three sons!" That's why she named him Levi (Connect).

She became pregnant a final time and had a fourth son. She said, "This time I'll praise GOD." So she named him Judah (Praise-GOD). Then she stopped having children.

Genesis 29:31–35 MSG

When Jacob ran from Esau, he stayed with his uncle Laban. He promptly fell in love with Laban's beautiful younger daughter, Rachel. He asked for her hand in marriage; Laban agreed, but first Jacob had to work seven years in his uncle's fields. Jacob gladly did the work, so great was his love for Rachel.

When the seven years were up, Laban gave Jacob not Rachel but her unattractive older sister, Leah. The trickster had been tricked. In the end, Jacob married both sisters. It was no secret, however, which one he really loved.

Leah's is a pitiable story of a woman striving to win the love of a man who simply did not love her. She bore him child after child, hoping that each would be the one that turned Jacob's heart toward her. It never happened. But God did love her, and he bestowed on her an honor that Jacob was unable to bestow on Rachel: through her firstborn son, Judah, the unloved, rejected wife of Jacob became the ancestor of Jesus, who was "despised and rejected by men, a Man of sorrows and acquainted with grief" (Isa. 53:3 NKJV).

THE MAN WHO HELD ON

A man came and wrestled with [Jacob] until the dawn began to break. When the man saw that he would not win the match, he touched Jacob's hip and wrenched it out of its socket. Then the man said, "Let me go, for the dawn is breaking!"

But Jacob said, "I will not let you go unless you bless me."

"What is your name?" the man asked.

He replied, "Jacob."

"Your name will no longer be Jacob," the man told him. "From now on you will be called Israel, because you have fought with God and with men and have won."

"Please tell me your name," Jacob said.

"Why do you want to know my name?" the man replied. Then he blessed Jacob there.

Jacob named the place Peniel (which means "face of God"), for he said, "I have seen God face to face, yet my life has been spared."

Genesis 32:24–30 NLT

Jacob was on the road again. He had worn out his welcome with Laban and his family and was headed back home after many years—fourteen at least—in the hope that it would be safe to face Esau again. It was a journey filled with fear.

One night on the journey, Jacob was visited by a mysterious stranger who wrestled with him in the darkness until close to daybreak. Jacob wrestled well, and the stranger, in order to escape before daylight, touched Jacob's hip and put his leg out of the socket. But still Jacob held on, insisting that he would not let go until the stranger blessed him. He had come to understand that this stranger was God himself.

Jacob was desperate. There was danger on every side, and he had run out of tricks. He had nothing to bring to God, but he had no one to turn to besides God. There could be no better picture of faith: a man at the end of himself holds to God like grim death and says, "I won't let you go until you bless me."

A New Man, a New Brotherhood

Esau ran toward Jacob and hugged and kissed him. Then the two brothers started crying.

When Esau noticed the women and children he asked, "Whose children are these?"

Jacob answered, "These are the ones the Lord has been kind enough to give to me, your servant." . . .

Leah and her children came and bowed down; finally, Joseph and Rachel also came and bowed down.

Esau asked Jacob, "What did you mean by these herds I met along the road?"

"Master," Jacob answered, "I sent them so that you would be friendly to me."

"But, brother, I already have plenty," Esau replied. "Keep them for yourself."

"No!" Jacob said. "Please accept these gifts as a sign of your friendship for me. When you welcomed me and I saw your face, it was like seeing the face of God."

Genesis 33:4–5, 7–10 CEV

As Jacob neared his old home, he saw Esau coming to out meet him—Esau and four hundred men. It appeared that his fears of Esau were well founded. Jacob had dealt with trouble all his life, most of it of his own making, and had always managed to sidestep it through one trick or another. This time, however, he left the bag of tricks in the baggage train. He faced Esau like a man—a humble man, to be sure, bowing to the ground seven times on his approach—but an open-faced and honest man nevertheless.

Recognizing Jacob, Esau ran to him and embraced him. Jacob had to insist before Esau would accept any of the peace offerings he had brought. The two brothers who had contended so selfishly with each other were now trying to outdo one another in selflessness. For the first time in the biblical record, the two men loved each other like brothers. God had indeed blessed Jacob; a big part of that blessing was Jacob's new character, earned at the expense of great hardship and rewarded with the love of a newfound brother.

New Consequences for Old Habits

[Joseph's brothers] took Joseph's robe and slaughtered a goat and dipped the robe in the blood. And they sent the robe of many colors and brought it to their father and said, "This we have found; please identify whether it is your son's robe or not." And he identified it and said, "It is my son's robe. A fierce animal has devoured him. Joseph is without doubt torn to pieces." Then Jacob tore his garments and put sackcloth on his loins and mourned for his son many days. All his sons and all his daughters rose up to comfort him, but he refused to be comforted and said, "No, I shall go down to Sheol to my son, mourning."

Thus his father wept for him. Meanwhile the Midianites had sold him in Egypt to Potiphar, an officer of Pharaoh, the captain of the guard.

Genesis 37:31–36 ESV

Jacob may have been a changed man when he went back to Canaan after his years of working for his father-in-law, Laban, but he and his family still lived with the consequences of some of his habits and choices from earlier in his life. Round two of the old rivalry between Rachel and Leah, for example, played out in dramatic fashion in the lives of Jacob's sons.

It was no secret that Joseph was Jacob's favorite among his twelve sons. Joseph, after all, was the son of Jacob's favored wife, Rachel. The brothers' jealousy of Joseph grew into resentment and then into a hatred so fierce that they seriously considered killing him. In the end, they decided to sell him into slavery and fake his death.

Jacob was the victim of a trick that was crueler than any he had ever performed himself. Seeing his favorite son's cloak covered in blood, he descended into a deep and lasting mourning. It was a pitiful scene, but there was a peculiar justice in it; Joseph was reaping what he had sown.

CHARACTER AND CIRCUMSTANCE

Although she spoke to Joseph day after day, he refused to go to bed with her. Now one day he went into the house to do his work, and none of the household servants was there. She grabbed him by his garment and said, "Sleep with me!" But leaving his garment in her hand, he escaped and ran outside. . . .

She put Joseph's garment beside her until his master came home. Then she told him the same story: "The Hebrew slave you brought to us came to me to make fun of me, but when I screamed for help, he left his garment with me and ran outside."

When his master heard the story his wife told him . . . he was furious and had him thrown into prison, where the king's prisoners were confined. So Joseph was there in prison.

Genesis 39:10–12, 16–20
HCSB

Joseph had always been a young man of excellence and character. When he was shipped off to Egypt as a slave, it wasn't long before Potiphar, his master, recognized that the Lord was with Joseph and that everything he touched prospered. Potiphar put Joseph in charge of everything he owned.

Potiphar's wife also noticed that there was something special about Joseph, and she noticed that he was good-looking too. She tried to seduce him; she was persistent about it. But Joseph wouldn't think of it; Potiphar had placed too much trust in him. He asked. "How then could I do this great evil and sin against God?" (Gen. 39:9 NASB).

In her frustration, Potiphar's wife falsely accused Joseph of attempted rape, and he was thrown into prison. Ironically, it was his excellence and character that landed Joseph in prison, for it attracted the attention of Potiphar's wife and then guarded him against her advances. Even in prison, however, he rose to the top of the heap. Character isn't determined by circumstances. Joseph was Joseph, in whatever situation he found himself.

A Blessing to the Nations

Pharaoh asked them, "Can we find anyone like this man, one in whom is the spirit of God?"

Then Pharaoh said to Joseph, "Since God has made all this known to you, there is no one so discerning and wise as you. You shall be in charge of my palace, and all my people are to submit to your orders. Only with respect to the throne will I be greater than you."

So Pharaoh said to Joseph, "I hereby put you in charge of the whole land of Egypt." Then Pharaoh took his signet ring from his finger and put it on Joseph's finger. He dressed him in robes of fine linen and put a gold chain around his neck. . . .

Then Pharaoh said to Joseph, "I am Pharaoh, but without your word no one will lift hand or foot in all Egypt."

Genesis 41:38–42, 44 NIV

Pharaoh asked, "Can we find anyone like this man, one in whom is the spirit of God?" It's an interesting question, coming from a man who didn't worship Joseph's God—indeed, a man who set himself up as a god on earth. But he was a man in whom the spirit of the true God was a blessing to everyone around him.

When God promised to make a great nation out of Abram, he promised that Abram's descendants would be a blessing to all nations. Then, three generations later, the promise was coming true. Joseph's God-given ability to interpret dreams attracted Pharaoh's attention. By interpreting one of Pharaoh's dreams, Joseph accurately predicted a coming drought. Pharaoh put Joseph in charge of preparing Egypt's food stores in advance of the drought.

The wisdom granted by God is not strictly "spiritual." It touches on every area of human life—even, as in Joseph's case, agricultural policy! And, like rainfall and sunshine, the wisdom of his people is one of the ways that God blesses the world at large.

GOD'S OVERRULING MERCY

[Joseph] cried out, "Leave!" . . . So there was no one with Joseph when he identified himself to his brothers. But his sobbing was so violent that the Egyptians couldn't help but hear him. . . .

Joseph spoke to his brothers: . . . "I am Joseph your brother whom you sold into Egypt. But don't feel badly, don't blame yourselves for selling me. God was behind it. . . . God sent me on ahead to pave the way and make sure there was a remnant in the land, to save your lives in an amazing act of deliverance. So you see, it wasn't you who sent me here but God. He set me in place as a father to Pharaoh, put me in charge of his personal affairs, and made me ruler of all Egypt."

Genesis 45:1–5, 7–8 MSG

Consider what Joseph had been through. He had been sold into slavery. He had been falsely accused and thrown into prison. He had been separated for decades from his family and all because of a willful, malicious act on the part of his brothers. Then, in the middle of a famine, those same brothers went hat-in-hand to buy surplus grain from Egypt. They had no idea that the man in charge of the surplus was the brother they had betrayed so many years before.

Joseph was in a position to have revenge on his brothers. But instead, he initiated a tender family reunion. Why? In spite of his hardships, Joseph had never let himself grow bitter. Now at last he was able to see what God had been doing all those years.

Joseph's brothers had meant to do him evil, but God brought good out of the whole episode. Joseph had the wisdom to wait things out; he didn't assume he knew what God was up to. When we bring an eternal perspective to earthly events, we are freed from the bitterness that enslaves us and prevents us from being who God wants us to be.

A JOURNEY

It has been said that there are only two kinds of story: a stranger comes to town, or a person takes a trip. A good portion of the Old Testament is taken up with a trip—the Israelites' departure from Egypt, their forty years of wandering in the wilderness, and their occupation of the land that God had promised to their ancestor Abraham. What a long, strange trip it was! But through those struggles, a nation was

The LORD said [to Moses], "I have indeed seen the misery of my people in Egypt. I have heard them crying out because of their slave drivers, and I am concerned about their suffering. So I have come down to rescue them from the hand of the Egyptians and to bring them up out of that land into a good and spacious land, a land flowing with milk and honey—the home of the Canaanites, Hittites, Amorites, Perizzites, Hivites and Jebusites. And now the cry of the Israelites has reached me, and I have seen the way the Egyptians are oppressing them. So now, go. I am sending you to Pharaoh to bring my people the Israelites out of Egypt."

Exodus 3:7–10 NIV

The Pharaoh Who Forgot—and the God Who Didn't

A new king, who did not know about Joseph, came to power in Egypt. "Look," he said to his people, "the Israelites have become much too numerous for us. Come, we must deal shrewdly with them or they will become even more numerous and, if war breaks out, will join our enemies, fight against us and leave the country."

So they put slave masters over them to oppress them with forced labor, and they built Pithom and Rameses as store cities for Pharaoh. But the more they were oppressed, the more they multiplied and spread; so the Egyptians came to dread the Israelites and worked them ruthlessly. They made their lives bitter with hard labor in brick and mortar and with all kinds of work in the fields; in all their hard labor the Egyptians used them ruthlessly.

Exodus 1:8–14 NIV

Sometimes we seem to suffer for no reason. The Israelites had done nothing to show themselves disloyal or disobedient to Pharaoh. God blessed them as he had promised, giving them large and healthy families. Still, their oppression increased at the hands of the Egyptians. The Egyptians feared them, it seems, simply because there were so many of them.

We don't always know why we struggle and suffer. We try to lie low, keep under the radar, mind our own business; but sometimes the world just seems to have it in for us. That doesn't mean God has forgotten us, though. The new pharaoh did not know Joseph, or Abraham, Isaac, or Jacob, and certainly not the God they served. But God still knew his people, and he had not forgotten his promise to make them a great nation.

God has not forgotten us either. When we are in the midst of struggles, when we stagger under burdens, it helps to know that God has not forgotten. He has a plan to lead us into freedom. If we can hold on to hope, we will see God do great things.

SURPRISING DELIVERANCE

Pharaoh commanded all his people, saying, "Every son who is born you shall cast into the river." . . . And a man of the house of Levi went and took as wife a daughter of Levi. So the woman conceived and bore a son. . . . But when she could no longer hide him, she took an ark of bulrushes for him, daubed it with asphalt and pitch, put the child in it, and laid it in the reeds by the river's bank. . . .

Then the daughter of Pharaoh came down to bathe at the river. . . .

When she saw the ark among the reeds, she sent her maid to get it. And when she opened it, she saw the child, and behold, the baby wept. So she had compassion on him, and said, "This is one of the Hebrews' children."

Exodus 1:22–2:3, 5–6 NKJV

Suffering may come as a surprise, but that surprise is nothing compared to the surprise of God's deliverance. God delights in the unexpected twist. Moses' rescuer, after all, was the daughter of the very pharaoh who had ordered that all the Israelite boys be killed.

Plucked out of the water by a most unexpected heroine, Moses was just one of a long line of miracle babies in the Bible. God had promised Eve that the Savior to come would be one of her children. Abraham's son Isaac was a miracle baby. And ultimately, another miracle baby was born to Mary, and that baby became the promised Savior.

Moses' miraculous rescue was just one link in the chain that became the miraculous rescue of the Israelites—and ultimately the miraculous rescue of all God's people through Jesus. Sometimes a situation looks incredibly grim. But as in the case of Moses, God sends help from unexpected places, in large trouble and small. It may not come in the form of a miracle birth. It may not come from someone close to the source of our trouble. But God's help is just right and just in time.

GOD'S WORK, GOD'S WAY

Moses grew and became a man. One day [Moses] visited his people and saw that they were forced to work very hard. He saw an Egyptian beating a Hebrew man, one of Moses' own people. Moses looked all around and saw that no one was watching, so he killed the Egyptian and hid his body in the sand.

The next day Moses returned and saw two Hebrew men fighting each other. He said to the one that was in the wrong, "Why are you hitting one of your own people?"

The man answered, "Who made you our ruler and judge? Are you going to kill me as you killed the Egyptian?"

Moses was afraid and thought, "Now everyone knows what I did." . . . Moses ran away from the king and went to live in the land of Midian.

Exodus 2:11–15 NCV

"Moses looked all around and saw that no one was watching." That was the first clue that Moses was headed down the wrong path. As it turned out, Moses was wrong; one of his fellow Hebrews saw what he had done. And even if no other person had witnessed his act of murder, God would have seen it.

Moses' real problem wasn't that he was caught. The bigger problem was Moses' attempt to do God's work using human methods. He could have killed Egyptians all day, seven days a week, but he wasn't going to deliver the Israelites that way. God's plans did not involve popular revolt.

Throughout the story of redemptive history, God put his people in impossible situations—situations in which it was patently obvious that if things worked out all right, it was only because God intervened. It is hard to wait on God to do what only God can do. We want to take control. But God is forever putting us in situations that are beyond our control. In the end, we have no choice but to wait on God—we cannot deliver ourselves.

A Surprising Assignment

God called to him from out of the bush, "Moses! Moses!"

He said, "Yes? I'm right here!" . . .

Then he said, "I am the God of your father: The God of Abraham, the God of Isaac, the God of Jacob." Moses hid his face, afraid to look at God.

God said, "I've taken a good, long look at the affliction of my people in Egypt. I've heard their cries for deliverance from their slave masters; I know all about their pain. And now I have come down to help them, pry them loose from the grip of Egypt, get them out of that country and bring them to a good land with wide-open spaces, a land lush with milk and honey. . . .

"It's time for you to go back: I'm sending you to Pharaoh to bring my people, the People of Israel, out of Egypt."

Exodus 3:4, 6–10 MSG

Consider the amazing personal history of the man who stood before the burning bush. He had grown up in the court of the Egyptian pharaoh, the most powerful king on the planet at that time. In the decades since, he had been on the run, a disgraced criminal. When God appeared to him to assign him an impossible mission, Moses was an old man doing the menial work of herding sheep in the middle of nowhere.

But God didn't mention Moses' past. He didn't mention Moses' qualifications. God told Moses who God was, because that was all that mattered. He was the God who made—and kept—promises to the patriarchs. He was the God who was motivated now by compassion. And he was the God who still had blessings in store for his people.

When God lays a task before us, we sometimes look to ourselves and fret over our failures or our shortcomings. Sometimes we look at the size of the task and it seems impossible. But nothing is impossible for God. If we keep our eyes on him, we can do whatever he calls us to do.

WHO AM I, LORD? WHO ARE YOU?

Moses asked God, "Who am I that I should go to Pharaoh and that I should bring the Israelites out of Egypt?" . . . Then Moses asked God, "If I go to the Israelites and say to them: The God of your fathers has sent me to you, and they ask me, 'What is His name?' what should I tell them?"

God replied to Moses, "I AM WHO I AM. This is what you are to say to the Israelites: I AM has sent me to you." God also said to Moses, "Say this to the Israelites: Yahweh, the God of your fathers, the God of Abraham, the God of Isaac, and the God of Jacob, has sent me to you. This is My name forever; this is how I am to be remembered in every generation."

Exodus 3:11, 13–15 HCSB

When God first told Moses of the task he had for him, Moses' first question was "Who am I?" That question turned quickly, however, into "Who are you?" He asked God his name, in hopes that a name would give some clue as to who exactly was speaking to him. What kind of God speaks to men from burning bushes? What kind of God sends old men to challenge powerful kings and free entire nations from slavery?

"I AM WHO I AM," God answered. God's existence speaks for itself. He won't be bound or limited by any other name. But when God said, "I Am," he also said, "I was." He was the same God Abraham, Isaac, and Jacob knew. And he said, "I Will Be." I AM was a name for every generation.

The first truth to know about God is simply that HE IS. That can be hard, especially in a world that is always saying, "Show me." God is. He is the same yesterday, today, and forever. And he still cares about setting us, his people, free.

A Showdown in Pharaoh's Court

"The Egyptians will know that I am the Lord when I stretch out my hand against Egypt and bring the Israelites out of it. . . .

"When Pharaoh says to you, 'Perform a miracle,' then say to Aaron, 'Take your staff and throw it down before Pharaoh,' and it will become a snake."

So Moses and Aaron went to Pharaoh and did just as the Lord commanded. Aaron threw his staff down in front of Pharaoh and his officials, and it became a snake. Pharaoh then summoned wise men and sorcerers, and the Egyptian magicians also did the same things by their secret arts: Each one threw down his staff and it became a snake. But Aaron's staff swallowed up their staffs. Yet Pharaoh's heart became hard and he would not listen to them, just as the Lord had said.

Exodus 7:5, 9–13 NIV

God had a plan to see his people freed from slavery. But the plan wasn't just freedom for his people. He freed them so that it would be known that he was God. He was not content for the Israelites to sneak away in the middle of the night, or while Pharaoh was out of town. No, through Moses God challenged Pharaoh face-to-face, staff for staff, and snake for snake. God orchestrated a showdown in which he would challenge Pharaoh's authority in those areas where Pharaoh's authority was believed to be ultimate.

When God saves us, it is not enough that we be narrowly saved at the last minute. He challenges all authorities that might lay a claim to us in this life. We might feel bound by our culture, our circumstances, and our personal histories. These things can be powerful. But as God showed in the court of Pharaoh, he is more powerful than any earthly power, however ultimate it seems. As he stakes his claim on us, he wants the world to know his power and his rule. Through his people, God demonstrates that he alone is God.

Liberation Got Ugly

[God said,] "Moses, then command Aaron to hold his stick over the water. And when he does, every drop of water in Egypt will turn into blood." . . .

Moses and Aaron obeyed the Lord. Aaron held out his stick, then struck the Nile, as the king and his officials watched. The river turned into blood, the fish died, and the water smelled so bad that none of the Egyptians could drink it. Blood was everywhere in Egypt.

But the Egyptian magicians used their secret powers to do the same thing. The king did just as the Lord had said—he stubbornly refused to listen. Then he went back to his palace and never gave it a second thought. The Egyptians had to dig holes along the banks of the Nile for drinking water, because water from the river was unfit to drink.

Exodus 7:19–24 CEV

The liberation of the Israelites from slavery got ugly. The Egyptians viewed the Nile River as a source of life—and rightly so—not just for the drinking water, but because its annual floods created the bountiful harvests that fed the land. That the Nile turned to blood foreshadowed not life, but death.

In the daily lives of the Egyptians, the only bigger deal than the Nile would have been Pharaoh himself. All of this ugliness was a direct challenge to his authority. But his hired magicians could produce blood too. His power was confirmed, so he shrugged and walked away. The river was still polluted. It still stank of dead fish. The people had nothing to drink. But Pharaoh didn't care. He was still in charge.

Leaving behind our lives of bondage can get ugly too. Satan, the ruler of the land of our slavery, cares nothing for our well-being; he cares about only his own power. Satan does not give in without a fight. Sometimes old friends side with him and make it hard to follow God. But in the end, God delivers his people.

ISRAEL'S EMANCIPATION PROCLAMATION

Moses called all the elders of Israel together and said to them, "Go, pick out a lamb or young goat for each of your families, and slaughter the Passover animal. Drain the blood into a basin. Then take a bundle of hyssop branches and dip it into the blood. Brush the hyssop across the top and sides of the doorframes of your houses. And no one may go out through the door until morning. For the LORD will pass through the land to strike down the Egyptians. But when he sees the blood on the top and sides of the doorframe, the LORD will pass over your home. He will not permit his death angel to enter your house and strike you down.

"Remember, these instructions are a permanent law that you and your descendants must observe forever."

Exodus 12:21–24 NLT

The Passover was the defining event for the people of Israel. It was their emancipation proclamation, the day their Berlin wall came down, the end of their apartheid. Not only did it mark their freedom from slavery, but it also established their beginning as a nation.

That first Passover wasn't a party; it was a grisly blood sacrifice. This was not just a political liberation. God was changing things on a cosmic scale. The Israelites would now be free, yes, but in many other ways, the world would never be the same. What God was doing was not safe or tidy. The angel of death was not one to be trifled with. Only the blood of the sacrificial lamb kept him from the houses of God's people too.

The Passover was an early picture of God's plan to deliver his people. As the Lamb of God, Jesus spares us from the angel of death. We enjoy a new freedom and a new identity because of him. But we can never trivialize what it took to get us here. Instead, we worship in humble awe.

An Avoidable Tragedy

At midnight the Lord killed the first-born son of every Egyptian family, from the son of the king to the son of every prisoner in jail. He also killed the first-born male of every animal that belonged to the Egyptians. That night the king, his officials, and everyone else in Egypt got up and started crying bitterly. In every Egyptian home, someone was dead.

During the night the king sent for Moses and Aaron and told them, "Get your people out of my country and leave us alone! Go and worship the Lord, as you have asked. Take your sheep, goats, and cattle, and get out. But ask your God to be kind to me." The Egyptians did everything they could to get the Israelites to leave their country fast. They said, "Please hurry and leave. If you don't, we will all be dead."

Exodus 12:29–33 CEV

The slaying of the firstborn sons breaks our hearts even today. With nine plagues as warnings, it seemed such an avoidable tragedy. But Pharaoh's heart was hard. He was content to see his country decimated rather than admit his fault—until the destruction came to his house. He had to be broken. He had to learn the limits of his power and the limitlessness of God's. Once he learned where he stood, he chased Moses and the Israelites out of his country, and he begged that Moses ask his God to be kind to him.

This is sinful humanity's grasp of God. We want nothing to do with him when we are on top. When tragedy strikes, we would chase him away. But God is kind to us. He is more than kind. In yet another amazing reversal, God gave his own Firstborn to pay the penalty for our wrongdoing and to set us free.

Even in our most difficult hardships, we need not fight or resist as Pharaoh did; instead, God invites us to join with those singing songs of freedom as we travel to the promised land.

Fear Not, Stand Firm

When Pharaoh drew near, the people of Israel lifted up their eyes, and behold, the Egyptians were marching after them, and they feared greatly. And the people of Israel cried out to the LORD. They said to Moses, "Is it because there are no graves in Egypt that you have taken us away to die in the wilderness? What have you done to us in bringing us out of Egypt? Is not this what we said to you in Egypt, 'Leave us alone that we may serve the Egyptians'? For it would have been better for us to serve the Egyptians than to die in the wilderness."

And Moses said to the people, "Fear not, stand firm, and see the salvation of the LORD, which he will work for you today."

Exodus 14:10–13 ESV

Pharaoh had second thoughts about letting the people of Israel go, and so he pursued them. When the people saw Pharaoh and his army, their fear of their old enemy was stronger than their confidence in God. Pharaoh enslaved the people of Israel. He oppressed them. He killed their little boys. But at the Passover, the Lord clearly proved that he was more powerful than Pharaoh and that the Israelites were his people, not Pharaoh's people. How quickly Pharaoh forgot. But, tragically, God's people forgot too.

It's easy for us too to forget God's deliverance. Our enemies are tangible and familiar, while God's deliverance is supernatural, mysterious, and seemingly far away. But the invisible, as it turns out, is truer than the visible. God is all-powerful. He can and will defeat our enemies and deliver us from sin and bondage. He has already. No matter what Satan and the world stack up against us, God will never leave us or forsake us. We can have limitless confidence even in the face of impossible odds. Don't be afraid. Just watch the Lord at work.

HOPE AT THE BOTTOM OF THE SEA

Moses stretched out his hand over the sea; and the LORD caused the sea to go back by a strong east wind all that night, and made the sea into dry land, and the waters were divided. So the children of Israel went into the midst of the sea on the dry ground, and the waters were a wall to them on their right hand and on their left. And the Egyptians pursued [them]. . . .

The LORD said to Moses, "Stretch out your hand over the sea, that the waters may come back upon the Egyptians, on their chariots, and on their horsemen." And Moses stretched out his hand over the sea; and when the morning appeared, the sea returned to its full depth, while the Egyptians were fleeing into it. So the LORD overthrew the Egyptians in the midst of the sea.

Exodus 14:21–23, 26–27 NKJV

Behind the Israelites was the Egyptian army, perhaps the mightiest in the world. In front of them was a sea. Moses had hope, however. He urged the people to stand still, to watch for what God would do for them. And he was proven right. The Red Sea divided, and the people walked across to the other side. The pursuing army drowned in the sea.

Sometimes God's work is spectacular. It doesn't get much more dramatic than an ocean parting, and walls of water standing on either side as people walk on the sandy bottom of the sea. Usually, God's work is not so spectacular. But it is no less miraculous. The supernatural is forever exerting itself in the world where we live.

In spiritual terms, we face impossible odds—all of us. We exist in the spiritual as well as the bodily realm, and yet our spiritual resources are fundamentally lacking. Our enemies are immeasurably stronger than we are. We could no more save ourselves than the Israelites could save themselves from the Egyptians. But God intervenes. He splits the sea, and we walk to safety.

Moses' Song of Joy

Who is like You among the gods, O Lord? Who is like You, majestic in holiness, awesome in praises, working wonders?

You stretched out Your right hand, the earth swallowed them.

In Your lovingkindness You have led the people whom You have redeemed; in Your strength You have guided them to Your holy habitation.

The peoples have heard, they tremble; anguish has gripped the inhabitants of Philistia.

Then the chiefs of Edom were dismayed; the leaders of Moab, trembling grips them; all the inhabitants of Canaan have melted away.

Terror and dread fall upon them; by the greatness of Your arm they are motionless as stone; until Your people pass over, O Lord, until the people pass over whom You have purchased.

Exodus 15:11–16 NASB

Where there had been no hope, suddenly there was hope. The darkness gave way to brilliant light as Moses and the people stood on the far side of the sea. There on the seashore, Moses sang a song of irrepressible joy. "Who is like you among the gods?" he asked. The true God had exerted his authority over the Egyptian oppressors. He had wielded his authority over the sea itself, and even the sea obeyed.

The parting of the Red Sea changed the Israelites' perspective completely. God was on their side, and if God was for them, who could stand against them? The weak things of the world were putting the strong things to shame—or rather, through the weak things of the world, God was demonstrating just how strong he was.

There on the edge of the sea, sanity exerted itself. Moses and the Israelites stopped long enough to recognize what God had been doing. Terror gave way to praise and thanksgiving. That's an important skill—the ability to stop and say, "Thank you, God!" The God who delivered the Israelites delivers us too. If he is on our side, who can stand against us?

DAILY BREAD, RADICAL TRUST

When the layer of dew evaporated, behold, on the surface of the wilderness there was a fine flake-like thing, fine as the frost on the ground.

When the sons of Israel saw it, they said to one another, "What is it?" For they did not know what it was. And Moses said to them, "It is the bread which the LORD has given you to eat.

"This is what the LORD has commanded, 'Gather of it every man as much as he should eat; you shall take an omer apiece according to the number of persons each of you has in his tent.'"

The sons of Israel did so, and some gathered much and some little.

When they measured it with an omer, he who had gathered much had no excess, and he who had gathered little had no lack; every man gathered as much as he should eat.

Moses said to them, "Let no man leave any of it until morning."

But they did not listen to Moses, and some left part of it until morning, and it bred worms and became foul; and Moses was angry with them.

Exodus 16:14–20 NASB

In the wilderness, the traveling Israelites were in danger of starving. So God provided manna—a breadlike substance that the Israelites could gather in the morning for their daily sustenance.

There would always be enough, God promised. There was just one rule: the Israelites couldn't store the manna. They had to gather only as much as they needed each day and trust that God would provide the next day. The Sabbath was the exception; they could gather a double portion the day before to get them through the day of rest.

But some of the Israelites couldn't bring themselves to trust. They gathered extra manna and hid it away for later. And it got wormy and rotten in just one day!

God teaches us not to trust in our own resources.

Raised Hands of Support

At Rephidim the Amalekites came and fought the Israelites. So Moses said to Joshua, "Choose some men and go and fight the Amalekites. Tomorrow I will stand on the top of the hill, holding the walking stick of God in my hands."

Joshua obeyed Moses and went to fight the Amalekites, while Moses, Aaron, and Hur went to the top of the hill. As long as Moses held his hands up, the Israelites would win the fight, but when Moses put his hands down, the Amalekites would win. Later, when Moses' arms became tired, the men put a large rock under him, and he sat on it. Then Aaron and Hur held up Moses' hands—Aaron on one side and Hur on the other. They kept his hands steady until the sun went down. So Joshua defeated the Amalekites in this battle.

Exodus 17:8–13 NCV

From his place high on the hill, Moses could see the battle raging between the Israelites and the desert tribe of the Amalekites. He held in his hands the staff of God—a sign of his office, but more important, the symbol of God's power, for it was God who fought on behalf of his people. When Moses raised high the staff, he could see the line of Israelite fighters surge forward while the Amalekites fell back. When he lowered the staff, the Amalekites beat back the Israelites.

It was a long day of fighting, and Moses was an old man. As the sun got lower in the sky, he couldn't keep his arms up. That's when Moses' brother Aaron and a man named Hur stepped in and gave Moses the support he needed to finish the day.

Believers need one another. The days get long, and we get weary. We need fellow Christians to say, "Here, let me carry some of that burden for you." Like Aaron and Hur, we need to offer help; like Moses, we need to receive it. It's how God's work keeps moving forward.

REMEMBRANCE, HOPE, AND THE LAW

Moses went up [the mountain] to God, and the LORD called to him from the mountain: "This is what you must say to the house of Jacob, and explain to the Israelites: You have seen what I did to the Egyptians and how I carried you on eagles' wings and brought you to Me. Now if you will listen to Me and carefully keep My covenant, you will be My own possession out of all the peoples, although all the earth is Mine, and you will be My kingdom of priests and My holy nation." . . .

After Moses came back, he summoned the elders of the people, and put before them all these words that the LORD had commanded him. Then all the people responded together, "We will do all that the LORD has spoken." So Moses brought the people's words back to the LORD.

Exodus 19:3–8 HCSB

When he gave the law to his people, God might have started with "Here's what I'm going to do to you if you don't keep the rules I'm about to give you." But that's not where he started. He started with "Here's what I've done for you already." He had destroyed their Egyptian oppressors. He had carried the Israelites as if on the wings of eagles and brought them to himself.

Then, when God spoke of the future, he spoke of the rewards of obedience. It was his desire, he said, to make the Israelites his special possession among all the nations. He wanted to make of them a kingdom of priests. That's an amazing idea: an obedient, law-abiding people—a holy people—wouldn't need a king to rule over them. They would answer directly to God. Even the most average person would be a priest.

The basis of the law, in short, was relationship, not fear. In God's plan, the Israelites would obey out of gratitude for the things God had done for them and out of hope wrought by the benefits of obedience.

THE FIRST TABLE OF THE LAW

"I am the LORD your God, who brought you out of Egypt, out of the land of slavery.

"You shall have no other gods before me.

"You shall not make for yourself an idol in the form of anything in heaven above or on the earth beneath or in the waters below. . . .

"You shall not misuse the name of the LORD your God, for the LORD will not hold any-one guiltless who misuses his name.

"Remember the Sabbath day by keeping it holy. Six days you shall labor and do all your work, but the seventh day is a Sabbath to the LORD your God. On it you shall not do any work, neither you, nor your son or daughter, nor your manservant or maidservant, nor your animals, nor the alien within your gates."

Exodus 20:2–4, 7–10 NIV

Bible teachers sometimes divide the Ten Commandments into two "tables." The first table, the first through the fourth commandments, is concerned with our relationship with God. The second table, commandments six through ten, is about our relationship with one another. You might say the first four commandments are vertical, from earth to heaven, and the last six are horizontal, all about loving your neighbor.

People sometimes say there is nothing uniquely Judeo-Christian about the Ten Commandments. When it comes to the second table, that's true enough: almost all moral codes agree that it's bad to lie, steal, and murder. It's the first table that is specifically Judeo-Christian. Apart from a belief in the God of the Bible—indeed, apart from a relationship with him—those four commandments make no sense. There's no general-purpose morality here.

The "love your neighbor" commandments find their origin (and their motivation) in the imperative to love and revere God. If we honor God, we want to honor those who are made in his image. If we don't honor God, we're severely limited in our ability to love our neighbors; in fact, we can't love them in a truly meaningful way.

THUNDER AND GRACE

Honor your father and mother so that you'll live a long time in the land that GOD, your God, is giving you. No murder. No adultery. No stealing. No lies about your neighbor. No lusting after your neighbor's house—or wife or servant or maid or ox or donkey. Don't set your heart on anything that is your neighbor's.

All the people, experiencing the thunder and lightning, the trumpet blast and the smoking mountain, were afraid—they pulled back and stood at a distance. They said to Moses, "You speak to us and we'll listen, but don't have God speak to us or we'll die."

Moses spoke to the people: "Don't be afraid. God has come to test you and instill a deep and reverent awe within you so that you won't sin."

Exodus 20:12–20 MSG

After God laid down the law, he offered up a display that helped the Israelites understand what was at stake. Thunder boomed. Lightning streaked across the sky. Smoke rose in clouds, and, above it all, a trumpet horn blasted across the valley. The people were reminded of power, the majesty, the sheer otherness of God. *That* was the God they offended when they broke the law. The people were terrified. But Moses spoke with a voice of compassion. He urged them not to be afraid—to be in awe of God, yes, but not to be afraid.

God's law shows us how best to live with one another. But that's not the only purpose of the law—or even the most important purpose. Just as the lightning and smoke showed the Israelites how small they were before God, the law demonstrates just how far we fall short of God's plan for us. We cannot keep the whole law. We simply don't have it in us. The law shows us just how desperately we need the grace and mercy of God. Thankfully, he is a mighty God—and mighty to save.

SEAT OF MERCY

Tell the people to build a chest of acacia wood forty-five inches long, twenty-seven inches wide, and twenty-seven inches high. Cover it inside and out with pure gold and put a gold edging around the lid. . . . When I give you the Ten Commandments written on two flat stones, put them inside the chest.

Cover the lid of the chest with pure gold. Then hammer out two winged creatures of pure gold and fasten them to the lid at the ends of the chest. The creatures must face each other with their wings spread over the chest. Inside it place the two flat stones with the Ten Commandments and put the gold lid on top of the chest. I will meet you there between the two creatures and tell you what my people must do and what they must not do.

Exodus 25:10–11, 16–22 CEV

God's instructions for the design of the ark of the covenant were very specific. Not a single detail was left to chance. The same Creator God who chose the unique features of every plant and animal on the earth had strict requirements for the place in which his holy presence would come to visit.

The ark's lid was known as the atonement cover, or mercy seat. It was a royal throne, fit for the divine king. Carved from sturdy brownish-orange acacia wood and wrapped in pure gold, the seat covered and enveloped the stone tablets containing the law. God rested between them. That's an amazing picture. The law on those two tablets—the law that binds us—is covered by God's mercy.

The mercy seat provided a powerful symbol of God's protection. Through the law, God calls us to a high standard—higher than we can possibly keep in our own strength and morality. But over that stony law is the beautiful seat of mercy, enveloping and covering it—and protecting us from our own failures. Even in the laying down of the law, mercy sets the tone.

Worship at the Feet of an Idol

When the people saw that Moses delayed to come down from the mountain, the people assembled about Aaron and said to him, "Come, make us a god who will go before us; as for this Moses, the man who brought us up from the land of Egypt, we do not know what has become of him."

Aaron said to them, "Tear off the gold rings which are in the ears of your wives, your sons, and your daughters, and bring them to me."

Then all the people tore off the gold rings which were in their ears and brought them to Aaron.

He took this from their hand, and fashioned it with a graving tool and made it into a molten calf; and they said, "This is your god, O Israel, who brought you up from the land of Egypt."

Exodus 32:1–4 NASB

Fresh out of Egypt, the Israelites had a hard time letting go of that Fertile Crescent custom of idol worship. Moses had been gone for weeks meeting with God, and the people were impatient for a God they could see. They were surrounded by Canaanites who worshipped Baal, a god in the shape of a bull.

Aaron at last gave in to the crowd's pressure and suggested that they melt down their earrings and make an image of a calf out of the gold. There was a god that was manageable, easy—much more sensible than the invisible God that smoked and thundered from the mountaintops.

We're not so different from the Israelites who built the golden calf just weeks after God had given the command against idolatry. We're always tempted to shape God to our liking, to make him into something that we find convenient to worship—or to ignore. The true God isn't so easily controlled or manipulated. When we try to mold God to fit our own desires, we end up worshipping ourselves rather than the Almighty who created us.

IN THE CLEFT OF THE ROCK

Moses said, "If your presence doesn't take the lead here, call this trip off right now. How else will it be known that you're with me in this, with me and your people? . . .

"Please. Let me see your Glory."

GOD said, "I will make my Goodness pass right in front of you; I'll call out the name, GOD, right before you. I'll treat well whomever I want to treat well and I'll be kind to whomever I want to be kind."

GOD continued, "But you may not see my face. No one can see me and live."

GOD said, "Look, here is a place right beside me. Put yourself on this rock. When my Glory passes by, I'll put you in the cleft of the rock and cover you with my hand until I've passed by. Then I'll take my hand away and you'll see my back. But you won't see my face."

Exodus 33:15, 18–23 MSG

Moses was frustrated and furious when he came down from his lengthy conference with God on Mount Sinai to find the people dancing around the golden statue of a calf. In disgust, Moses threw down the holy tablets, tossed the calf into the fire, ground it into powder, and make the Israelites drink the whole nasty thing.

Eventually Moses' rage was spent, and he once again felt compassion for the Israelites. He prayed for God's mercy on the people. He was ready to pick up and move ahead. But he needed one thing if he was going to have the strength to continue. He needed to see God's glory, which is to say, Moses needed to be reminded why he was doing all this and why it was worth the trouble. It was all about God's glory.

It's easy to burn out when we lose sight of the big picture—when we get the idea that our efforts are for our own comfort or security or glory. If we're going to have the strength to carry on, every now and then we need to take a step back and see God's glory.

A Face That Shines

Moses did not know that the skin of his face shone while he talked with Him.

So when Aaron and all the children of Israel saw Moses, behold, the skin of his face shone, and they were afraid to come near him.

Then Moses called to them, and Aaron and all the rulers of the congregation returned to him; and Moses talked with them.

Afterward all the children of Israel came near, and he gave them as commandments all that the LORD had spoken with him on Mount Sinai.

And when Moses had finished speaking with them, he put a veil on his face.

But whenever Moses went in before the LORD to speak with Him, he would take the veil off until he came out; and he would come out and speak to the children of Israel whatever he had been commanded.

Exodus 34:29–34 NKJV

Moses went back up the mountain another forty days and forty nights. He was in the presence of God, and when he came back, his face was glowing. It was obvious he'd been with Someone other than a human. Instead of being comforted, the people felt afraid again. They had never seen a man's face lit up with dazzling brilliance.

Again, this came down to the Israelites' wanting a God who was a little more manageable, not so other. That God transcended, and he made much bigger, all-encompassing claims than the claims they were used to hearing. The polytheistic gods of the ancient Near East were exaggerated versions of things known from the natural world—animals, the sun, the moon. None of those things turned the worshipper's face into a scary light show.

Idols have no power to transform anyone with light. Neither do our idols—comfort, pleasure, money, self, or anything else we look to for meaning and significance. There is no light in those things. But as we spend time praying and worshipping the true God, it will be obvious to those around us that we have a light coming from within.

THE WORK OF SKILLED HANDS

Moses said to the people of Israel, "See, the LORD has called by name Bezalel the son of Uri, son of Hur, of the tribe of Judah; and he has filled him with the Spirit of God, with skill, with intelligence, with knowledge, and with all craftsmanship, to devise artistic designs, to work in gold and silver and bronze, in cutting stones for setting, and in carving wood, for work in every skilled craft.

"And he has inspired him to teach, both him and Oholiab the son of Ahisamach of the tribe of Dan. He has filled them with skill to do every sort of work done by an engraver or by a designer or by an embroiderer in blue and purple and scarlet yarns and fine twined linen, or by a weaver—by any sort of workman or skilled designer."

Exodus 35:30–35 ESV

The building of the tabernacle required a massive community effort. Those were times when every thread was spun by hand. Most people didn't have more than a couple of changes of clothing, unless they were wealthy. Skilled craftsmen were used to working on their own, making pieces they could sell individually to provide food for their own families.

When God called Bezalel to come forward as an artisan, he instilled in him talents beyond normal gifts. The Master Designer worked through Bezalel's hands to accomplish the goal of creating the tools and the setting for proper worship. Bezalel obeyed, and he went beyond his own efforts by teaching others, which served to multiply and magnify his artistry.

God is still building the tabernacle through the hands of his people today. No one skill is more important than another skill. A preacher's voice isn't more significant than a plumber's hands that install pipes to bring forth running water. Everyone has a talent that can be used to further the kingdom. The gifts of our unique design, brought into unity, continue God's movement of inhabiting every nation on earth.

BRINGING YOUR BEST TO GOD

Whatever man of the house of Israel . . . who offers his sacrifice for any of his vows or for any of his freewill offerings, which they offer to the LORD as a burnt offering—you shall offer of your own free will a male without blemish from the cattle, from the sheep, or from the goats. Whatever has a defect, you shall not offer, for it shall not be acceptable on your behalf. And whoever offers a sacrifice of a peace offering to the LORD, to fulfill his vow, or a freewill offering from the cattle or the sheep, it must be perfect to be accepted; there shall be no defect in it. Those that are blind or broken or maimed, or have an ulcer or eczema or scabs, you shall not offer to the LORD.

Leviticus 22:18–22 NKJV

When the tabernacle was set up for worship, God wanted his people to bring him animals without any defects. Only perfect animals could be accepted because they mirrored God's perfect, holy nature. Giving away the best cattle or sheep was a hard thing for the Hebrew farmers, who needed healthy animals to earn a living. Handing them over was one tangible way they could demonstrate their love for God.

God still requires that we bring him our best. It is tempting to give God the leftovers of our "real" lives—the lives of getting and spending. But God isn't fooled. Our time, energy, and earthly goods all come from him anyway; there's no sense in hoarding what never really belonged to us in the first place.

In a worldly sense, there's no return on the investment when we give our resources to God. But that's just the point. When we give to God, we acknowledge that there is something better and more important than the things the world considers valuable. When we turn our earthly goods over to God, they take on a new significance that transcends their earthly value.

THE WAGES OF SIN

[God said,] "If you will not listen to me and carry out all these commands, and if you reject my decrees and abhor my laws and fail to carry out all my commands and so violate my covenant, then I will do this to you: I will bring upon you sudden terror, wasting diseases and fever that will destroy your sight and drain away your life. You will plant seed in vain, because your enemies will eat it. I will set my face against you so that you will be defeated by your enemies; those who hate you will rule over you, and you will flee even when no one is pursuing you. . . .

"Your strength will be spent in vain, because your soil will not yield its crops, nor will the trees of the land yield their fruit."

Leviticus 26:14–17, 20 NIV

If the Israelites were wondering whether God was serious about their obedience, this passage clears it all up. No gray issues here—either they obeyed or they didn't. God promised them peace and longevity if they chose to do what he asked; on the other side, he made it clear that if they strayed, disaster would wipe them out.

Sin has consequences—natural, built-in consequences that ripple through our lives and the lives of those around us. This world is out of whack, subject to futility and hurt in the best of circumstances, and subject to even more futility and more hurt when our sin makes things worse.

In our own lives, it's not always possible to trace the source of tragedy. It could be the result of personal disobedience, someone else's mistakes, or merely the devastating result of natural disaster. Going through a hard time should make us want to search our hearts and be sure we're at peace with our heavenly Father. His Spirit will reveal those areas we need to sift through, digging out stubborn areas of sin so that we can move back closer to him, where he wants us to be.

GOD REMEMBERS

[God said,] "On the other hand, if they confess their sins and the sins of their ancestors, their treacherous betrayal, the defiance that set off my defiance that sent them off into enemy lands; if by some chance they soften their hard hearts and make amends for their sin, I'll remember my covenant with Jacob, I'll remember my covenant with Isaac, and, yes, I'll remember my covenant with Abraham. And I'll remember the land. . . .

"But in spite of their behavior, while they are among their enemies I won't reject or abhor or destroy them completely. I won't break my covenant with them: I am GOD, their God. For their sake I will remember the covenant with their ancestors whom I, with all the nations watching, brought out of Egypt in order to be their God. I am GOD."

Leviticus 26:40–42, 44–45
MSG

Slow to anger. Abounding in love. It's a pattern that pops up repeatedly in Scripture. In Exodus, Numbers, Nehemiah, Psalms, Jonah, and all the way to the book of James in the New Testament, that character trait—slowness in matters of anger and quickness in matters of love—is one that most defines the God of the universe.

Even if the Israelites chose to disobey, even if they were scattered among their enemies as a result, God promised he would still give them a chance to repent and return to him. His ultimate purpose was not to destroy them, but to help them rise up and flourish as a nation.

God's mercies are still new every morning, just as the sun rises after a night of darkness. He didn't give up on the Hebrew people, and he won't give up on us. Even though we forget, God remembers. When we can hold on to hope even in the midst of suffering, it shows we understand God's merciful ways of relating to us. And it makes us a little more like God—slower to anger and quicker to forgive.

CLOUD BY DAY, PILLAR BY NIGHT

On the day the Tabernacle was set up, the cloud covered it. But from evening until morning the cloud over the Tabernacle looked like a pillar of fire. This was the regular pattern—at night the cloud that covered the Tabernacle had the appearance of fire. Whenever the cloud lifted from over the sacred tent, the people of Israel would break camp and follow it. And wherever the cloud settled, the people of Israel would set up camp. In this way, they traveled and camped at the LORD's command wherever he told them to go. Then they remained in their camp as long as the cloud stayed over the Tabernacle. . . .

So they camped or traveled at the LORD's command, and they did whatever the LORD told them through Moses.

Numbers 9:15–18, 23 NLT

When Moses led the Israelites out of Egypt, they were in a hurry to get out. Four hundred years of bondage can do that to you. It seemed the Promised Land was just around the corner. Except that it wasn't.

Weeks passed, then months, then years. Their sandals didn't wear out, and most of them stayed hopeful that someday they'd be settled in a land flowing with milk and honey. But for the time being, the Israelites pitched their tents and broke them down, ready to move whenever the cloud or the fiery pillar of God's presence let them know it was time to move on.

It's harder to follow God when we can't see him. Most of us aren't navigating with a miracle cloud hovering over the next step in our journey. And nights without a pillar of fire can seem long and lonely indeed. But we don't have to be summoned by cloud or fire to know he's there because we have God's Word, the Bible. When we remain in his presence, we can trust we're following God. Even if it seems that we're staying in one place, God is still accomplishing his work.

Two Ways of Complaining to God

Moses heard the people weeping throughout their clans, everyone at the door of his tent. And the anger of the Lord blazed hotly, and Moses was displeased.

Moses said to the Lord, "Why have you dealt ill with your servant? And why have I not found favor in your sight, that you lay the burden of all this people on me? Did I conceive all this people? Did I give them birth, that you should say to me, 'Carry them in your bosom, as a nurse carries a nursing child,' to the land that you swore to give their fathers? Where am I to get meat to give to all this people? For they weep before me and say, 'Give us meat, that we may eat.' I am not able to carry all this people alone; the burden is too heavy for me."

Numbers 11:10–14 ESV

In spite of all God had done for them, the Israelites seemed to have the impression that God was stingy or forgetful in the matter of providing for their needs. Turning up their noses at the manna God faithfully provided, they longed for the food they had eaten when they were still slaves in Egypt.

Moses was exhausted with them. His frustration expressed itself in a complaint to God. "Why are you doing this to me?" he wanted to know. Moses seemed to have an attitude problem. Maybe he *did* have an attitude problem. But he brought his attitude problem to God. He didn't hide from God or put on a false happy face and then go try to solve his problem without God's help. He said, in effect, "These are your people, God, and I need you to deal with them."

God can work with that kind of honesty when we pray, "Lord, I'm angry and frustrated and flummoxed, and I need you to step in here." When we bring ourselves to God—the good, the bad, and the ugly—God shows up and does amazing things.

MOSES' ZEAL FOR GLORY

Moses went out and told the people the words of the LORD, and he gathered the seventy men of the elders of the people and placed them around the tabernacle. Then the LORD came down in the cloud, and spoke to him, and took of the Spirit that was upon him, and placed the same upon the seventy elders. . . .

Two men had remained in the camp: the name of one was Eldad, and the name of the other Medad. And the Spirit rested upon them. . . . They prophesied in the camp. . . . So Joshua the son of Nun, Moses' assistant, one of his choice men, answered and said, "Moses my lord, forbid them!"

Then Moses said to him, "Are you zealous for my sake? Oh, that all the LORD's people were prophets and that the LORD would put His Spirit upon them!"

Numbers 11:24–26, 28–29
NKJV

Moses was in serious danger of burning out. It was a big job that God had given him, and it was apparent that he wouldn't be able to do it alone. So God placed his Spirit on seventy men—deputies, you might say. When two of the men came out of the tabernacle and began prophesying out in public, Joshua saw a problem. Those men, he believed, were a threat to Moses' authority. Moses did the prophesying around there, and Joshua was protective of his boss's unique role. Perhaps Joshua also saw Eldad and Medad as threats to his own position. He urged Moses to correct the rogue prophets. But Moses didn't feel threatened. He welcomed any manifestation of God's presence.

Even in spiritual matters, ego exerts itself. The story of Moses reminds us, however, that we need not be zealous for our own glory, but for God's. We need to encourage and equip others to serve, and to see the kingdom of God move forward and expand, not to protect our spiritual turf. Besides, in any case, we can't take credit for the work of God's Spirit.

OUTRAGEOUS ABUNDANCE

Before Moses sent them into Canaan, he said: After you go through the Southern Desert of Canaan, continue north into the hill country and find out what those regions are like. Be sure to remember how many people live there, how strong they are, and if they live in open towns or walled cities. See if the land is good for growing crops and find out what kinds of trees grow there. It's time for grapes to ripen, so try to bring back some of the fruit that grows there.

The twelve men left to explore Canaan. . . . When they got to Bunch Valley, they cut off a branch with such a huge bunch of grapes, that it took two men to carry it on a pole. That's why the place was called Bunch Valley.

Numbers 13:17–21, 23–24
CEV

God had promised a good land for his people to dwell in. It was a good land indeed, abundant almost to an outlandish degree. Imagine a bunch of grapes so big that it would take two men to carry it! That's the kind of land God invited his people into. He offered an abundance that they couldn't hope to lay hold of by themselves.

The Promised Land is a picture of what God offers us even now. But it's a spiritual prosperity represented here, not the material prosperity that Americans imagine when they hear the phrase "God's blessings." There are plenty of godly people who don't have two nickels to rub together—a truth that is most evident to anyone who has visited believers in parts of the world that are less wealthy than America.

In fact, the inward abundance of the Christian life is often *more* evident in people who cannot put their hope in any earthly prosperity. The irrepressible joy of a third-world Christian who deals every day with poverty and hunger and disease—that's an abundance even more outlandish than a two-man bunch of grapes.

ANOTHER KIND OF VISION

"We went to the land where you sent us. It truly flows with milk and honey, and this is its fruit. Nevertheless the people who dwell in the land are strong; the cities are fortified and very large; moreover we saw the descendants of Anak there." . . .

Then Caleb quieted the people before Moses, and said, "Let us go up at once and take possession, for we are well able to overcome it."

But the men who had gone up with him said, "We are not able to go up against the people, for they are stronger than we are. . . .

"The land through which we have gone as spies is a land that devours its inhabitants, and all the people whom we saw in it are men of great stature. . . . We were like grasshoppers in our own sight, and so we were in their sight."

Numbers 13:27–28, 30–33
NKJV

Caleb believed what God had told the people. He knew they would be able to take the land of Canaan because God had told them, generations before, that he would give it to them. The people there were strong. Fine. God is stronger. For Caleb, the unseen was more real than that which he could see.

But of the twelve spies sent out to scope out the land, only Joshua saw things the way Caleb saw them. The other ten couldn't see past the fortifications of the cities and the strength of the armies. No doubt, they thought of themselves as being "realistic." Caleb and Joshua must have seemed like dreamers to them.

But consider how skewed those "realistic" spies' vision really was. "We were like grasshoppers in our own sight," they said. *In their own sight.* They thought they were taking a realistic view, but they were the ones whose vision was skewed. When we have a small view of God, we have a shrunken view of our own place in the scheme of things. When we believe God, we are ready to slay giants.

THE LOGICAL END OF GRUMBLING

[God said,] "How long will these evil people complain about me? I have heard the grumbling and complaining of these Israelites. So tell them, 'This is what the LORD says. I heard what you said, and as surely as I live, I will do those very things to you: You will die in this desert. Every one of you who is twenty years old or older and who was counted with the people—all of you who complained against me—will die. Not one of you will enter the land where I promised you would live; only Caleb son of Jephunneh and Joshua son of Nun will go in. You said that your children would be taken away, but I will bring them into the land to enjoy what you refused. As for you, you will die in this desert.'"

Numbers 14:27–32 NCV

To grumble is to replace God's truth about the world with our own pitiful version of things. God says, "I know the plans I have for you—plans to prosper you and not to harm you" (Jer. 29:11 NIV). The grumbler looks at a difficult situation and says, "God must be out to get me." Grumbling seems like a harmless outlet for our frustrations, a way to blow off some steam. In reality, grumbling is a way of saying, "God, I know how things work better than you do. You say one thing, but I know how things really are."

As he so often does throughout the Bible, God punished the Israelites by making their words come true. Their grumblings became reality. God brought them to the very edge of the Promised Land, and they said, "We wish we had died in Egypt, or in the desert." God said, "You wish you could have died in the desert? All right then. You will die in this desert."

Our grumblings aren't just words. They become realities. They shrink our souls; they make this world of wonder a less wonderful place. That's the logical end of grumbling.

SECOND THOUGHTS

When Moses reported these words to all the Israelites, the people were overcome with grief.

They got up early the next morning and went up the ridge of the hill country, saying, "Let's go to the place the LORD promised, for we were wrong."

But Moses responded, "Why are you going against the LORD's command? It won't succeed. Don't go, because the LORD is not among you and you will be defeated by your enemies. . . .

But they dared to go up the ridge of the hill country, even though the ark of the LORD's covenant and Moses did not leave the camp. Then the Amalekites and Canaanites who lived in that [part of the] hill country came down, attacked them, and routed them as far as Hormah.

Numbers 14:39–42, 44–45
HCSB

It was a bad case of second thoughts. The Israelites didn't want to accept the consequences of their own choice. They chose to nurse their fears rather than moving with purpose into the beautiful land that God was giving them. So God said, in effect, "Have it your way. Don't enter the Promised Land. Wander here in the wilderness for the rest of your lives." That's when the Israelites changed their tune. "All right. We'll go! We'll go!"

But they wouldn't be going with God's covering. And that was a problem. The Israelites weren't going to win against the Canaanites in their own strength. They were roundly defeated. After all, going into Canaan had nothing to do with their faith in God, only their desire to avoid punishment.

God calls us to an abundant life, just as he called the Israelites. Laying hold of it requires that we deny ourselves, serve others, and seek God's kingdom first. Sometimes that seems even harder than fighting giants. What God calls us to do, however, he also equips us to do. And apart from his equipping, we can never expect to lay hold of the abundance we desire.

Look Up and Live

[The Israelites] spoke against God and against Moses, and said, "Why have you brought us up out of Egypt to die in the desert? There is no bread! There is no water! And we detest this miserable food!"

Then the LORD sent venomous snakes among them; they bit the people and many Israelites died. The people came to Moses and said, "We sinned when we spoke against the LORD and against you. Pray that the LORD will take the snakes away from us." So Moses prayed for the people.

The LORD said to Moses, "Make a snake and put it up on a pole; anyone who is bitten can look at it and live." So Moses made a bronze snake and put it up on a pole. Then when anyone was bitten by a snake and looked at the bronze snake, he lived.

Numbers 21:5–9 NIV

Picture it. Venomous serpents were everywhere. People were being bitten. They were suffering terribly. They were dying. In such a situation, where would you look? Your natural reaction would be to look down. You'd be watching to be sure you weren't about to step on a snake. You'd be looking at friends and neighbors who had fallen and died. You might be looking at the swollen calf of your leg where you had been bitten yourself, trying to assess the damage, hoping it wouldn't kill you.

God's cure was a surprising one: a bronze serpent raised high on a pole. It looks suspiciously like one of those graven images that God forbade in the Ten Commandments. But the bronze serpent wasn't an idol. It was God's way of saying, "Look up here! Get your eyes off the ground, off your circumstances, and look to me for your salvation." There was no power in the bronze sign of the snake; the healing came from God—and it came when people were willing to resist that overwhelming temptation to keep their eyes glued to the ground. The people were healed when they looked up to God for healing. And so are we.

HEAR, O ISRAEL

Hear, O Israel, and be careful to obey so that it may go well with you and that you may increase greatly in a land flowing with milk and honey, just as the LORD, the God of your fathers, promised you.

Hear, O Israel: The LORD our God, the LORD is one. Love the LORD your God with all your heart and with all your soul and with all your strength. These commandments that I give you today are to be upon your hearts. Impress them on your children. Talk about them when you sit at home and when you walk along the road, when you lie down and when you get up. Tie them as symbols on your hands and bind them on your foreheads. Write them on the doorframes of your houses and on your gates.

Deuteronomy 6:3–9 NIV

Hear, O Israel." This call was more than God's rapping the podium and saying, "Listen up, everybody." "Hear, O Israel," had been the Israelites' call to worship since God spoke those words through Moses. And it sets the tone for God's relationship with his people, and his people's relationship with one another. "Hear, O Israel" wasn't just a command. It was also a promise: Hear and obey, and there will be blessing. It was a declaration: Hear and know that God is one. It was an invitation: Hear and love completely. And it was a charge: Hear and teach.

The instruction to teach our children shows this best. Hear, O Israel, and listen well enough that you can teach someone else what you learn. Learn God and his commands so thoroughly that you can talk about them all day, in every situation, and make them fixtures in your home. This is part of obeying him, part of knowing him, part of loving him. Once we are serious about loving God with all our hearts, souls, and strength, we will be equipped—and, more to the point, motivated—to obey his commands.

Remember — and Fear

[Moses said,] "When your son asks you in time to come, saying, 'What do the testimonies and the statutes and the judgments mean which the Lord our God commanded you?' then you shall say to your son, 'We were slaves to Pharaoh in Egypt, and the Lord brought us from Egypt with a mighty hand. . . .

"'He brought us out from there in order to bring us in, to give us the land which He had sworn to our fathers.'

"So the Lord commanded us to observe all these statutes, to fear the Lord our God for our good always and for our survival, as it is today.

"It will be righteousness for us if we are careful to observe all this commandment before the Lord our God, just as He commanded us."

Deuteronomy 6:20–21, 23–25 NASB

Keeping commandments was central to the spiritual lives of the Israelites. Obedience was—and is—important to God too. But the order of things is vitally important. Consider the way God instructed parents to tell their children about the importance of obedience. Tell them this, he said: first we were slaves; then God delivered us; then God gave us a new life; *then* we obey his statutes.

We can't obey our way to freedom or to new life. To think we can is to misunderstand our slavery to sin. God initiated our deliverance and accomplished it on his own. For us now to do his will is the only right and grateful response.

Moses too talked of fearing the Lord for our good and our survival. But the fear of God isn't merely a fear that he will catch us breaking a commandment. We fear the God who took Pharaoh's firstborn and parted the Red Sea, lest he find us ungrateful for all he's done on our behalf. Christ, our Passover Lamb, has delivered us from slavery worse than Egypt and at greater cost. We keep his commands out of gratitude and love.

GOD'S BLESSING ON THE STUBBORN

This very day you are crossing the Jordan to enter the land and dispossess nations that are much bigger and stronger than you are. . . .

But when GOD pushes them out ahead of you, don't start thinking to yourselves, "It's because of all the good I've done that GOD has brought me in here to dispossess these nations." . . . No, it's nothing good that you've done, no record for decency that you've built up, that got you here; it's because of the vile wickedness of these nations that GOD, your God, is dispossessing them before you so that he can keep his promised word to your ancestors, to Abraham, Isaac, and Jacob.

Know this and don't ever forget it: It's not because of any good that you've done that GOD is giving you this good land to own. Anything but! You're stubborn as mules.

Deuteronomy 9:1, 4–6 MSG

It's easy for us to measure our performance, to evaluate our goodness or righteousness, by comparing ourselves to others. And if we choose the other guy carefully enough—a Hitler or a Stalin, maybe—we can come off looking quite good. We don't have to be perfect, just better than he is.

God knows better. His holiness is the only standard of comparison, and no one measures up. That doesn't keep him from giving us his blessings. He made promises to Abraham, Isaac, and Jacob, and he made good on those promises even though the children of Israel didn't deserve it. God brought the Israelites into the Promised Land in spite of themselves. Yes, the Canaanites were wicked, but Moses warned the people of Israel not to think of themselves as much better.

We also receive many and great blessings from God. But those blessings aren't evidence that we have earned anything. We should receive God's gifts and enjoy them, but they should keep us humble and make us grateful. If we are honest, the fact that we in no way deserve God's blessings makes them more precious.

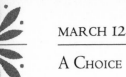

A Choice

[Moses said,] "See, I have set before you today life and good, death and evil. If you obey the commandments of the LORD your God that I command you today . . . then you shall live and multiply, and the LORD your God will bless you in the land that you are entering to take possession of it. But if your heart turns away, and you will not hear, but are drawn away to worship other gods . . . you shall surely perish. You shall not live long in the land that you are going over the Jordan to enter and possess. . . . I have set before you life and death, blessing and curse. Therefore choose life, that you and your offspring may live, loving the LORD your God, obeying his voice and holding fast to him, for he is your life and length of days."

Deuteronomy 30:15–20 ESV

Wisdom makes choices based on results. Not "How will this choice make me feel?" but "What will come of this choice?" Not "Does this taste good?" but "Is this healthy?" When God laid a choice before the Israelites, he also set forth the results: life or death. He made it easy for them by spelling out for them the true nature of their decision. He might have said, "Choose to obey, or not," or "Choose the Lord, and not false gods." And the Israelites might have shrugged and said, "We'll take our chances." That's exactly what they did, actually, even though God gave them every opportunity to know better—even though he showed them the result of their choices—life or death.

How would your choices be different if you always focused on ultimate outcomes? Not "Does this activity/experience/relationship bring me pleasure?" but "Does it bring me closer to God, enable me better to love and serve him?" Each decision we make without considering God will take us further away from him. But the choices ultimately are not "God, or not God," but "the God of life, or death without him."

SEEING FROM A DISTANCE

Moses climbed Mount Nebo from the plains of Moab to the top of Pisgah, across from Jericho. There the LORD showed him the whole land—from Gilead to Dan, all of Naphtali, the territory of Ephraim and Manasseh, all the land of Judah as far as the western sea, the Negev and the whole region from the Valley of Jericho, the City of Palms, as far as Zoar. Then the LORD said to him, "This is the land I promised on oath to Abraham, Isaac and Jacob. . . . I have let you see it with your eyes, but you will not cross over into it."

And Moses the servant of the LORD died there in Moab, as the LORD had said. He buried him in Moab, in the valley opposite Beth Peor, but to this day no one knows where his grave is.

Deuteronomy 34:1–6 NIV

On the top of Mount Nebo God showed Moses the vastness of the width and breadth of the entire Promised Land. It was a miraculous sight. But Moses had to see it from a distance. God didn't permit Moses to enter the Promised Land and see it personally. Moses had sinned at a place called Meribah, taking some of God's glory for himself by providing water from a rock. To us it may seem a harsh punishment. But God was merciful even in that punishment. He showed Moses something greater than a land flowing with milk and honey. On Mount Nebo, God showed Moses that he really was making good on his promises. They were there!

We don't get everything we long for. Sometimes God denies us because of our sin, sometimes simply because he knows it isn't best for us. The Bible gives us a vision of promises fulfilled. We see even more in Christ, the promised Savior and Victor over sin and death. And we see from a distance the promised land that will be ours one day because we are his. And that's enough.

COURAGE BEYOND OUR COMFORT ZONE

[God said to Joshua,] "I will not fail you or abandon you.

"Be strong and courageous, for you are the one who will lead these people to possess all the land I swore to their ancestors I would give them. Be strong and very courageous. Be careful to obey all the instructions Moses gave you. Do not deviate from them, turning either to the right or to the left. Then you will be successful in everything you do. Study this Book of Instruction continually. Meditate on it day and night so you will be sure to obey everything written in it. Only then will you prosper and succeed in all you do. This is my command—be strong and courageous! Do not be afraid or discouraged. For the LORD your God is with you wherever you go."

Joshua 1:5–9 NLT

Joshua was a brave man. He was a mighty warrior. When ten of twelve spies had been afraid to enter the Promised Land, Joshua had been ready to go in and fight giants. Forty years later, he was again standing on the east bank of the Jordan River on the eve of the campaign to take the land in God's name. Was Joshua afraid? He may have been. After all, God felt the need to give him a pep talk: "Be strong and courageous."

Joshua had a new job there. He was not just a warrior anymore. After Moses' death, it was Joshua's job to lead the people—not just to conquer the land, but to "possess it." It isn't hard to imagine him being more anxious about governing than he was about defeating the Canaanites and taking the land. But God promised to be with him.

Do you find yourself facing tasks that you never asked for? God gives you what you need to complete the work he has put before you. Be strong and courageous. The Lord your God is with you wherever you go.

WHY WE CARRY STONES

[The Israelites] camped in Gilgal on the east border of Jericho. And those twelve stones which they took out of the Jordan, Joshua set up in Gilgal. Then he spoke to the children of Israel, saying: "When your children ask their fathers in time to come, saying, 'What are these stones?' then you shall let your children know, saying, 'Israel crossed over this Jordan on dry land'; for the LORD your God dried up the waters of the Jordan before you until you had crossed over, as the LORD your God did to the Red Sea, which He dried up before us until we had crossed over, that all the peoples of the earth may know the hand of the LORD, that it is mighty, that you may fear the LORD your God forever."

Joshua 4:19–24 NKJV

When God stopped the flow of the Jordan River, it was miraculous. The Jordan was a major obstacle for the throng of Israelites preparing to enter Canaan, and it was an advantage to pass into the Promised Land on dry ground, ready to fight if necessary.

Even as they saw the miracle, the Israelites probably wanted to get across quickly—just in case. But God commanded them to stop and collect stones. Furthermore, they would have been slowed by the extra weight. The stones they would build into a monument—a reminder to the Israelites and their children that they had come this far by God's help. It was a reminder also to the Canaanites, who could see and fear the God who fought for the Israelites.

Have you ever experienced a miracle? It wasn't just for you. When God works miracles, he does it not just for those who immediately benefit, but for a wider audience too. Are you embarrassed to tell someone? Sometimes monument stones are heavy, but they serve as a reminder to us, to our children, and to the unbelieving world too that God is still at work.

REMEMBER RAHAB

On the seventh day, the army got up at daybreak. They marched slowly around Jericho the same as they had done for the past six days, except on this day they went around seven times. Then the priests blew the trumpets, and Joshua yelled:

Get ready to shout! The LORD will let you capture this town. But you must destroy it and everything in it, to show that it now belongs to the LORD. The woman Rahab helped the spies we sent, so protect her and the others who are inside her house. But kill everyone else in the town. . . .

The priests blew their trumpets again, and the soldiers shouted as loud as they could. The walls of Jericho fell flat. Then the soldiers rushed up the hill, went straight into the town, and captured it.

Joshua 6:15–17, 20 CEV

When we think of the battle of Jericho, we think of the miraculous collapse of the walls that made it possible for the Israelites to conquer the first enemies they encountered in the Promised Land. We think of the blasting trumpets, the shouting, the sound of massive stones crumbling and tumbling. But in the midst of all that was Joshua's quieter reminder to save Rahab and her family.

Rahab was the prostitute who protected the Israelite men who spied out Jericho before the Israelites crossed the Jordan River. She begged the men to remember her when the invasion came, for she knew that the God of the Israelites was all-powerful.

Rahab married an Israelite and settled among God's people. Her great-grandson was King David, which makes her an ancestor of Jesus. Rahab is a beautiful reminder that it is not our business to judge who is worthy of God's rescue and who isn't. No one is beyond God's grace. Rahab was not just a pagan; she was a prostitute. Nevertheless, when she submitted to God, he saved her. She was more than rescued; she was granted the honor of being the ancestor of the promised Messiah!

INTENTIONAL COURAGE

[Joshua said,] Be very courageous to keep and to do all that is written in the Book of the Law of Moses, lest you turn aside from it to the right hand or to the left, and lest you go among these nations, these who remain among you. You shall not make mention of the name of their gods, nor cause anyone to swear by them; you shall not serve them nor bow down to them, but you shall hold fast to the LORD your God, as you have done to this day. For the LORD has driven out from before you great and strong nations; but as for you, no one has been able to stand against you to this day. One man of you shall chase a thousand, for the LORD your God is He who fights for you."

Joshua 23:6–10 NKJV

The Israelites' wandering was over. They had settled in the Promised Land. Through much struggle, they had survived battle after battle with their Canaanite neighbors. But now they faced an even greater danger from the pagan locals: their friendship. In Joshua's farewell speech just before his death, one of his chief concerns was the possibility that the Israelites, now that they had settled down, would start blending in with the other nations who inhabit Canaan. The natural drift would be toward assimilation. So Joshua called them to be intentional: "Be very courageous to keep and to do all that is written in the Book.

"Be very courageous," Joshua said. Obedience to God's Word isn't meek or slavish. It requires courage. The Israelites needed courage throughout their battles to occupy the Promised Land. They—and we—need just as much courage to live everyday life in obedience to God. It takes courage to stand firm against the current of the world around us. That courage comes from remembering what God has already done for us. God is faithful. Take courage.

CLEAR-EYED FAITH

[Joshua said,] "Fear the LORD and worship Him in sincerity and truth . . . But if it doesn't please you to worship the LORD, choose for yourselves today the one you will worship: the gods your fathers worshiped beyond the Euphrates River, or the gods of the Amorites in whose land you are living. As for me and my family, we will worship the LORD."

The people replied, "We will certainly not abandon the LORD to worship other gods! For the LORD our God brought us and our fathers out of the land of Egypt, the place of slavery and performed these great signs before our eyes. He also protected us all along the way we went and among all the peoples whose lands we traveled through. . . . We too will worship the LORD, because He is our God."

Joshua 24:14–18 HCSB

To choose is to shape the future even though we can't see it. When it comes to matters of faith, we choose by looking at the past. Israel's leaders never asked the people to choose anything on blind faith. Joshua's call for the Israelites to choose came after yet another long recounting of everything God had done for them. God afflicted their Egyptian oppressors. He split the Red Sea. He gave the Israelites great victories over powerful armies in Canaan. He gave them cities they hadn't built, orchards they hadn't planted. Now, Joshua said, in light of all that, what will you choose?

We all have to choose. There's no need to try to see into the future. Just look at the past. How has God delivered? How well has he kept his promises? Here's an equally important question: How has the world kept its promises? The world promises to make you happy and give you security. Has it? "Choose this day," Joshua said. Decide who has been more faithful to you—God, or the world and its gods. And choose accordingly.

A Vicious Cycle

The Israelites did evil in the Lord's sight and served the images of Baal. They abandoned the Lord. . . .

This made the Lord burn with anger against Israel, so he handed them over to raiders who stole their possessions. He turned them over to their enemies all around, and they were no longer able to resist them. . . .

Then the Lord raised up judges to rescue the Israelites from their attackers. Yet Israel did not listen to the judges. . . .

Whenever the Lord raised up a judge over Israel, he was with that judge and rescued the people from their enemies throughout the judge's lifetime. For the Lord took pity on his people, who were burdened by oppression and suffering. But when the judge died, the people returned to their corrupt ways, behaving worse than those who had lived before them.

Judges 2:11–12, 14, 16–19 NLT

The last chapter of the book of Joshua contains the people's rousing proclamation: "We will certainly not abandon the Lord to worship other gods!" (24:16 HCSB). It sounded great. Flip a page or two—literally—and the people have already fallen off the wagon. They did evil, and they worshipped the Baals. And so began the cycle that defines the book of Judges. The people slipped into idolatry and immorality. God punished them by sending a neighboring tribe or nation to defeat and oppress them. The people prayed to God to deliver them. God sent a judge who delivered them from their oppressors. The people straightened up for a little while. Then they slipped back into idolatry and immorality, and the cycle started again.

The Israelites were incredibly slow on the uptake. How did they not learn their lesson? But they were no more foolish than the rest of us. We don't have it in us to straighten up and fly right. We don't learn our lesson. In the end, the most important lesson is this: every day we have to repent and turn back to God and rely on him for our righteousness.

God's Special Forces

The LORD said to Gideon, "The people who are with you are too many for Me to give Midian into their hands, for Israel would become boastful, saying, 'My own power has delivered me.' . . .

So [Gideon] brought the people down to the water. And the LORD said to Gideon, "You shall separate everyone who laps the water with his tongue as a dog laps, as well as everyone who kneels to drink."

Now the number of those who lapped, putting their hand to their mouth, was 300 men; but all the rest of the people kneeled to drink water.

The LORD said to Gideon, "I will deliver you with the 300 men who lapped and will give the Midianites into your hands; so let all the other people go, each man to his home."

Judges 7:2, 5–7 NASB

God had already cut Gideon's force from thirty-two thousand to ten thousand by sending home every soldier who admitted to being afraid. Even at thirty-two thousand, the Israelites were outnumbered by their Midianite enemies. It seemed that bravery was more important to God than numbers. There's a certain logic in that. But then God ordered Gideon to cut the force again—down to the three hundred men who dipped water and drank out of their hands rather than lapping it up like a dog.

Three hundred men against tens of thousands. There is no logic in that. There is no explaining it in terms of God's looking for the most skilled and vigilant warriors. No, God wanted Gideon's fighting force to be outrageously puny so that when they defeated the enemy, nobody could possibly believe they had done it in their own strength.

God doesn't need our strength or our ability. He is all-powerful. Nevertheless, he grants us the privilege of being used by him when we make ourselves available. God's kingdom is moving forward and expanding. What joy when he includes us in his plans.

THE STRONG MADE WEAK

[Delilah] kept at it day after day, nagging and tormenting [Samson]. Finally, he was fed up—he couldn't take another minute of it. He spilled it.

He told her, "A razor has never touched my head. I've been God's Nazirite from conception. If I were shaved, my strength would leave me; I would be as helpless as any other mortal."

When Delilah realized that he had told her his secret, she sent for the Philistine tyrants, telling them, "Come quickly—this time he's told me the truth." They came, bringing the bribe money.

When she got him to sleep, his head on her lap, she motioned to a man to cut off the seven braids of his hair. Immediately he began to grow weak. His strength drained from him.

Judges 16:16–19 MSG

What made Samson weak? Technically, it was having his hair cut. But what made him have his hair cut? An even greater weakness than the loss of physical strength was his loss of self-control. He wasn't stupid. Delilah didn't trick him, but she wore him down by constant nagging. The worst part was that Samson had fooled Delilah in the past; whenever she thought she knew how to weaken him, she tried to do it. Samson knew what to expect. But he thought he could get out of her traps. He forgot that his strength came from God, and he thought he could take care of himself. Perhaps his greatest weakness was his pride.

Samson was God's Nazirite, set apart since conception for a special role and purpose. He had come to think he was just strong. As a strong man, he thought he could do what he wanted, associate with people he should have recognized as a threat.

We have to be honest about our own strengths and weaknesses. What strength we have, we have from God, to use for his purposes, not our own pleasure.

NEVER TOO LATE

The Philistine rulers were celebrating in a temple packed with people and with three thousand more on the flat roof. They had all been watching Samson and making fun of him.

Samson prayed, "Please remember me, LORD God. The Philistines poked out my eyes, but make me strong one last time, so I can take revenge for at least one of my eyes!"

Samson was standing between the two middle columns that held up the roof. He felt around and found one column with his right hand, and the other with his left hand.

Then he shouted, "Let me die with the Philistines!" He pushed against the columns as hard as he could, and the temple collapsed with the Philistine rulers and everyone else still inside. Samson killed more Philistines when he died than he had killed during his entire life.

Judges 16:27–30 CEV

Before he was born, God chose Samson to become a great deliverer of Israel. An angel visited his desperate, childless parents to announce his upcoming birth. With great joy, they tried to raise him purely, as a Nazirite. Their son was amazing—with his bare hands, he tore a lion to pieces, and he killed a thousand Philistines in one day with the jawbone of a donkey.

Yet Samson had a flaw: when he saw a beautiful woman, he wanted her. It didn't matter if she shared his faith in God. It didn't matter if she came from the Philistines, Israel's enemy during this forty-year period of oppression. Eventually, he met his match in the deceptive Delilah, who tricked him into disclosing the secret of his strength.

Samson, the mighty warrior, became a slave and a laughingstock. His eyes were gouged out, and his enemies taunted him. In a last desperate act, he begged God to remember him. God heard his prayer. Samson destroyed more Philistines in his final act than he ever did while alive. God can still use you for his purpose no matter what you've been through. It's never too late to make an impact.

THE WILL TO FOLLOW

[Naomi said,] "Turn back, my daughters; go your way. . . . It is exceedingly bitter to me for your sake that the hand of the LORD has gone out against me." Then they lifted up their voices and wept again. And Orpah kissed her mother-in-law, but Ruth clung to her.

And she said, "See, your sister-in-law has gone back to her people and to her gods; return after your sister-in-law."

But Ruth said, "Do not urge me to leave you or to return from following you. For where you go I will go, and where you lodge I will lodge. Your people shall be my people, and your God my God. Where you die I will die, and there will I be buried." . . . And when Naomi saw that she was determined to go with her, she said no more.

Ruth 1:12–18 ESV

The book of Ruth serves an important purpose: it establishes the genealogical link between Jesus and the tribe of Judah. Through the story of these two women, Naomi and Ruth, we gain a glimpse into the lives of Jesus' ancestry. Although it was a dark and evil time in Israel's history, a few never abandoned their faith.

Naomi's devastating loss of her husband and two sons brought her to a tragic point in life. Yet she showed her kind heart in setting her two daughters-in-law free to remarry and start over in the land of Moab, east of the Dead Sea. She knew the hard road of poverty that lay before a widow whose lifestyle depended on her husband's provision. Yet Ruth surprised her by showing a deep and compassionate love.

Ruth didn't want to abandon her newfound faith in the God of Israel, the God of her mother-in-law. She could never go back to the ways of her past. Her loyalty to Naomi reminds us that we may have to make the choice to follow God even when our circumstances don't make any sense. His love compels us, and we will never regret following in the footsteps of true believers.

The Fruits of a Good Reputation

Boaz said to Ruth, "You will listen, my daughter, will you not? Do not go to glean in another field, nor go from here, but stay close by my young women. . . . And when you are thirsty, go to the vessels and drink from what the young men have drawn."

So she fell on her face, bowed down to the ground, and said to him, "Why have I found favor in your eyes, that you should take notice of me, since I am a foreigner?"

And Boaz answered and said to her, "It has been fully reported to me, all that you have done for your mother-in-law since the death of your husband, and how you have left your father and your mother and the land of your birth, and have come to a people whom you did not know before. The LORD repay your work."

Ruth 2:8–12 NKJV

Ruth chose to make a clean break from her people, and her actions were noticed. Right away, Boaz let her know she was welcome to glean in his fields and to take what she needed. God protected Ruth from possible starvation by interceding with her kinsman-redeemer, Boaz. Yet she did her part as well, by being humble and willing to work hard, even if it meant picking up other people's leftovers.

Instead of waiting around, Ruth showed initiative. She exhibited the character of a noble woman—by being diligent, loyal, and brave. These qualities earned her a good reputation, but only because she displayed them consistently in all areas of her life. Wherever she went, Ruth's character remained the same.

People who demonstrate good character stand out in our culture today. Proverbs 22:1 tells us, "A good name is more desirable than great riches" (NIV). A good name comes from consistently living out the character traits we believe in, no matter where we are or whom we're with. A good name is worth more than great wealth, and through small acts of faith, God will reward those who serve him.

BLESSED WITH JOY

Boaz took Ruth home as his wife and had sexual relations with her. The LORD let her become pregnant, and she gave birth to a son. The women told Naomi, "Praise the LORD who gave you this grandson. May he become famous in Israel. He will give you new life and will take care of you in your old age because of your daughter-in-law who loves you. She is better for you than seven sons, because she has given birth to your grandson."

Naomi took the boy, held him in her arms, and cared for him. The neighbors gave the boy his name, saying, "This boy was born for Naomi." They named him Obed. Obed was the father of Jesse, and Jesse was the father of David.

Ruth 4:13–17 NCV

When Naomi grieved the sudden deaths of her husband and two sons, she thought she'd spend the rest of her life in sorrow. Her grief was so deep, she even wanted to change her name to Mara, for bitterness. Yet Naomi didn't give up. She moved to a new season, choosing to focus on the needs of others. In time, God blessed her abundantly in ways she could never have imagined.

The events recorded in the book of Ruth were part of God's plan for redemption through Jesus Christ. But Naomi had no way of knowing that. She lived each day as faithfully as she could, taking the next step without knowing exactly where or how God would lead her. Her day of great joy came at last when she became a grandmother. Her role in the house of David forever marked her as one of the most blessed women in history.

Even when sorrow and tragedy strike our lives, we can still look to the Bible for strength. Paul wrote that we can "rejoice in our sufferings, because we know that suffering produces perseverance; perseverance character; and character, hope" (Rom. 5:3–4 NIV). Instead of asking why God allows something bad to happen, we can learn to trust him.

A Kingdom

In earthly terms, it didn't seem possible. That ragtag crowd of travelers became one of the most important kingdoms in the Near East. They were indeed a light to the nations. It didn't last long, that era of glory. But one thing was abundantly clear: God was at work in the midst of his people.

This is what makes you so great, Master God! There is none like you, no God but you, nothing to compare with what we've heard with our own ears. And who is like your people, like Israel, a nation unique in the earth, whom God set out to redeem for himself (and became most famous for it), performing great and fearsome acts, throwing out nations and their gods left and right as you saved your people from Egypt? You established for yourself a people—your very own Israel!—your people permanently. And you, God, became their God.

2 Samuel 7:22–24 MSG

The Heart's Deepest Cry

"O Lord of hosts, if you will indeed look on the affliction of your servant and remember me and not forget your servant, but will give to your servant a son, then I will give him to the Lord all the days of his life." . . .

Hannah was speaking in her heart; only her lips moved, and her voice was not heard. Therefore Eli took her to be a drunken woman. . . . But Hannah answered, "No, my lord, I am a woman troubled in spirit. I have drunk neither wine nor strong drink, but I have been pouring out my soul before the Lord." . . . Then Eli answered, "Go in peace, and the God of Israel grant your petition that you have made to him."

I Samuel 1:11, 13–17 ESV

During Eli's time of priesthood, Israel had been ruled by judges for more than two hundred years. Yet the governing authority was about to change, and Hannah would play a key role in ushering Israel into the era of kingship. But at that point, she was a woman in agony. Childless year after year, she shared her husband with a rival who had already borne him several children.

In her distress, she turned to the Giver of all life. Her pain was so deep that she wept and moved her lips with no sound emerging. She prayed with such passion, Eli assumed she was under the influence of alcohol. Yet she wasn't drunk on wine, but overcome with the Holy Spirit, who intercedes in times of great distress, beyond the ability of language.

When we're in pain, the world offers plenty of substitutes to dull our hearts—we can turn to food or drink, worldly pleasures, sports and entertainment, or even bury ourselves in busy schedules. But as Hannah discovered, prayer opens the way for God to work. Hannah's story shows us where we should go—to God, who can transform our desperation into hope. He's always waiting to listen and bring us into his fullness of joy.

ANSWERED PRAYERS

Hannah prayed and said: "My heart rejoices in the LORD; my horn is exalted in the LORD. I smile at my enemies, because I rejoice in Your salvation. . . . Those who were full have hired themselves out for bread, and the hungry have ceased to hunger. Even the barren has borne seven, and she who has many children has become feeble. . . . He brings low and lifts up. He raises the poor from the dust and lifts the beggar from the ash heap, to set them among princes and make them inherit the throne of glory. For the pillars of the earth are the LORD's, and He has set the world upon them."

1 Samuel 2:1, 5, 7–8 NKJV

God answered Hannah's earnest prayers by opening her womb and blessing her with a son. She named him Samuel, which sounds like the Hebrew for "heard of God." After about three years, she weaned Samuel and took him back to the temple, giving him up for a lifetime of service to God. How hard this must have been for her! Yet she gave him up willingly, by faith.

Samuel became one of Israel's greatest prophets. He was a humble man who anointed Israel's first king. His mother's prayer was recorded for eternity. She had gone from being a barren woman to becoming the joyful mother of a son. Her poetic words echo her confidence in God's sovereignty and her gratitude for everything he had done.

Later, God continued to bless Hannah by allowing her to bear five more children—three sons and two daughters. Her story inspired Mary, the mother of Jesus, to model her own praise song, known as the Magnificat, after Hannah's prayer (see Luke 1:46–55). Like Hannah's and Mary's prayers, our prayers show God how thankful we are for all his blessings. When we share answered prayers with our family and friends, we help others grow in faith. Our stories should be treasured as well.

Falling Down before the Almighty

[After the battle against the Philistines,] the Benjaminite answered, "Israel ran away from the Philistines, and the Israelite army has lost many soldiers. Your two sons are dead and the Philistines have taken the Ark of God." . . .

After the Philistines had captured the Ark of God, they took it from Ebenezer to Ashdod. They carried it into Dagon's temple and put it next to Dagon. When the people of Ashdod rose early the next morning, they found that Dagon had fallen on his face on the ground before the Ark of the LORD. So they put Dagon back in his place. The next morning when they rose, they again found Dagon fallen on the ground before the Ark of the LORD. His head and hands had broken off and were lying in the doorway. Only his body was still in one piece.

1 Samuel 4:17; 5:1–4 NCV

Without consulting Samuel, the armies of Israel attacked the Philistines. Eli's sons, Hophni and Phinehas, entered the Holy of Holies to remove the ark. They carried it onto the battlefield, thinking it would scare the Philistines and bring success to Israel. For their heinous sin, Eli's sons were slain in battle, and when Eli heard the news, he fell over and died. Within hours, his daughter-in-law died giving birth to his grandson as well.

The Philistines celebrated the victory by triumphantly displaying the ark in the temple of their god Dagon. They figured that if it had brought such good luck to the Israelites, maybe it would reward them as well. When the Israelites discovered they'd lost the ark, they wailed in agony, thinking God had deserted them forever.

But God isn't an idol. He can't be contained in a box! Three times, three nights in a row, the Dagon statue crashed before the throne of God. The third time, Dagon's head and hands fell off. The Philistines were terrified. Our God has no boundaries. We can't package him up into a method of teaching or a set of rules to follow. He's living and almighty. Before him, every knee will bow.

Give Us a King!

One day the nation's leaders came to Samuel at Ramah and said. . . . "We want a king to be our leader, just like all the other nations. Choose one for us!" Samuel was upset to hear the leaders say they wanted a king, so he prayed about it. The Lord answered:

Samuel, do everything they want you to do. I am really the one they have rejected as their king. Ever since the day I rescued my people from Egypt, they have turned from me to worship idols. Now they are turning away from you. Do everything they ask, but warn them and tell them how a king will treat them. . . .

The people would not listen to Samuel. "No!" they said. "We want to be like other nations. We want a king to rule us and lead us in battle."

1 Samuel 8:4–9, 19–20 CEV

God called Israel out from the nations around them to be holy, separate, and unique. He did it because he loved them and wanted them to survive. But the Israelites were tired of being different, of serving a God nobody could see. They wanted a human monarch to rule the nation, even though only God could cause them to flourish in the hostile land of Canaan.

But Samuel warned them that having a king wouldn't make all their problems go away. He would reign over them and force their sons and daughters into servitude. Still, they begged. In reality, they were rejecting God as their leader. Had the Israelites submitted to God's ultimate leadership, they would have thrived beyond their expectations. Instead, they set themselves up for disaster.

Often, we let others' values and actions dictate our behavior. When we pay lip service to God on Sunday but continue to live by the world's standards, we'll blend into our culture too much. Faith in God must permeate every area of our lives. We need to stand out and worship God alone. We live under his kingship.

Chosen

Samuel had all the tribes of Israel come forward, and the tribe of Benjamin was selected. Then he had the tribe of Benjamin come forward by its clans, and the Matrite clan was selected. Finally, Saul son of Kish was selected. But when they searched for him, they could not find him. They again inquired of the LORD, "Has the man come here yet?"

The LORD replied, "There he is, hidden among the supplies."

They ran and got him from there. When he stood among the people, he stood a head taller than anyone else. Samuel said to all the people, "Do you see the one the LORD has chosen? There is no one like him among the entire population."

And all the people shouted, "Long live the king!"

1 Samuel 10:20–24 HCSB

Israel wanted a king, and God picked a man who would look the part. Saul had movie-star attributes—he stood a head taller than the rest, and his good looks commanded attention. But it wasn't in his heart to be a king. Instead of coming forward, he hid among the baggage. He already knew he'd been chosen, and he hid from the responsibility.

Pagan kings were considered gods in the ancient Near East. They made up laws and answered to no one. But Israel's king would submit to the higher authority of God. Saul didn't think he could handle that role. He looked the part, but he had flaws that would cause him trouble all his life.

Our culture is dominated by people who look good on TV and magazine covers. We listen to what they have to say because they have a nice smile and attractive physical features. But this puts us in a dangerous position. We can be led astray by looking at the outside of a person more than his or her heart. God values the opposite. We need to look for leaders who are humble and submissive to God's laws.

A New Direction for Prayer

The people all said to Samuel, "Pray to the Lord your God for your servants so that we will not die, for we have added to all our other sins the evil of asking for a king."

"Do not be afraid," Samuel replied. "You have done all this evil; yet do not turn away from the Lord, but serve the Lord with all your heart. Do not turn away after useless idols. They can do you no good, nor can they rescue you, because they are useless. For the sake of his great name the Lord will not reject his people, because the Lord was pleased to make you his own. As for me, far be it from me that I should sin against the Lord by failing to pray for you. And I will teach you the way that is good and right."

1 Samuel 12:19–23 NIV

It was time for Samuel to move on. The people had made their choice, and he needed to step down to allow Saul to rise up as their first king. They gathered to hear his farewell speech, a bittersweet ending to a life dedicated to God's service. He'd been raised in the temple as a young boy and had always been in the spotlight of leadership.

Samuel reminded Israel of their long journey, how God had rescued them from slavery in Egypt to the point of victory over their enemies time and time again. He shared the stories of human leaders who bowed to God's authority and thrived according to his purpose. There was still hope for Israel. Even with a king, they still had a chance to worship God as their ultimate monarch.

Although Samuel disagreed with the Israelites' demand for a king, he assured them he would continue to pray for them and teach them. He was disappointed, but he still loved his people and wanted the best for them. We may disagree with others, but we shouldn't stop praying for them. God can take any situation and use it for his glory.

Waiting on God

Saul said, "Bring to me the burnt offering and the peace offerings." And he offered the burnt offering.

As soon as he finished offering the burnt offering, behold, Samuel came. . . . Samuel said, "What have you done?" And Saul said, "Because I saw that the people were scattering from me, and that you did not come within the appointed days, and that the Philistines were assembling at Michmash, therefore I said, 'Now the Philistines will come down against me at Gilgal, and I have not asked the favor of the Lord.' So I forced myself and offered the burnt offering."

Samuel said to Saul, "You have acted foolishly; you have not kept the commandment of the Lord your God, which He commanded you, for now the Lord would have established your kingdom over Israel forever.

"But now your kingdom shall not endure."

1 Samuel 13:9–14 NASB

Wait for me at Gilgal," Samuel had said on the day he anointed Saul king. The king wasn't to go to battle until the prophet returned. It probably didn't make sense to Saul at the time. He waited seven days for Samuel, but when Samuel didn't come that morning, Saul rushed to action. And he paid a price.

It's hard to wait on God. He does things in his time. We have come to expect things instantly, on demand, just in time, or yesterday. But some things in life we still have to wait for. Plants don't bear fruit until they mature. And if we rush or push or try to hurry, we will be disappointed, if not harmed. It's true if we rush to intimacy in relationships. It's true if we spend before we have money.

God's timing is not an arbitrary delay; he does not make us wait without reason—whether we understand the reason or not. When everything else is right, then the time is right for action. We learn God's priorities by reading the Bible and praying. And waiting. It helps to remember that God waits with us.

THE LORD GIVES US VICTORY

When the Philistines saw [Jonathan and his armor-bearer] coming, they shouted, "Look! The Hebrews are crawling out of their holes!" Then the men from the outpost shouted to Jonathan, "Come on up here, and we'll teach you a lesson!"

"Come on, climb right behind me," Jonathan said to his armor bearer, "for the LORD will help us defeat them!"

So they climbed up using both hands and feet, and the Philistines fell before Jonathan, and his armor bearer killed those who came behind them. They killed some twenty men in all, and their bodies were scattered over about half an acre.

Suddenly, panic broke out in the Philistine army, both in the camp and in the field, including even the outposts and raiding parties. And just then an earthquake struck, and everyone was terrified.

1 Samuel 14:11–15 NLT

Jonathan was a faithful, God-fearing man. And those qualities made him a great soldier. He might have even made a great king, but because of his father's sin, he would never get the chance. Where Saul feared the Philistines, Jonathan knew God would give him victory over his enemies. Saul saw his own army shrinking and panicked. Jonathan was not afraid to attack an entire Philistine garrison with only his armor-bearer—while climbing a cliff!

Jonathan was not tougher, meaner, or more strategic than his father. The real difference was that Jonathan understood that God decides battles. Saul arrogantly took the rights of Samuel the prophet and offered a sacrifice to try to turn God to his side. Jonathan, on the other hand, genuinely sought the Lord. When God answered, Jonathan confidently knew he would win this battle.

No matter how much we might seem to be outnumbered, no matter how steep our climb, no matter how late things seem to be getting for us, when God has promised us victory—victory over sin and temptation, loneliness or fear—we can press on in faith, confident that victory will come.

THE STUFF KINGS ARE MADE OF

The LORD said to Samuel, "How long will you grieve over Saul, since I have rejected him from being king over Israel? Fill your horn with oil and go; I will send you to Jesse the Bethlehemite, for I have selected a king for Myself among his sons." . . .

So Samuel did what the LORD said, and came to Bethlehem . . . He also consecrated Jesse and his sons and invited them to the sacrifice.

When they entered, he looked at Eliab and thought, "Surely the LORD's anointed is before Him."

But the LORD said to Samuel, "Do not look at his appearance or at the height of his stature, because I have rejected him; for God sees not as man sees, for man looks at the outward appearance, but the LORD looks at the heart."

1 Samuel 16:1, 4–7 NASB

Samuel anointed Israel's first and most famous kings. But Samuel did not choose these men; he only confirmed God's selection. In the case of Saul, God gave the people exactly what they asked for, and that was a punishment in itself.

When God was ready to replace Saul, he again told Samuel, "I'll show you the man." Upon seeing Jesse's sons, Samuel—surprisingly, uncharacteristically—went straight for big, strong, handsome Eliab, the one who was most like Saul.

But God has a completely different set of priorities. Looks and natural abilities are not enough. They weren't for Saul. Not that there is anything wrong with those things: David was strong and handsome too. But the important thing is the condition of the heart, and only God can see that. The person who will love and serve and obey is God's man or woman.

The good news is that God can use us all. We cannot change our size or strength or appearance. But we can soften our hearts. And if we submit our hearts to him, he will like what he sees.

RECKLESS FAITH?

"Master," said David, "don't give up hope. I'm ready to go and fight this Philistine."

Saul answered David, "You can't go and fight this Philistine. You're too young and inexperienced." . . .

David said, "I've been a shepherd, tending sheep for my father. Whenever a lion or bear came and took a lamb from the flock, I'd go after it, knock it down, and rescue the lamb. If it turned on me, I'd grab it by the throat, wring its neck, and kill it. Lion or bear, it made no difference—I killed it. And I'll do the same to this Philistine pig who is taunting the troops of God-Alive. GOD, who delivered me from the teeth of the lion and the claws of the bear, will deliver me from this Philistine."

Saul said, "Go. And GOD help you!"

1 Samuel 17:32–37 MSG

David's stories of extreme shepherding sound exaggerated, like the bragging of a reckless adolescent. But David wasn't saying, "Hey, watch this!" He was saying, "Don't give up hope!" He was bearing witness to God's greatness, not his own. The killing of lions and bears was God's doing.

David was still young. He hadn't yet acquired the cynicism that afflicted the adults around him. God's promises were real to David; he had seen God work in his own life, so when he heard how God had worked throughout the Israelites' history, he believed it. And he believed that God would work in the future. When he looked around at God's people trembling in the face of the giant, he was no less astonished at their fear than they were astonished at his bravery. It was as if it had never occurred to David to doubt God.

The world is hard. Things don't always go our way. That doesn't mean that God has abandoned us or that he is unable to keep his promises. We are blessed when we have the childlike faith of David, who said, "I'm ready to go and fight this Philistine."

WITHOUT A SWORD

David replied to the Philistine, "You come to me with sword, spear, and javelin, but I come to you in the name of the LORD of Heaven's Armies—the God of the armies of Israel, whom you have defied. Today the LORD will conquer you, and I will kill you and cut off your head. And then I will give the dead bodies of your men to the birds and wild animals, and the whole world will know that there is a God in Israel! And everyone assembled here will know that the LORD rescues his people, but not with sword and spear. This is the LORD's battle, and he will give you to us!" . . .

So David triumphed over the Philistine with only a sling and a stone, for he had no sword.

1 Samuel 17:45–50 NLT

Look at swords in this short passage. Goliath had one, the Lord didn't need one, and David didn't have one. The Lord works with the simplest tools, or even without tools if he deems that way better. He can do his work with puny people, and he can do his work with robust people.

There's nothing wrong with having tools or using them. David used Goliath's own sword against him. Even the sling David used to drop Goliath was a human device, not a magic wand. But our tools need to be kept in perspective. The most powerful of human devices will not always be best for God's people or his work.

David's victory was clean and simple. It clearly showed that God rescues his people. When we do the Lord's work in the Lord's way, God gets all the glory, and we get all the benefits of victory. We choose our tools because they honor God and they work. Finances, technology, strategy, and worldly wisdom have not built God's kingdom. Love, faith, hope, and obedience do.

People Love a Winner

By the time David had finished reporting to Saul, Jonathan was deeply impressed with David—an immediate bond was forged between them. He became totally committed to David. From that point on he would be David's number-one advocate and friend.

Saul received David into his own household that day, no more to return to the home of his father.

Jonathan, out of his deep love for David, made a covenant with him. He formalized it with solemn gifts: his own royal robe and weapons—armor, sword, bow, and belt.

Whatever Saul gave David to do, he did it—and did it well. So well that Saul put him in charge of his military operations. Everybody, both the people in general and Saul's servants, approved of and admired David's leadership.

1 Samuel 18:1–5 MSG

Everything David did went well. When others saw how God blessed David, they were attracted to him, from the crown prince in the palace to the average person, and from government officials to servants. Even King Saul saw how having David around would be to his advantage. But when he saw how David's popularity might hurt more than help him, Saul turned against David.

Jonathan, on the other hand, allied himself with David at his own expense. In political terms, David's rising fortunes couldn't help but cause a decline in Jonathan's fortunes. But Jonathan valued his friendship with David more than he valued his own claim to the throne. He made a covenant, a solemn promise, and confirmed it by making a gift of his weapons and royal robes.

Godly friendship is a serious business and, in David and Jonathan's case, a life-and-death matter. David owed his very life to Jonathan's friendship. Jonathan and David were like-minded, facing in the same direction and working toward the same goals and hopes. Theirs was a friendship that demonstrated to the world what God's love is like.

THE BETTER MAN

Once again an evil spirit from the LORD rushed upon Saul as he was sitting in his house with his spear in his hand. David was playing the harp. Saul tried to pin David to the wall with his spear, but David jumped out of the way. So Saul's spear went into the wall, and David ran away that night.

Saul sent messengers to David's house to watch it and to kill him in the morning. But Michal, David's wife, warned him, saying, "Tonight you must run for your life. If you don't, you will be dead in the morning." So she let David down out of a window, and he ran away and escaped. Then Michal took an idol, laid it on the bed, covered it with clothes, and put goats' hair at its head.

Saul sent messengers to take David prisoner, but Michal said, "He is sick."

1 Samuel 19:9–14 NCV

No matter how faithless Saul was to David, David never betrayed him. When Saul ordered David to go to war, David went. When Saul sent him on dangerous missions, David went. When Saul was out of his head, David tried to soothe him.

David's wife, Michal, is a bit of a mystery. She was Saul's daughter; the king reluctantly gave her to David after David completed one of Saul's deadly challenges. She was not apparently a woman of faith. She knew how to get her hands on an idol, and she later mocked David for his faith. However, she could see clearly that between David and her father, David was the better man. When she had to choose between her father and her husband, she chose David. She was one of a long line of people who kept alive the line that eventually gave rise to Jesus, the Deliverer whom God had promised from Genesis on.

Michal is yet another example of a person through whom God worked quite independently of his or her faithfulness. God always finds a way to do his will.

CRAZY, DISHONEST, OR LOYAL?

David ran away from Saul and went to Achish king of Gath. But the servants of Achish said to him, "This is David, the king of the Israelites. He's the man they dance and sing about, saying: 'Saul has killed thousands of his enemies, but David has killed tens of thousands.' "

David paid attention to these words and was very much afraid of Achish king of Gath. So he pretended to be crazy in front of Achish and his servants. . . . He acted like a madman and clawed on the doors of the gate and let spit run down his beard.

Achish said to his servants, "Look at the man! He's crazy! Why do you bring him to me? I have enough madmen. . . . Don't let him in my house!"

1 Samuel 21:10–15 NCV

David was desperate indeed when he ran away to Gath to get away from Saul. Gath was the hometown of Goliath. Furthermore, it was the Philistines' capital. But he soon realized that his enemy's enemy would not necessarily be his friend. He couldn't consider Saul his enemy anyway. How could he be an enemy of the anointed king of God's people?

David could have saved his own skin by telling King Achish the truth. Yes, he had been Saul's champion, but he and Saul had had a falling-out. He could have offered to be Achish's new champion; there were a hundred ways he could have joined forces with the Philistines to get even with the king who had run him off.

David would have to be crazy, as a matter of fact, to be in Gath if he wasn't there with the intention of hurting Saul. So crazy is what David pretended to be. It was a risky move, and it threatened to destroy his dignity and reputation. Dignity and reputation are sometimes casualties of the fight to stay true to our principles. Are you willing to sacrifice yours if necessary for the sake of doing what's right?

ENDS AND MEANS

There were some sheep pens along the side of the road, and one of them was built around the entrance to a cave. Saul went into the cave to relieve himself.

David and his men were hiding at the back of the cave. They whispered to David, "The LORD told you he was going to let you defeat your enemies. . . . This must be the day the LORD was talking about."

David sneaked over and cut off a small piece of Saul's robe, but Saul didn't notice a thing. Afterward, David was sorry that he had even done that, and he told his men, "Stop talking foolishly. We're not going to attack Saul. He's my king, and I pray that the LORD will keep me from doing anything to harm his chosen king." Saul left the cave and started down the road.

1 Samuel 24:3–7 CEV

There are times we experience a conflict between what we want and what God appears to be giving us. Or sometimes it might look as if God is giving us some good thing in a way that just doesn't seem right.

David had one of those situations when he came upon Saul in the cave. David's friends meant well when they told him that God was giving David what he had promised. Yes, God had promised to make David king. But David also knew that it was wrong to kill a king. So he refused.

Sometimes we encounter circumstances that look like a chance to take what is coming to us. But like David, we need to keep in mind the bigger picture. It doesn't please God when we try to get the right thing in the wrong way. The end does not justify the means. God promises to make things come out right in the end. At the same time, he cares about the means we use to get them. David got it right by being faithful. And eventually he was blessed. God will reward our faithfulness too.

A GHOST STORY

The king said to [the fortune-teller], "What do you see?"

The woman said, "I see a spirit coming up out of the ground." . . .

Saul knew it was Samuel, and he bowed down and prostrated himself with his face to the ground.

Samuel said to Saul, "Why have you disturbed me by bringing me up?"

"I am in great distress," Saul said. "The Philistines are fighting against me, and God has turned away from me. He no longer answers me, either by prophets or by dreams. So I have called on you to tell me what to do."

Samuel said, "Why do you consult me, now that the LORD has turned away from you and become your enemy? . . . The LORD has torn the kingdom out of your hands and given it to one of your neighbors—to David."

1 Samuel 28:13–17 NIV

It's one of the stranger scenes in the Bible. Once again taking matters into his own hands, Saul found a witch and summoned up the ghost of the dead Samuel to get answers he didn't feel he was getting from God. He was in the middle of a military crisis, but God no longer answered him.

When Saul said that God no longer answered him, what he really meant was that he didn't like what God had to say; God no longer answered Saul the way Saul wanted to be answered. Saul often wanted confirmation from God, but he also wanted to do exactly what he wanted to do. He was never one for obedience, and he always had an explanation why the rules didn't apply to him. God had said he would turn his back on Saul for his disobedience, and then he did. But Saul wanted a different answer. He wanted God to bless his plans.

The Bible says some hard things about denying ourselves, loving our enemies, putting God first. We are foolish if we think we can live any way we please and still get a good result.

Finding Strength

David and his men reached Ziklag on the third day. Now the Amalekites had raided the Negev and Ziklag. They had attacked Ziklag and burned it, and had taken captive the women and all who were in it, both young and old. They killed none of them, but carried them off as they went on their way.

When David and his men came to Ziklag, they found it destroyed by fire and their wives and sons and daughters taken captive. So David and his men wept aloud until they had no strength left to weep. David's two wives had been captured—Ahinoam of Jezreel and Abigail, the widow of Nabal of Carmel. David was greatly distressed because the men were talking of stoning him; each one was bitter in spirit because of his sons and daughters. But David found strength in the Lord his God.

1 Samuel 30:1–6 NIV

Things were not going well for David. He was running for his life from his own king. He lived among people whom he used to fight and kill and who now didn't trust him. He had to pretend to be insane to escape with his life, and then he found the city where he and his men plundered and took families captive.

David was likely feeling a failure at that point. He couldn't serve the king he wanted to serve and the nation he loved. The Philistines wouldn't have him. And since roving bandits kidnapped his family and the families of his men, even his loyal troops were starting to consider him more of a liability than an asset.

David hit rock bottom. But he still found strength. It wasn't because he had a new plan. It wasn't because he looked deep inside himself for an inner resolve. He found his strength in God. David's circumstances were hopeless. He was personally spent. But God's love and protection and provision are infinite, a never-ending source of strength. He can be our strength too, no matter what our situation.

Whom Do We Believe?

The Philistines fought against Israel, and Israel's men fled from them. Many were killed on Mount Gilboa. The Philistines overtook Saul and his sons and killed his sons, Jonathan, Abinadab, and Malchishua. When the battle intensified against Saul, the archers caught up with him and severely wounded him. Then Saul said to his armor-bearer, "Draw your sword and run me through with it, or these un- circumcised men will come and run me through and tor- ture me." But his armor-bearer would not do it because he was terrified. Then Saul took his sword and fell on it. When his armor-bearer saw that Saul was dead, he also fell on his own sword and died with him. So on that day, Saul died to- gether with his three sons, his armor-bearer, and all his men.

1 Samuel 31:1–6 HCSB

Saul died as he had lived: doing things his own way, and do- ing them badly. God had told him he would die in battle with the Philistines, but he went anyway. When he was injured and his death seemed inevitable, he still wanted things on his own terms. When his armor-bearer wouldn't kill him, he killed himself. But there was no victory in being master of his own death. Saul ended up a dis- grace to his family and to his nation.

Saul revealed something in his fear of dying by a Philistine's hand. He feared his enemies more than he trusted God. David took on Goliath rather than let the uncircumcised Philistines trash-talk his God. Saul believed their talk rather than believing in the God who promises to rescue and defend those who faithfully follow him.

We do not have to deal with wild-eyed barbaric Philistines, though we will meet those who oppose our God and us—sometimes strongly. But we shouldn't be afraid. That would only play into their hands and work against us, just as Saul's fear did him in. Instead, we need to put our trust in God and in his cause and his promises.

The Forever King

All the tribes of Israel came to David at Hebron and said, "Behold, we are your bone and your flesh.

"Previously, when Saul was king over us, you were the one who led Israel out and in. And the LORD said to you, 'You will shepherd My people Israel, and you will be a ruler over Israel.'"

So all the elders of Israel came to the king at Hebron, and King David made a covenant with them before the LORD at Hebron; then they anointed David king over Israel.

David was thirty years old when he became king, and he reigned forty years.

At Hebron he reigned over Judah seven years and six months, and in Jerusalem he reigned thirty-three years over all Israel and Judah.

2 Samuel 5:1–5 NASB

David was the standard against which the kings of Israel and Judah were measured. That wasn't just nostalgia of later generations looking back to Israel's golden age. In his own lifetime, David was recognized as the ideal king. "You have always been our king," said the Israelites. "Even when Saul was on the throne, you were the one who acted like the king."

The people knew that David had been chosen by God and that they were God's people, not the king's people. They knew that David was their shepherd, and David knew it too. And so his coronation did not celebrate him; rather, it was a covenant of David with Israel before God.

Whether as a lowly shepherd, a warrior, or a king, David always pursued excellence. While a shepherd, he was as noble as a king. While a king, he exercised the tender care of a shepherd, doing what was best for the people rather than oppressing them. He served God's people as a shepherd, doing what was best for them. David understood that he lived his life under the eye of God and that all of it mattered.

When Good Intentions Are Not Enough

[David led his troops] to Baalah of Judah to bring back the Ark of God, which bears the name of the LORD of Heaven's Armies, who is enthroned between the cherubim. They placed the Ark of God on a new cart and brought it from Abinadab's house, which was on a hill. Uzzah and Ahio, Abinadab's sons, were guiding the cart as it left the house, carrying the Ark of God. . . . David and all the people of Israel were celebrating before the LORD, singing songs and playing all kinds of musical instruments. . . .

But when they arrived at the threshing floor of Nacon, the oxen stumbled, and Uzzah reached out his hand and steadied the Ark of God. Then the LORD's anger was aroused against Uzzah, and God struck him dead because of this. So Uzzah died right there beside the Ark of God.

2 Samuel 6:2–7 NLT

David meant well; really, he did. The ark was to him a holy, sacred object, not a common thing. When he took it into battle, he put it on a new cart, probably built especially for this purpose. The people worshipped God as the ark rolled along. And when Uzzah touched it, it was out of concern, not disrespect.

But God had given Moses specific instructions for how the ark was to be moved. It was to be carried by Levites using poles attached to either side. Did it really matter? To God, yes. Why did he want the ark transported on poles rather than on a cart? The Bible never specifies, but that's not the point of the story.

This story is ultimately about God's holiness. We must not forget that God is not like us. He is not a god of "close enough." When he gives specific commands, we must follow them, now no less than in Uzzah's time. And as in Uzzah's time, we disobey. The good news is that for those who believe, Jesus suffered the punishment we deserved. God still demands holiness. Thankfully, Jesus is our holiness.

WHO'S IN CHARGE?

[God said,] "I took you from the pasture, tagging along after sheep, and made you prince over my people Israel. I was with you everywhere you went and mowed your enemies down before you. Now I'm making you famous, to be ranked with the great names on earth. . . . GOD himself will build you a house! When your life is complete and you're buried with your ancestors, then I'll raise up your child, your own flesh and blood, to succeed you, and I'll firmly establish his rule. He will build a house to honor me, and I will guarantee his kingdom's rule permanently. I'll be a father to him, and he'll be a son to me. When he does wrong, I'll discipline him in the usual ways, the pitfalls and obstacles of this mortal life."

2 Samuel 7:8–14 MSG

David looked around his beautiful palace, and a thought came to him: the king's dwelling place was more luxurious than God's place. God was still dwelling in a tent. David wanted to build a temple for God. But God said, "No, David, you won't be establishing the house of God. God will establish the house of David."

The promise in this passage is sometimes referred to as the Davidic Covenant. God promised to establish the line of David forever. We know from history that the line of David as a political institution did not last forever. The monarchy was in serious trouble by the time David's grandson ascended the throne, and a few hundred years later there wasn't even a semblance left of the house of David.

Nevertheless, God established the line of David in an eternal way. David was the ancestor of Jesus, the Lion of the tribe of Judah. We have seen throughout the Old Testament that the Israelites' true King was God, not human beings. In Jesus, the God-man, we have a King who far outshines even David, the greatest of human kings.

SOMETHING BIGGER

[David said,] "Who am I, O Sovereign LORD, and what is my family, that you have brought me this far? And now, Sovereign LORD, in addition to everything else, you speak of giving your servant a lasting dynasty! Do you deal with everyone this way, O Sovereign LORD?

"What more can I say to you? You know what your servant is really like, Sovereign LORD. Because of your promise and according to your will, you have done all these great things and have made them known to your servant.

"How great you are, O Sovereign LORD! There is no one like you. We have never even heard of another God like you! What other nation on earth is like your people Israel? What other nation, O God, have you redeemed from slavery to be your own people?"

2 Samuel 7:18–23 NLT

David's response to God's covenant was sheer wonder. *Who am I that you would extend this kind of blessing to me?* "You know what your servant is really like," he says. It's as if David is shrugging his shoulders—*I don't get it, but I suppose you know what's best, Lord.* David knew his success and glory were God's doing, not because of his abilities or efforts. Many psalms are about how good God had been to David. But David saw that God had blessed him not only for his own benefit but also for all of humanity. God gets bigger in David's eyes, if that is possible, and David in turn grows more humble.

Just as David had gone from shepherd boy to king, the Israelites had gone from slaves to a great nation. God was at work showing the whole world what kind of God he was. He still is. When we too are blessed, it's not because we deserve it, but for God's glory. And it's not just for our benefit, but so we might be a blessing to others.

Power Doesn't Always Corrupt

The king said, "Is there not still someone of the house of Saul, that I may show the kindness of God to him?" Ziba said to the king, "There is still a son of Jonathan; he is crippled in his feet." . . .

Mephibosheth the son of Jonathan. . . . fell on his face and paid homage. And David said, "Mephibosheth!" And he answered, "Behold, I am your servant." And David said to him, "Do not fear, for I will show you kindness for the sake of your father Jonathan, and I will restore to you all the land of Saul your father, and you shall eat at my table always." And he paid homage and said, "What is your servant, that you should show regard for a dead dog such as I?" . . .

Mephibosheth ate at David's table, like one of the king's sons.

2 Samuel 9:3, 6–8, 11 ESV

David's character showed forth in his desire to bless a member of Saul's family. In the ancient world, it was often a messy, violent transition when the crown passed from one family to another. It was standard practice for the new king to kill any relatives of the old king so they couldn't try to take back the throne. Mephibosheth feared that kind of treatment.

But this was no ordinary transition. David did not take the crown from Saul; the crown was given to him. David had been loyal even when Saul tried to kill him. He loved Saul, and he loved Saul's son, Jonathan, even more. Becoming king had not changed David. He would have a lapse later, but at that moment, power had not corrupted David. He wasn't so interested in preserving his own authority as he was about using his authority to do what was right.

It was completely in David's power to kill Mephibosheth or make his life more miserable than it already was. We reflect David's character—and God's—if we do the right thing because it's right, whether or not we have the power or authority to act otherwise.

WRONG PLACE, WRONG TIME, WRONG ACTIONS

It happened in the spring of the year, at the time when kings go out to battle, that David sent Joab and his servants with him, and all Israel; and they destroyed the people of Ammon and besieged Rabbah. But David remained at Jerusalem.

Then it happened one evening that David arose from his bed and walked on the roof of the king's house. And from the roof he saw a woman bathing, and the woman was very beautiful to behold. . . . Then David sent messengers, and took her; and she came to him, and he lay with her. . . . And the woman conceived; so she sent and told David, and said, "I am with child."

Then David sent to Joab, saying, "Send me Uriah the Hittite." And Joab sent Uriah to David.

2 Samuel 11:1–2, 4–6 NKJV

David was the standard by which kings in Israel and Judah were measured for nearly five hundred years. He was a man after God's own heart. We read the Psalms and wish we had faith like David's, but David was a man who sinned and failed in a big way.

Why couldn't David see temptation coming? He set himself up to fail in several ways. He should have been at war, but he stayed home. He should have been in bed, but he was on the roof. He should have turned away, but his eyes lingered on a woman bathing. Those were mistakes. Once David sinned, though, it snowballed. He called for her and had sex with her. When consequences became apparent, he called for her husband, Uriah. He could have confessed at that point, but he chose to charge ahead instead.

We all need to be alert to temptation and resist it early. We should avoid situations and circumstances that tempt us. The longer we continue, the harder it gets until we're out of control. But even when we sin, it's never too late to confess.

Sin and Self-Preservation

David called Uriah to come to see him, so Uriah ate and drank with David. David made Uriah drunk, but he still did not go home. That evening Uriah again slept with the king's officers.

The next morning David wrote a letter to Joab and sent it by Uriah. In the letter David wrote, "Put Uriah on the front lines where the fighting is worst and leave him there alone. Let him be killed in battle."

Joab watched the city and saw where its strongest defenders were and put Uriah there. When the men of the city came out to fight against Joab, some of David's men were killed. And Uriah the Hittite was one of them. . . .

When Bathsheba heard that her husband was dead, she cried for him.

2 Samuel 11:13–17, 26 NCV

It is astonishing how quickly David's sin grew from lust to adultery to murder. This tragic episode in David's life shows the destructive nature of sin. Sin turned David from a life of love and obedience to a life of self-preservation at any cost.

David tried to cover up his adultery with Bathsheba by bringing her husband, Uriah, home from battle and treating him to a state dinner. This supposed honor was really a trick to cover David's dishonor. The further irony is that Uriah was too honorable to sleep with his wife while his soldiers were in the field. David had Uriah killed in battle. To accomplish that, however, he had to jeopardize the battle and Israel's army in order to put Uriah in harm's way.

The guilt of his sin ate at David and interfered with his being a good king, a commander, and a shepherd of God's people. He wasn't even a decent human being. His every action was calculated and selfish. Sin keeps us from doing our duty, from showing love and thinking of others before ourselves. Sin turns us inward, not outward—a sad, pathetic way to live.

THE MORAL OF THE STORY

[Nathan said to David,] "A rich man and a poor man lived in the same town. The rich man owned a lot of sheep and cattle, but the poor man had only one little lamb that he had bought and raised. The lamb became a pet for him and his children. He even let it eat from his plate and drink from his cup and sleep on his lap. The lamb was like one of his own children.

"One day someone came to visit the rich man, but the rich man didn't want to kill any of his own sheep or cattle and serve it to the visitor. So he stole the poor man's little lamb and served it instead."

David was furious with the rich man and said to Nathan, "I swear by the living LORD that the man who did this deserves to die!"

2 Samuel 12:1–5 CEV

We know from several of the psalms that the guilt of his sins tore David up. He had not completely lost his moral compass. He still knew right from wrong. He just needed some help seeing how it applied to him.

The prophet Nathan told David a story with such an obvious moral that it infuriated the king. The contrasts were obvious, between rich and poor, between having and taking, between nurturing and killing. David clearly saw the rich man was wrong, so wrong that he pronounced a death sentence on the guilty.

But as clearly as he could see the wrong that the man in the story had committed, David failed to see that he was the man. We can be huge sinners and not realize it, yet still have twenty-twenty vision regarding other people's faults.

We all need Nathans in our lives, people who are willing to step in and help us step outside ourselves to see who we really are. It takes a true friend to point out our faults and failures and to point us toward the God who offers forgiveness and relief.

A NASTY SPIRAL

[Amnon grabbed Tamar] and said, "Come to bed with me, sister!"

"No, brother!" she said, "Don't hurt me! This kind of thing isn't done in Israel! Don't do this terrible thing! Where could I ever show my face? And you—you'll be out on the street in disgrace. Oh, please! Speak to the king—he'll let you marry me."

But he wouldn't listen. Being much stronger than she, he raped her.

No sooner had Amnon raped her than he hated her—an immense hatred. The hatred that he felt for her was greater than the love he'd had for her. "Get up," he said, "and get out!"

"Oh no, brother," she said. "Please! This is an even worse evil than what you just did to me!"

But he wouldn't listen to her.

2 Samuel 13:11–16 MSG

It was a sad and sorry episode, a shocking and prurient reminder that the Israelites, God's chosen people, were capable of sinking as low as anybody else was. Tamar begged Amnon to leave her alone. She made a cogent, reasoned case, but Amnon was a slave to his desire. He raped his own half sister.

One of the saddest things about the story is that once he got what he wanted, Amnon hated Tamar. "Get up!" he told her. "Get out!" as if it were her fault that he raped her. Amnon's hatred was greater than his desire had ever been. It was surely a projection of his self-loathing.

That's a picture of how sin works in our lives. The enemy tempts us, and when we succumb, he beats us up for having given in. When we've been beaten up, we look for someone else to whom we can pass along the hurt. The egregious wrong that Amnon did to his sister was multiplied by his behavior afterward. Sin, small and large, sets in motion a nasty spiral of wrong and hurt.

FAKING IT

Absalom got a chariot and horses for himself and fifty men to run before him. Absalom would get up early and stand near the city gate. Anyone who had a problem for the king to settle would come here. When someone came, Absalom would call out and say, "What city are you from?"

The person would answer, "I'm from one of the tribes of Israel."

Then Absalom would say, "Look, your claims are right, but the king has no one to listen to you." Absalom would also say, "I wish someone would make me judge in this land! Then people with problems could come to me, and I could help them get justice."

People would come near Absalom to bow to him. When they did, Absalom would reach out his hand and take hold of them and kiss them. . . . In this way, Absalom stole the hearts of all Israel.

2 Samuel 15:1–6 NCV

If Absalom had a bumper sticker on his chariot, it would have read "Fake it till you make it." His plot to steal his father's kingdom hinged not on open violence (that would come later) but on creating the appearance of kingliness. He put on a fantastic show, with his fifty men running in front of his chariot, his subtle criticism of his father's rule, and his false expressions of concern for the people.

The people were fooled. They forgot about the leadership that David had given them. They saw the young, beautiful Absalom and thought he would make a fine king.

Absalom's lust for power caused him to deceive a nation and take up arms against his own father. It's the way of the world: We fake it in hopes of someday making it. We seize what isn't ours for the taking. We manipulate others, put up false fronts.

God calls us to a higher standard. He calls us to be motivated by love and honesty, not by power or greed. And he calls us to trust that it is possible to get what we need and still leave our integrity intact.

A NEAR MISS, A FORCED RETIREMENT

The Philistines again waged war against Israel. David went down with his soldiers, and they fought the Philistines, but David became exhausted. Then Ishbi-benob, one of the descendants of the giant, whose bronze spear weighed about eight pounds and who wore new armor, intended to kill David. But Abishai son of Zeruiah came to his aid, struck the Philistine, and killed him. Then David's men swore to him: "You must never again go out with us to battle. You must not extinguish the lamp of Israel." . . .

At Gath there was still another battle. A huge man was there with six fingers on each hand and six toes on each foot—24 in all. He, too, was descended from the giant. When he taunted Israel, Jonathan, son of David's brother Shimei, killed him.

2 Samuel 21:15–17, 20–21
HCSB

With a few notable exceptions, David had always done his duty with regard to his army and his nation. He was by nature a man of war and a man of action—first in the attack and last in the retreat. Even though he was getting on in years, it should be no surprise that David found himself in the thick of things with the Philistines—Israelites' perennial foes.

David no doubt had a flood of memories being in the field against the Philistines. The Philistines certainly remembered him. A relative of David's old enemy Goliath was laying in wait for him and might have killed him if one of David's soldiers hadn't come to the rescue.

That's when David's men sat him down. They said, in effect, "You have a new duty to your kingdom: to stay away from the battlefield and keep yourself alive."

Sometimes our duty is to disengage, to recover, to take on a support role away from the front lines. Our duty, sometimes, is simply to live to fight another day.

JOY OVER DIGNITY

David, the elders of Israel, and the commanders of thousands started out to get the Chest of the Covenant of GOD and bring it up from the house of Obed-Edom. And they went rejoicing. . . . They were all dressed in elegant linen—David, the Levites carrying the Chest, the choir and band, and Kenaniah who was directing the music. David also wore a linen prayer shawl (called an ephod). On they came, all Israel on parade bringing up the Chest of the Covenant of GOD, shouting and cheering, playing every kind of brass and percussion and string instrument.

When the Chest of the Covenant of GOD entered the City of David, Michal, Saul's daughter, was watching from a window. When she saw King David dancing ecstatically she was filled with contempt.

1 Chronicles 15:25, 27–29
MSG

When the ark of the covenant was brought back from the Philistines, it ended up in the house of a man named Obed-Edom. There it remained for twenty years. As David was establishing Jerusalem as the center of Israelite life, he brought the ark to the city. There was a huge and joyful procession as the ark took its place in the City of David.

In the midst of the celebration, David let himself go. He danced in the streets with an abandon that showed he loved God more than he loved his own dignified reputation.

From an upper-story window high above the celebration, Michal, David's wife, watched. She saw her husband dancing like a crazy man, and she despised him. No doubt she thought that she, a princess herself, deserved a more dignified husband. It isn't hard to imagine Michal asking, "Is this really necessary?"

Being fully sold out to God can be costly. It can cost us some dignity—and those who are closest to us won't always like it. But David experienced joy that day. Michal resisted God's joy—and that's costly too.

DAVID'S PLAN—AND GOD'S

Soon after David moved into his new palace, he said to Nathan the prophet, "Look around! I live in a palace made of cedar, but the sacred chest is kept in a tent." . . .

That night, the LORD told Nathan to go to David and tell him:

David, you are my servant, so listen carefully: You are not the one to build a temple for me. I didn't live in a temple when I brought my people out of Egypt, and I don't live in one now. A tent has always been my home wherever I have gone with them. I chose special leaders and told them to be like shepherds for my people Israel. But did I ever say anything to even one of them about building a cedar temple for me?

1 Chronicles 17:1–6 CEV

It was a strange moment. David appeared to be motivated by sincere devotion and gratitude when he offered to build a house for God. David wanted to do something nice for God; he wanted God to be honored at least as well as the false gods of neighboring tribes were honored. They all had temples. Why shouldn't the true God? God said, in effect, "Who said anything about a house?"

David showed remarkable restraint. He had the resources to move forward with a building project that would have brought plenty of glory—to David if not to God. The time would come—and quite soon—when God would have his temple built. But that wasn't work for David to do.

God is forever doing things differently from the way we would do things. His motives are wholly other. In our efforts to please God, we offer to do better, be better, build this monument, perform that grand gesture. God says, "I'm the One at work here. I do. I build. You believe. You obey." Sometimes obedience is a matter of holding back on our best ideas.

A ROYAL MESS

Adonijah, whose mother was Haggith, put himself forward and said, "I will be king." . . . (His father had never interfered with him by asking, "Why do you behave as you do?" . . .)

Nathan asked Bathsheba, Solomon's mother, "Have you not heard that Adonijah, the son of Haggith, has become king without our lord David's knowing it? Now then, let me advise you how you can save your own life and the life of your son Solomon. Go in to King David and say to him, 'My lord the king, did you not swear to me your servant: "Surely Solomon your son shall be king after me, and he will sit on my throne"? Why then has Adonijah become king?' While you are still there talking to the king, I will come in and confirm what you have said."

1 Kings 1:5–6, 11–14 NIV

David's last days weren't tidy at all. It was as if all David's sins and heartaches came back for one last visit before he left this life. Adonijah, David's third son, was in line for David's throne because both of his elder brothers were dead. Absalom had killed Amnon after Amnon raped Tamar. Then Absalom was killed in the battle in which he attempted to wrest power from David. The very fact that Adonijah had a legitimate claim to the throne was a reminder of two of the most painful episodes of David's life.

Into the mix came Bathsheba, demanding that David keep his promise to make their son Solomon the king. David's sin with Bathsheba had started the whole mess in the first place. Things got complicated fast.

Even on his deathbed, David was still plagued by the consequences of his sin decades earlier. David was a passionate pursuer of God, and God showed him huge mercies. There is always forgiveness, but that forgiveness doesn't keep the earthly consequences of our sins from rippling through our lives for years.

A FATHER'S BLESSING

As David's time to die drew near, he charged Solomon his son, saying, "I am going the way of all the earth. Be strong, therefore, and show yourself a man.

"Keep the charge of the LORD your God, to walk in His ways, to keep His statutes, His commandments, His ordinances, and His testimonies, according to what is written in the Law of Moses, that you may succeed in all that you do and wherever you turn, so that the LORD may carry out His promise which He spoke concerning me, saying, 'If your sons are careful of their way, to walk before Me in truth with all their heart and with all their soul, you shall not lack a man on the throne of Israel.'" . . .

Then David slept with his fathers and was buried in the city of David.

1 Kings 2:1–4, 10 NASB

David kept his promise to Bathsheba. He confirmed their son Solomon as his successor even though Solomon wasn't his oldest living son. The last meeting between the two men was a tender one. The older man gave a blessing in the form of challenge: "Be strong, therefore, and show yourself a man."

David assured Solomon that there was a place for him at the table. He also reminded him of God's promises. And he handed over unfinished business to his son, entrusting him with scores that hadn't been settled and reminding him to show kindness to certain people. In short, David assured Solomon that he was indeed a worthy successor. The biblical record suggests that David's conversation with Solomon was David's last order of business. They were his last recorded words.

It is one thing to say, "Be a man." It is quite another to say, "I know you have what it takes to be a man. I believe in you. And God is faithful to support you." That kind of blessing and affirmation is one of the most significant things a father can do for his son.

A GREAT CHOICE

GOD appeared to Solomon in a dream: God said, "What can I give you? Ask."

Solomon said, "You were extravagantly generous in love with David my father. . . . And you have persisted in this great and generous love by giving him . . . a son to sit on his throne. . . .

"Give me a God-listening heart so I can lead your people well, discerning the difference between good and evil. For who on their own is capable of leading your glorious people?" . . .

And God said to him, "Because you have asked for this and haven't grasped after a long life, or riches, or the doom of your enemies, but you have asked for the ability to lead and govern well, I'll give you what you've asked for—I'm giving you a wise and mature heart. . . . As a bonus, I'm giving you both the wealth and glory you didn't ask for."

1 Kings 3:5–6, 9–13 MSG

He could have had anything he wanted—wealth, health, success. Instead, Solomon asked for wisdom to know the difference between bad and good, between good and best. He realized that he didn't have it in him to lead the Israelites. God was pleased.

God was so pleased with Solomon's request that he threw in health and wealth. Indeed, the outlandish success that Solomon enjoyed was an outgrowth of his wisdom. He made good choices, and those choices paid off not just for Solomon but also for all his subjects. The fact that Solomon asked God for wisdom suggests that he had a measure of wisdom already.

"If any of you lacks wisdom," wrote James in the New Testament, "let him ask of God . . . and it will be given to him" (James 1:5 NASB). A prayer for wisdom is one that always gets a yes from God. God wants nothing more than to see his people be wise. Was there ever a parent who refused a child's request for more vegetables? When we ask God for what is best for us, God is eager to give it.

A GRUESOME TEST

[One of two prostitutes before Solomon said], "One night while we were all asleep, she rolled over on her baby, and he died. Then while I was still asleep, she got up and took my son out of my bed. She put him in her bed, then she put her dead baby next to me.

"In the morning when I got up to feed my son, I saw that he was dead. But when I looked at him in the light, I knew he wasn't my son."

"No!" the other woman shouted. "He was your son. My baby is alive!" . . .

They argued back and forth in front of Solomon, until finally he said, "Both of you say this live baby is yours. Someone bring me a sword."

A sword was brought, and Solomon ordered, "Cut the baby in half! That way each of you can have part of him."

1 Kings 3:19–25 CEV

Solomon had no way of looking at a baby and knowing for sure who its mother was. Nor were there any reliable witnesses in this case of she-said-she-said. But the wise king knew people, and he could see that there was real bitterness between the two women who stood before him.

How would he figure out to whom the baby belonged? He devised a test. He offered to cut the baby in two and give a half to each woman. The test put the women's hearts on full display. The first woman thought it was an okay plan. The second woman said she would rather see the baby go away than be harmed. It was obvious that it was the second woman who loved the baby like a mother.

The two women claimed to want the same thing. Perhaps they even believed they wanted the same thing. But only one of them loved the baby. The other only wanted to feel better after losing her own baby. We don't always want what we think we want. It takes wisdom to see through to our deepest motives.

A BUILDER'S PRAYER

[Solomon prayed,] "Now therefore, O God of Israel, let Your word, I pray, be confirmed which You have spoken to Your servant, my father David.

"But will God indeed dwell on the earth? Behold, heaven and the highest heaven cannot contain You, how much less this house which I have built!

"Yet have regard to the prayer of Your servant and to his supplication, O LORD my God, to listen to the cry and to the prayer which Your servant prays before You today; that Your eyes may be open toward this house night and day, toward the place of which You have said, 'My name shall be there,' to listen to the prayer which Your servant shall pray toward this place.

"Listen to the supplication of Your servant and of Your people Israel, when they pray toward this place; hear in heaven Your dwelling place; hear and forgive."

1 Kings 8:26–30 NASB

At the end of one of the most incredible building projects in human history, Solomon stood before God and the people of Israel and acknowledged that this building wasn't enough. The whole earth couldn't contain the God of the universe. How could a temple built by human hands?

Consider the difference between Solomon's position here and that of his father, David. David wanted to build a dwelling place for God. He begged for the opportunity to build a temple. But he wasn't the man for the job. Solomon, on the other hand, *was* the man for the job of building the temple. God equipped him and provided everything he needed to complete the task. The process humbled Solomon. He was fully aware that even this magnificent edifice couldn't truly be God's dwelling place. Nevertheless, the temple would be a meeting place between God and his people. God would be present as he promised—present, but not contained.

We give God our best in the humble realization that God doesn't *need* anything from us. But he invites us to work alongside him, honoring our obedience and filling in the gaps we inevitably leave.

WHAT DO YOU GIVE SOMEONE WHO HAS EVERYTHING?

The Queen of Sheba heard how famous Solomon was, so she went to Jerusalem to test him with difficult questions. She took along several of her officials, and she loaded her camels with gifts of spices, jewels, and gold. When she arrived, she and Solomon talked about everything she could think of. He answered every question, no matter how difficult it was.

The Queen was amazed at Solomon's wisdom. She was breathless when she saw his palace, the food on his table, his officials, his servants in their uniforms, the people who served his food, and the sacrifices he offered at the LORD's temple. . . .

Solomon gave her the gifts he would have given any other ruler, but he also gave her everything else she wanted. Then she and her officials went back to their own country.

1 Kings 10:1–5, 11–13 CEV

Of all the state visits to all the kings of Israel and Judah recorded in the Bible, this one is unique. It wasn't the huge and fabulously expensive exchanges of gifts on both sides; that wasn't uncommon. What was rare about this visit was the reason the queen of Sheba came. Kings and queens always had motives and agendas when they made state visits. Sometimes they wanted to form alliances, for peace or for war. Sometimes they wanted to marry off their sons and daughters. But the queen of Sheba came to ask Solomon hard questions.

The queen of Sheba came to Jerusalem with the intent of stumping Solomon. Instead, Solomon wowed her with his wisdom—both in his ability to answer questions and in the ways he ordered his life and kingdom. That was God-given wisdom that Solomon displayed, and it made an impression on his visitor. Her wonder climaxed, it is worth noting, with Solomon's temple and the worship there.

That's what happens when we use God's gifts for God's glory. People notice, and they are drawn to the God who gives us every good thing.

Wisdom in All of Life

King Solomon became richer and wiser than any other king on earth. People from every nation came to consult him and to hear the wisdom God had given him. . . .

Solomon built up a huge force of chariots and horses. . . . He stationed some of them in the chariot cities and some near him in Jerusalem. The king made silver as plentiful in Jerusalem as stone. And valuable cedar timber was as common as the sycamore-fig trees that grow in the foothills of Judah. Solomon's horses were imported from Egypt and from Cilicia; the king's traders acquired them from Cilicia at the standard price. At that time chariots from Egypt could be purchased for 600 pieces of silver, and horses for 150 pieces of silver. They were then exported to the kings of the Hittites and the kings of Aram.

1 Kings 10:23–24, 26–29 NLT

Only a few generations earlier, it appeared that the children of Israel weren't going to amount to much. They were a half-million escaped slaves wandering through a wilderness, hoping somehow to make a home in a strip of land already occupied by great tribes and nations. Then, under Solomon's wise leadership, they were a miracle among the nations. They had tremendous military might, but they were at peace with all their enemies. And they did it without incurring any national debt! Silver was as common as stones. And inflation was under control: chariots and horses could be bought for a song and sold for a profit to other nations.

In short, Solomon's wisdom was not limited to "spiritual" matters. As Solomon turned his face toward God, God gave him the kind of wisdom that benefited a whole nation. This whole world is God's—not just the churches, not just Sunday mornings and Wednesday nights, but all of it. As we pray for our leaders, Solomon is worth bearing in mind. His wisdom worked its way into every decision; as a result, his nation became a light to the world.

The Center and Focus of Our Worship

The trumpeters and singers joined together to praise and thank the LORD with one voice. They raised [their] voices, accompanied by trumpets, cymbals, and musical instruments, in praise to the LORD: For He is good; His faithful love endures forever; the temple, the LORD's temple, was filled with a cloud. And because of the cloud, the priests were not able to continue ministering, for the glory of the LORD filled God's temple.

Then Solomon said: The LORD said He would dwell in thick darkness, but I have built an exalted temple for You, a place for Your residence forever.

Then the king turned and blessed the entire congregation of Israel while they were standing. He said: May the LORD God of Israel be praised!

2 Chronicles 5:13–6:4 HCSB

The world had never seen anything like Solomon's temple. Set high on a hill, it was massive, with gold everywhere, and intricate carving and painting. The combination of sheer size and tiny detail was a wonder in itself.

Solomon had reason to be proud. He had amassed the tremendous national wealth that made such a project conceivable. He had shown the leadership that made it a reality. Any king would be proud to have such an architectural wonder as his legacy.

The dedication ceremony celebrated the amazing achievement that was the temple. The people sang and shouted praise to God; the musicians played their hearts out. Then God's presence entered the temple in the form of a cloud, and it was so overwhelming that the priests couldn't even continue with their worship. They were overawed by God's presence. And suddenly the achievement of the temple was put in context. The offering of all that skill, all that artistry, was really an invitation to God. And when God showed up, all that beauty and art was swept up into something even bigger and more awe-inspiring.

A HOUSE OF PRAYER FOR ALL NATIONS

The LORD appeared to Solomon in the night and said to him: "I have heard your prayer and have chosen this place for myself as a house of sacrifice. When I shut up the heavens so that there is no rain, or command the locust to devour the land, or send pestilence among my people, if my people who are called by my name humble themselves, and pray and seek my face and turn from their wicked ways, then I will hear from heaven and will forgive their sin and heal their land. Now my eyes will be open and my ears attentive to the prayer that is made in this place. For now I have chosen and consecrated this house that my name may be there forever. My eyes and my heart will be there for all time."

2 Chronicles 7:12–16 ESV

Solomon had prayed that God would inhabit the temple he had built, even though God was not obliged to take up residence there. Solomon had built it in good faith. It had been his father's dream, and God was pleased with David. So when the Lord chose Solomon's temple it meant something. It did not mean that Solomon was perfect, as the biblical record shows. It did not mean Israel was perfect either. But God chose to dwell with them nevertheless.

Notice that when God speaks of future punishment for Israel's future sin, he says, "*When* I shut up the heavens," not "*If*." He knew his people would disobey and disappoint. And yet he chose to dwell with them anyway. He is a God of grace.

When the Lord consecrated Solomon's temple, he confirmed that he planned to save people, despite their sin and rebellion. This temple was to be a place where God exercised and demonstrated his salvation. We need God's grace as desperately as the Israelites ever did. And God still gives it.

DANGEROUS LIAISONS

King Solomon . . . loved many foreign women besides Pharaoh's daughter—Moabites, Ammonites, Edomites, Sidonians and Hittites. They were from nations about which the LORD had told the Israelites, "You must not intermarry with them, because they will surely turn your hearts after their gods." Nevertheless, Solomon held fast to them in love. He had seven hundred wives of royal birth and three hundred concubines, and his wives led him astray. As Solomon grew old, his wives turned his heart after other gods, and his heart was not fully devoted to the LORD his God, as the heart of David his father had been. He followed Ashtoreth the goddess of the Sidonians, and Molech the detestable god of the Ammonites. So Solomon did evil in the eyes of the LORD.

1 Kings 11:1–6 NIV

What happened to Solomon's wisdom? By following his heart and not his head, Solomon let himself be led away from faithfully following God. No doubt, Solomon's trouble with foreign women started out as a strategic move. His first wife was Pharaoh's daughter: the marriage would have solidified Israel's relationship with the Egyptians. He probably continued that line of thought as he took wives from smaller nations nearby, gaining the loyalty of their fathers and brothers. "Make love, not war," as the old saying goes.

But somewhere along the way, Solomon let a love for those women replace his love for God. Solomon was a wise man. How had he gotten himself in that mess? It may have been the proud thought that he was too smart to have to pay the consequences for breaking God's rules about marrying foreigners. He was used to getting what he wanted; perhaps he thought he could pursue his own pleasure without getting in over his head.

Solomon was smart. But sin usually goes for the heart, not the head. Putting God first will keep us both humble and safe from ourselves.

DISSOLUTION

One thing the Israelites never quite got in their heads: it was God, and God only, who held their little kingdom together. They turned away from God, yet God pursued them repeatedly, rescuing them from war and famine and earthly trouble of every kind. In the end, however, God let them have their own way, and their way meant dissolution and eventually destruction. Even then, however, there was hope and the promise of a Deliverer.

In the wilderness prepare the way of the Lord; make straight in the desert a highway for our God. Every valley shall be lifted up, and every mountain and hill be made low; the uneven ground shall become level, and the rough places a plain. And the glory of the Lord shall be revealed, and all flesh shall see it together, for the mouth of the Lord has spoken.

Isaiah 40:3–5 ESV

WHO IS IN CONTROL?

[Rehoboam] did not listen to the people; for the turn of events was from the LORD, that He might fulfill His word. . . .

Now when all Israel saw that the king did not listen to them, the people answered the king, saying:

"What share have we in David? We have no inheritance in the son of Jesse. To your tents, O Israel! Now, see to your own house, O David!"

So Israel departed to their tents. But Rehoboam reigned over the children of Israel who dwelt in the cities of Judah.

Then King Rehoboam sent Adoram, who was in charge of the revenue; but all Israel stoned him with stones, and he died. Therefore King Rehoboam mounted his chariot in haste to flee to Jerusalem. So Israel has been in rebellion against the house of David to this day.

1 Kings 12:15–19 NKJV

When Solomon died and his son Rehoboam came to the throne, the people asked the new king to lighten their workload. They felt that Solomon had worked them too hard with his many building projects. But Rehoboam's advisers had told him that he should start his reign by showing people who was boss. He refused to lighten their load. When the ten northern tribes rebelled, he sent not an emissary but a tax collector, whom the people promptly stoned. And just like that, the dream of a united Israel was over. Only the tribes of Judah and Benjamin remained loyal to the house of David. The ten tribes of the north became their own kingdom.

The people wanted an easier life. The king wanted to fill the royal treasury. But neither side considered the main character in Israel's drama. No one asked what God wanted.

It would appear that things were spinning into chaos because of the people's rebellion. And yet the Bible is clear: "the turn of events was from the LORD." God remained in control. And he remains in control, no matter how chaotic the world around us appears to be.

Remembering the Giver of the Gift

Go, tell Jeroboam that this is what the Lord, the God of Israel, says: "I raised you up from among the people and made you a leader over my people Israel. . . . But you have not been like my servant David, who kept my commands and followed me with all his heart, doing only what was right in my eyes. You have done more evil than all who lived before you. You have made for yourself other gods, idols made of metal; you have provoked me to anger and thrust me behind your back.

"Because of this, I am going to bring disaster on the house of Jeroboam. I will cut off from Jeroboam every last male in Israel—slave or free. I will burn up the house of Jeroboam as one burns dung, until it is all gone."

1 Kings 14:7–10 NIV

To Jeroboam, it may have felt like a setup. He never asked to be king; he had been a faithful servant to Solomon until the prophet Ahijah announced that he would be the first king of the new northern kingdom of Israel. Now the kingdom was being taken from him? His descendants would be destroyed?

When God gives titles or offices, gifts or opportunities, he gives them for a purpose. He cares what is done with them. The whole reason the northern tribes were taken from Solomon's son was Solomon's sin of idolatry. Jeroboam should have known that. Whatever other mistakes he might have made, surely he would have avoided idolatry. But he didn't. He took the gifts, and rather than worshipping the Giver, he worshipped false gods.

There were kings of Israel and Judah who were rich, wise, and brave. But the only ones who pleased God were the ones who followed him, as David had. For us too, every opportunity, every position is a gift from God. He cares how we use those gifts, and he is forever looking for those who, like David, will be faithful to use them in obedience.

God Provides in Hard Times

Elijah, who was from Tishbe in Gilead, told King Ahab, "As surely as the Lord, the God of Israel, lives—the God I serve—there will be no dew or rain during the next few years until I give the word!"

Then the Lord said to Elijah, "Go to the east and hide by Kerith Brook, near where it enters the Jordan River. Drink from the brook and eat what the ravens bring you, for I have commanded them to bring you food."

So Elijah did as the Lord told him and camped beside Kerith Brook, east of the Jordan. The ravens brought him bread and meat each morning and evening, and he drank from the brook. But after a while the brook dried up, for there was no rainfall anywhere in the land.

1 Kings 17:1–7 NLT

Elijah was a man of great faith. He was going to need it. He himself would suffer in the drought that he prophesied. He had been faithful in the midst of an idolatrous nation, but he too would be affected by God's judgment on the land.

Elijah never complained, though, because he believed in God's promises. He followed God's instruction to hide by the Kerith Brook, and there God provided food and water as he promised. The ravens that brought his food were ceremonially "unclean" for Jews, but Elijah didn't complain. When the water dried up, he still didn't complain. He knew that the Lord who had provided so far would continue to be faithful. In truth, the drought itself—and the fact that it continued—meant that God was keeping his promises.

We often suffer trials and difficulties in this life. The world is broken because of sin. Even when they are faithful, God's people can be caught up in the consequences of the world's brokenness. But God is faithful to his promises, and we can continue to hope in him.

What Have I Done to You?

The son of the woman who owned the house got sick, and he kept getting worse, until finally he died. The woman shouted at Elijah, "What have I done to you? I thought you were God's prophet. Did you come here to cause the death of my son as a reminder that I've sinned against God?"

"Bring me your son," Elijah said. . . . Elijah laid the boy on his bed and prayed, "Lord God, why did you do such a terrible thing to this woman? She's letting me stay here, and now you've let her son die." Elijah stretched himself out over the boy three times, while praying, "Lord God, bring this boy back to life!" . . .

The boy started breathing again. Elijah picked him up and carried him downstairs. He gave the boy to his mother and said, "Look, your son is alive."

1 Kings 17:17–23 CEV

We don't know why the Lord does things the way he does. When the brook at the Kerith Ravine dried up, the Lord sent Elijah to Zarephath, where he lived with a widow and her son. The Lord provided for them miraculously so Elijah's stay with them would not be a hardship. But then the boy died.

There's no reason to believe that Elijah himself understood why the boy died. When the mother shouted at him, he had no answer. But even as she questioned God's logic—God's very goodness— Elijah prayed for the boy to be healed.

One of the most striking things about this story is Elijah's matter-of-factness. He didn't launch into grand theological explanations. He didn't try to read God's mind. He just told God what he wanted and waited for God to do what God does: "Lord God, bring this boy back to life!"

Bringing us back to life—it's what God does. Dead in our sin, dead in our sorrows and disappointments and sufferings, we come back to life when God enters in. He invites us to ask: "Lord, bring me back to life!"

Hearts on Fire

The water flowed around the altar and he also filled the trench with water. . . .

Elijah the prophet came near and said, "O Lord, the God of Abraham, Isaac and Israel, today let it be known that You are God in Israel and that I am Your servant and I have done all these things at Your word.

"Answer me, O Lord, answer me, that this people may know that You, O Lord, are God, and that You have turned their heart back again."

Then the fire of the Lord fell and consumed the burnt offering and the wood and the stones and the dust, and licked up the water that was in the trench.

When all the people saw it, they fell on their faces; and they said, "The Lord, He is God; the Lord, He is God."

1 Kings 18:35–39 NASB

Ahab gathered four hundred prophets together on Mount Carmel and told them to do whatever it took to make the gods bring the rain again. It was amazing that Elijah even showed his face there. It was amazing that he would challenge four hundred prophets to a showdown to see whose god would bring down fire to consume the sacrifices they laid out.

It was even more amazing that Elijah would douse his sacrifice with bucket after bucket of precious water during this severe drought.

But fire from heaven was not the greatest miracle Elijah expected or witnessed that day. Elijah had prayed that the people would know that God had "turned their heart back again." A change in the human heart is an even greater miracle than overcoming the laws of nature, but it's exactly what Elijah expected.

And God did it. When the people saw the fire from heaven, they confessed, "The Lord, He is God." They had lived in rebellion for years, and were skeptical even this day. But God is merciful, and he used even fire from heaven to draw his people back to himself. That was the real miracle.

What We Need between Battles

Jezebel immediately sent a messenger to Elijah with her threat: "The gods will get you for this and I'll get even with you! By this time tomorrow you'll be as dead as any one of those prophets."

When Elijah saw how things were, he ran for dear life to Beersheba, far in the south of Judah. . . .

He came to a lone broom bush and collapsed in its shade, wanting in the worst way to be done with it all—to just die: "Enough of this, God! Take my life—I'm ready to join my ancestors in the grave!" Exhausted, he fell asleep. . . .

Suddenly an angel shook him awake and said, "Get up and eat!" He looked around and, to his surprise, right by his head were a loaf of bread baked on some coals and a jug of water.

1 Kings 19:2–6 MSG

The showdown with the prophets of Baal on Mount Carmel was a high point of Elijah's ministry. And immediately after it came the crash that often follows success. He had won, but the queen now wanted him dead. He probably wondered if anything had really changed. So he ran for his life, miles and miles into the wilderness of the southern kingdom.

Finally, he collapsed, discouraged, emotionally spent, and physically exhausted. He told God he couldn't fight anymore and was ready to die. But God was not finished with him yet. Instead, he let him sleep. A good night's rest can revive even a despairing heart. And in case this sounds too ordinary, God also fed Elijah. Food is common too, but Elijah needed it. God provided it miraculously with a home-cooked meal in the desert.

Sometimes our spiritual struggles overwhelm us, often just when we think we've succeeded. We deal with forces larger than ourselves. But the reminder of God's provision even of food and rest gives us perspective. He created everything. He created us to need sleep and sustenance. And he gives them to us, sometimes when we least expect it.

SUITABLE REPLACEMENTS

As [Elijah and Elisha] still went on and talked, behold, chariots of fire and horses of fire separated the two of them. And Elijah went up by a whirlwind into heaven. And Elisha saw it and he cried, "My father, my father! The chariots of Israel and its horsemen!" And he saw him no more.

Then he took hold of his own clothes and tore them in two pieces. And he took up the cloak of Elijah that had fallen from him and went back and stood on the bank of the Jordan. Then he took the cloak of Elijah that had fallen from him and struck the water, saying, "Where is the LORD, the God of Elijah?" And when he had struck the water, the water was parted to the one side and to the other, and Elisha went over.

2 Kings 2:11–14 ESV

Elijah was one of the most significant prophets in the Bible. Though he didn't write like Isaiah or Jeremiah, more is written about him than about many other prophets. And he worked miracles throughout his ministry. So perhaps it shouldn't be surprising that he left this life in a miraculous way. It's such a miracle, in fact, that he is one of two people in the Bible never to have died. He was taken straight to heaven.

Elijah was amazing, but only because his God was amazing. When Elijah left this life, there was still work to be done. When Elijah was gone, his assistant, Elisha, was there to take his place. It must have been intimidating, but God equipped Elisha to do what he would need to do. In case Elisha doubted it, God worked a miracle through him, right on the spot.

It's humbling to look at the great spiritual heroes of the past. Who can measure up to Elijah? But God alone enabled those great figures to do what they did. And as long as the work of making known God's kingdom remains unfinished, God will enable us too.

God's Endless Provision

[Elisha said to the poor widow who had nothing but a little oil,] "Go, borrow vessels from everywhere, from all your neighbors—empty vessels; do not gather just a few. And when you have come in, you shall shut the door behind you and your sons; then pour it into all those vessels, and set aside the full ones."

So she went from him and shut the door behind her and her sons, who brought the vessels to her; and she poured it out. Now it came to pass, when the vessels were full, that she said to her son, "Bring me another vessel."

And he said to her, "There is not another vessel." So the oil ceased. Then she came and told the man of God. And he said, "Go, sell the oil and pay your debt; and you and your sons live on the rest."

2 Kings 4:3–7 NKJV

Do not gather just a few." The poor widow was used to thinking small. All she wanted was enough to get by. But Elisha encouraged her to think big. God is a God of abundance, and he delights to give us more than we can ask or imagine. Why ask for just enough, when God is ready to give so much more? It took faith for the widow to go around and ask her neighbors for jars. Imagine the scene: "Now, what exactly do you need all my jars for? The stranger told you what?"

When God came through, it wasn't just the widow and her family who were blessed, but everybody in the neighborhood. Surely, for the rest of their lives, they told the story: "You remember the old widow who used to live in the third house on the right. One day she came asking for jars, and you won't believe what happened. . . ."

Sometimes you're the poor widow in need of help. Sometimes you're the neighbor who spares a jar or two. Either way, it is a joy and a privilege to participate in God's provision for his people.

MIRACLES FOR THE STATUS-CONSCIOUS

Elisha sent someone outside to say to him, "Go wash seven times in the Jordan River. Then you'll be completely cured."

But Naaman stormed off, grumbling, "Why couldn't he come out and talk to me? I thought for sure he would stand in front of me and pray to the LORD his God, then wave his hand over my skin and cure me. What about the Abana River or the Pharpar River? Those rivers in Damascus are just as good as any river in Israel. I could have washed in them and been cured." His servants went over to him and said, "Sir, if the prophet had told you to do something difficult, you would have done it. So why don't you do what he said? Go wash and be cured."

2 Kings 5:10–13 CEV

Naaman was the commander of the army of Assyria. He was used to being treated with respect. How many times a day did his soldiers salute him? He had access to the king, and that was in his own country. The Israelites were weak at that time, while Assyria was strong. Israel did what Assyria said. Anyone in Israel should have groveled before Naaman.

So Naaman was upset when Elisha sent a message by a servant instead of rushing out of the house to see him. And he didn't like his instructions either, and he didn't like the rivers in Israel.

But one of Naaman's servants was brave enough to remind him that he had come for a miracle. Miracles are not about our status or about what we deserve. They are not about elaborate ritual or magical waters. Miracles come from a God who is greater than his creation. The simplicity of Elisha's instructions is what made them beautiful. They showed Naaman the God of Israel heals, and not rituals, rivers, or prophets.

When we need God to work in our lives, there's no need for elaborate solutions, only the willingness to see God work in his own way.

The Eyes of Faith

One night the king of Aram sent a great army with many chariots and horses to surround the city.

When the servant of the man of God got up early the next morning and went outside, there were troops, horses, and chariots everywhere. "Oh, sir, what will we do now?" the young man cried to Elisha.

"Don't be afraid!" Elisha told him. "For there are more on our side than on theirs!" Then Elisha prayed, "O Lord, open his eyes and let him see!" The Lord opened the young man's eyes, and when he looked up, he saw that the hillside around Elisha was filled with horses and chariots of fire.

As the Aramean army advanced toward him, Elisha prayed, "O Lord, please make them blind." So the Lord struck them with blindness as Elisha had asked.

2 Kings 6:14–18 NLT

All night long, the chariots and horses pulled into position. Aramean spears bristled. Aramean swords glinted in the first light of dawn. Elisha's servant awoke to the terror of it. The Aramean army in all its cruelty was right there on Jerusalem's doorstep.

But even as the Arameans pulled into position, the armies of the Lord were pulling into position just behind them. God's people were surrounded all right: they were surrounded by the love and power of a God who had no intention of turning them over to the depredations of the Arameans.

Elisha knew that the unseen was truer than that which he could see. The Arameans had them surrounded—true. But there was something truer, and Elisha had eyes to see it. He prayed that his servant would have the same sight; and then he prayed that the Arameans would be blinded.

This world is full of dangers and enemies. But they don't get the last word. God's people can always say, "There are more on our side than on theirs!" For when God is for us, who can stand against us?

ANY OTHER GOD

[The Assyrian commander shouted,] "Listen to what the great king, the king of Assyria, says! The king says you should not let Hezekiah fool you, because he can't save you from my power. Don't let Hezekiah talk you into trusting the Lord by saying, 'The Lord will surely save us. This city won't be handed over to the king of Assyria.'

"Don't listen to Hezekiah. The king of Assyria says, 'Make peace with me, and come out of the city to me. Then every-one will be free to eat the fruit from his own grapevine and fig tree and to drink water from his own well. . . . Choose to live and not to die!'

"Don't listen to Hezekiah. He is fooling you when he says, 'The Lord will save us.' Has a god of any other nation saved his people from the power of the king of Assyria?"

2 Kings 18:28–33 NCV

The Assyrian commander spoke with a certain authority. He had already taken many towns of Judah, and now he was besieging Jerusalem itself. He made a very smooth-sounding appeal—and a barely veiled threat—directly to the people of the city. Hezekiah, one of the few faithful kings of Judah, had urged the people to trust in the Lord's deliverance. The Assyrian pointed to his horses, his chariots, his fighting men. Were the people of Jerusalem sure they wanted to put their trust in an invisible God when such a visible threat was outside their gates?

Sometimes falsehood can be very convincing. That's why it's important to learn to listen to the truth of God. The Assyrian army would have been extremely persuasive. No other god had succeeded in saving its people from the Assyrians. Those who oppose God may offer greater benefits and more freedom than following God's way. The commander's promise of eating their own fruit and drinking their own water must have appealed to the Jews. But when those promises contradict what God has said, we know they are wrong. If we follow him with our hearts, like Hezekiah, we will know the difference.

A FRESH START FOR JUDAH

Go to the king of Judah [Josiah] who sent you to seek the LORD and tell him: "This is what the LORD, the God of Israel, says concerning the message you have just heard: You were sorry and humbled yourself before the LORD when you heard what I said against this city and its people—that this land would be cursed and become desolate. You tore your clothing in despair and wept before me in repentance. And I have indeed heard you, says the LORD. So I will not send the promised disaster until after you have died and been buried in peace. You will not see the disaster I am going to bring on this city." . . .

Never before had there been a king like Josiah, who turned to the LORD with all his heart and soul and strength, obeying all the laws of Moses. And there has never been a king like him since.

2 Kings 22:18–20; 23:25 NLT

It had been generations since the people of Israel and Judah had worshipped God. The temple had fallen into disrepair. Worse than that, there were altars to pagan gods in the temple.

Then Josiah came along. Eighteen years into Josiah's reign, the temple in Jerusalem was being renovated, and Hilkiah the high priest found a copy of the Book of the Law, or the Bible. The high priest gave the scroll to a scribe named Shaphar, who read it and gave it to the king, who was only twenty-six years old at the time.

When King Josiah read the words that were written in the Book of the Law, he tore his clothes for sorrow at what had been lost. After generations of hard-heartedness and neglect of the things of God, Josiah's heart was tender, and he began taking steps to restore his people to the true worship of God.

It's hard to imagine how the people of God could have lost the Bible, and it's hard to imagine how a young man who grew up in such an environment could be so sensitive to God's leading. But there is always hope, no matter how dark things appear.

Ruling by the Book

The king commanded all the people, "Keep the Passover to the Lord your God, as it is written in this Book of the Covenant." For no such Passover had been kept . . . during all the days of the kings of Israel or of the kings of Judah. . . .

Moreover, Josiah put away the mediums and the necromancers and the household gods and the idols and all the abominations that were seen in the land of Judah and in Jerusalem, that he might establish the words of the law that were written in the book. . . . Before him there was no king like him, who turned to the Lord with all his heart and with all his soul and with all his might, according to all the Law of Moses, nor did any like him arise after him.

2 Kings 23:21–22, 24–25 ESV

The celebration of the Passover was all about remembering. Josiah lived in a generation that had completely forgotten—about the Passover and about the deliverance from Egypt that the Passover celebrated. Josiah was all about remembering. The amazing thing about Josiah was that he committed to remembering even before he knew what had been forgotten. He knew something was wrong in Judah, and he wanted something better.

When he read about the Passover in the Scriptures, he was eager to implement it. And for the first time since the break between the two kingdoms—about three hundred years—the Jewish people came back to the most treasured of their holiday traditions.

If Josiah had failed as a king, who would have blamed him? He was only eight years old when he was made king. His father and grandfather before him were scoundrels and idolaters. But Josiah was determined to bring something new to Judah—or rather, something old—and he transformed his culture. God honors our desire to be faithful, and he will make good on our first steps, however awkward, toward obedience.

KNOWING OUR PLACE

On the military side, Uzziah had a well-prepared army ready to fight. . . . The roster of family leaders over the fighting men accounted for 2,600. Under them were reinforcement troops numbering 307,000, with 500 of them on constant alert—a strong royal defense against any attack. Uzziah had them well-armed with shields, spears, helmets, armor, bows, and slingshots. He also installed the latest in military technology on the towers and corners of Jerusalem for shooting arrows and hurling stones. He became well known for all this—a famous king. Everything seemed to go his way.

But then the strength and success went to his head. Arrogant and proud, he fell. One day, contemptuous of GOD, he walked into The Temple of GOD like he owned it and took over, burning incense on the Incense Altar.

2 Chronicles 26:11–16 MSG

Uzziah had succeeded in the things important to kings. He had military might and success. He had a large and well-equipped army and a well-fortified kingdom. He was even famous for the strength he had brought to Judah. His enemies feared him.

Then he got it into his head to enter the temple and offer incense. Just in case he simply didn't know better, the priests confronted him and told him burning incense was forbidden to him. But he shouted them down. And the Lord afflicted him with leprosy.

Uzziah did not know his place. He was a capable man as a commander and as a king. But God had consecrated priests, not kings, to offer incense in the temple. A good businessman will not necessarily make a good church leader. A good church leader will not necessarily make a good politician.

Success can be an obstacle. We can never succeed our way to favor with God. Only Christ's sacrifice is sufficient for us. There is nothing we can add to or improve. Only by following God's Word will we have his blessing in what we do, whether we have worldly success or not.

Interchangeable Gods

In the time of his distress he became yet more faithless to the Lord—this same King Ahaz. For he sacrificed to the gods of Damascus that had defeated him and said, "Because the gods of the kings of Syria helped them, I will sacrifice to them that they may help me."

But they were the ruin of him and of all Israel. And Ahaz gathered together the vessels of the house of God and cut in pieces the vessels of the house of God, and he shut up the doors of the house of the Lord, and he made himself altars in every corner of Jerusalem. In every city of Judah he made high places to make offerings to other gods, provoking to anger the Lord, the God of his fathers.

2 Chronicles 28:22–25 ESV

Even by the atrocious standards of the kings of Israel and Judah, Ahaz was remarkably atrocious. He had setback after setback, but they never turned him toward God. They only led him further astray.

Ahaz lost battles to nations all around him. Never once did it occur to him that his unfaithfulness might have been the cause. He decided, instead, that God had betrayed him. He got even by desecrating and shutting down the temple, then going after the gods of the nations that had defeated him. He believed there were many gods, and their aid and support could be bought by whoever offered the best sacrifices.

Many in the ancient world believed this way, but it was especially foolish for the children of Israel. The Lord had always made it clear that he was the one true God and that all others were imaginary and powerless. Furthermore, he made it clear that his salvation wasn't something to be bought; it came by grace.

Ahaz looked at the world around him and drew his own conclusions about God. That was the basis of his many blunders.

SINS OF THE FATHERS

Hezekiah was twenty-five years old when he became the king of Judah. . . . He did what was pleasing in the LORD's sight, just as his ancestor David had done.

In the very first month of the first year of his reign, Hezekiah reopened the doors of the Temple of the LORD and repaired them. He summoned the priests and Levites to meet him at the courtyard east of the Temple. He said to them,

"Listen to me, you Levites! Purify yourselves, and purify the Temple of the LORD, the God of your ancestors. Remove all the defiled things from the sanctuary. Our ancestors were unfaithful and did what was evil in the sight of the LORD our God. They abandoned the LORD and his dwelling place; they turned their backs on him."

2 Chronicles 29:1–6 NLT

Hezekiah made worship of the Lord a priority in Israel and in his reign. One of the first things he did as king was clean up the temple. This wasn't just a public works project, beautifying a symbolic historic building. He didn't just repair the building; he told the Levites to purify themselves, and to take anything spiritually impure out of the temple.

In so doing, Hezekiah swam against the tide of family history. As Hezekiah said in his speech to the priests, his recent ancestors, in contrast to his distant ancestor David, had been unfaithful and disobedient.

Many of us may have similar stories. There may be a grandparent or distant relative who was a faithful servant of the Lord, but closer family might not have been so faithful. Or the roles may be switched. Family can have a profound influence on us. But God's influence is greater. Hezekiah turned out very different from his immediate ancestors. Rather than following their example, he followed God. Hezekiah had his own story. And God was pleased with it.

RIGHTEOUS PREPARATIONS

Sennacherib king of Assyria came and entered Judah; he encamped against the fortified cities, thinking to win them over to himself. . . .

And [Hezekiah] strengthened himself, built up all the wall that was broken, raised it up to the towers, and built another wall outside; also he repaired the Millo in the City of David, and made weapons and shields in abundance. Then he set military captains over the people . . . and gave them encouragement, saying, "Be strong and courageous; do not be afraid nor dismayed before the king of Assyria, nor before all the multitude that is with him; for there are more with us than with him. With him is an arm of flesh; but with us is the LORD our God, to help us and to fight our battles."

2 Chronicles 32:1, 5–8 NKJV

Hezekiah had begun his reign by concentrating on worship of the Lord and purification of the temple. That put him in distinct contrast to many of the kings who preceded him. They seemed especially vulnerable to false worship when they were under military threat. Hezekiah's own father had sacrificed to idols when the king of Assyria threatened.

When Hezekiah was threatened, he did what any good king would do to prepare for war. He fortified his city. He prepared his soldiers with offensive and defensive weapons. And he gave rousing speeches to encourage and motivate them.

But the most important thing Hezekiah did was to continue to believe in the Lord. He knew God would fight for his people. For the faithful, the Lord is not just a secret weapon. The Lord is the God of history who makes things happen; the God who makes and keeps promises to his people; and the God of the covenant, who has taken a people for his own and will protect and defend them.

When threatened, we do what we can to prepare, but most important, we know that God rescues, defends, and saves us.

THE GOD OF HISTORY

God brought the king of Babylon to attack them. The king killed the young men even when they were in the Temple. He had no mercy on the young men or women, the old men or those who were sick. God handed all of them over to Nebuchadnezzar. Nebuchadnezzar carried away to Babylon all the things from the Temple of God, both large and small, and all the treasures from the Temple of the LORD. . . . Nebuchadnezzar and his army set fire to God's Temple and broke down Jerusalem's wall and burned all the palaces. They took or destroyed every valuable thing in Jerusalem.

Nebuchadnezzar took captive to Babylon the people who were left alive, and he forced them to be slaves for him and his descendants. They remained there as slaves until the Persian kingdom defeated Babylon.

2 Chronicles 36:17–20 NCV

Nebuchadnezzar seems to be ultimately powerful, and ultimately evil. He was merciless when attacking the people of Israel, killing them even in the temple, and forcing them into slavery. He was irreverent in looting and destroying God's temple. And he was shameless in destroying every other valuable thing in Jerusalem.

But Nebuchadnezzar was not invincible. God brought him to Jerusalem to punish the people for their sins. There are cruel and ambitious men around the world and throughout history. But God controls history. For all of Nebuchadnezzar's might and cruelty, the empire he built was later defeated by the Persians.

Why did God permit such a wicked man to abuse his people and even destroy his temple? Because he was willing to suffer the desecration of his temple, rather than to have his own people live wickedly and give him a bad name.

When we suffer injustice at the hands of rulers of this age, it helps to remember that they have no power except what God has given them. So we put our trust in God. At the same time, we should never forget that he is holy and deserves our service in humility and obedience.

Keeping Our Focus

When the adversaries of Judah and Benjamin heard that the descendants of the captivity were building the temple of the LORD God of Israel, they came to Zerubbabel and the heads of the fathers' houses, and said to them, "Let us build with you, for we seek your God as you do." . . .

But Zerubbabel and Jeshua and the rest of the heads of the fathers' houses of Israel said to them, "You may do nothing with us to build a house for our God; but we alone will build to the LORD God of Israel." . . .

Then the people of the land tried to discourage the people of Judah. They troubled them in building, and hired counselors against them to frustrate their purpose all the days of Cyrus king of Persia, even until the reign of Darius king of Persia.

Ezra 4:1–5 NKJV

The Jews rebuilding the temple in Jerusalem could have used some extra help from stonemasons and builders. But the physical labor wasn't the most important thing. The rebuilding of the temple was spiritual work, a task for God's people.

Some enemies of Benjamin and Judah offered to come alongside the Jews returning from exile and help them rebuild the temple. They said they worshipped the same God. But the Jewish leaders counted the costs and decided to decline the offer. In terms of local politics, it looked like a mistake. They needed all the friends they could get. As the record shows, those who "offered" friendship quickly became enemies.

Building the church—not the bricks and mortar, but the community—is something that only God's people can do. There are times when we have to separate ourselves from the world. There are times when we have to say the true worship of God is more important than "success," if that success would lead us to dilute or compromise the truth. God will build his kingdom in his own ways. We can trust him for that.

THREE KINGS

King Darius gave the order, and they searched in the library of Babylon in the archives. But it was in the fortress of Ecbatana in the province of Media that a scroll was found with this record written on it: In the first year of King Cyrus, he issued a decree concerning the house of God in Jerusalem:

Let the house be rebuilt as a place for offering sacrifices, and let its [original] foundations be retained. Its height is to be 90 feet and its width 90 feet, with three layers of cut stones and one of timber. The cost is to be paid from the royal treasury. The gold and silver articles of God's house that Nebuchadnezzar took from the temple in Jerusalem and carried to Babylon must also be returned. They are to be brought to the temple in Jerusalem, where they belong.

Ezra 6:1–5 HCSB

A bureaucratic hall of records is not the first place you would expect to find Israel's deliverance. But God can do all things. When people of Israel tried to return to their homeland after two generations in exile, the locals opposed them. They petitioned King Darius to make them stop. But Darius found the earlier decree of Cyrus and upheld it.

Cyrus, king of Persia, granted permission for the exiles to return and rebuild the temple. He even specified the dimensions of the temple so that it would be as grand and as prominent as Solomon's had been. What's more, he provided resources for the rebuilding.

It was God's plan to return his people to the land. Like the gold and silver articles Nebuchadnezzar had taken from the first temple, the people were to be returned to the Promised Land, "where they belonged."

God used Nebuchadnezzar to punish, Cyrus to restore, and Darius to confirm his purposes. When he has plans to bless and protect, he does so. We should not be afraid of rulers or authorities we fear might oppose us. God is bigger.

For Better or Worse

Hanani, one of my brothers, came from Judah with some other men, and I [Nehemiah] questioned them about the Jewish remnant that survived the exile, and also about Jerusalem.

They said to me, "Those who survived the exile and are back in the province are in great trouble and disgrace. The wall of Jerusalem is broken down, and its gates have been burned with fire."

When I heard these things, I sat down and wept. For some days I mourned and fasted and prayed before the God of heaven. Then I said: . . .

"O Lord, let your ear be attentive to the prayer of this your servant and to the prayer of your servants who delight in revering your name. Give your servant success today by granting him favor in the presence of [the king]."

I was cupbearer to the king.

Nehemiah 1:2–5, 11 NIV

Nehemiah was an exceptional man. The Persians saw it, and he was made cupbearer to the king. He also distinguished himself later as a skillful leader and administrator during the return of the exiles to Jerusalem.

Though Nehemiah was an exceptional man, his response to the tragic news of the destruction of Jerusalem was very human. He wept. He prayed. And he planned how he could remedy the situation. His response involved his heart, his spirit, and his mind—all of him.

The news from Jerusalem affected Nehemiah comprehensively as a man, but he gave all aspects of his grief over to God. His tears sustained him while he fasted. He persisted in his prayers. And he committed his plans to God, asking that God hear his prayer and grant him favor with the king.

Nehemiah was driven by his love for God, for his people, for his nation. And that affected everything he did, everything he was.

Sometimes we find ourselves in mourning, sometimes we find ourselves in a position of favor with people of power and influence. Like Nehemiah, let us give it all to God, and live the results for his glory.

Israel's Second Chance

I said to them, "You see the bad situation we are in, that Jerusalem is desolate and its gates burned by fire. Come, let us rebuild the wall of Jerusalem so that we will no longer be a reproach."

I told them how the hand of my God had been favorable to me and also about the king's words which he had spoken to me. Then they said, "Let us arise and build." So they put their hands to the good work.

But when Sanballat the Horonite and Tobiah the Ammonite official heard it, they mocked us and despised us and said, "What is this thing you are doing? Are you rebelling against the king?"

So I answered them and said to them, "The God of heaven will give us success; therefore we His servants will arise and build, but you have no portion, right or memorial in Jerusalem."

Nehemiah 2:17–20 NASB

The Lord is a God of second chances. From Adam and Eve down to us, he does not treat people as their sins deserve. He shows grace and forgives. The nation of Israel had sinned, and the people were exiled as punishment. But God gave them a second chance.

There were already Jews in Jerusalem when Nehemiah arrived. Nehemiah gave them a pep talk and told them how he had the blessing of the king. When the leaders of the nearby nations objected to the rebuilding project, Nehemiah did not appeal to Artaxerxes, but to God.

Nehemiah knew that the Jews had been exiled for following the false gods of the Canaanites. And they could not make the same mistake again. Their beginnings would be more humble. Their numbers were few. Making friends with their new neighbors might have seemed sensible. But this time they could not mix with the other nations and be led astray in their worship.

God is still gracious. He still gives second chances. Let us learn from our mistakes and not take his grace for granted.

FIRST I PRAYED

The king said, "Why does your face look sad even though you are not sick? Your heart must be sad."

Then I was very afraid. I said to the king, "May the king live forever! My face is sad because the city where my ancestors are buried lies in ruins, and its gates have been destroyed by fire."

Then the king said to me, "What do you want?"

First I prayed to the God of heaven. Then I answered the king, "If you are willing and if I have pleased you, send me to the city in Judah where my ancestors are buried so I can rebuild it." . . .

He asked me, "How long will your trip take, and when will you get back?" It pleased the king to send me, so I set a time.

Nehemiah 2:2–6 NCV

Nehemiah knew what he had to do, and he did it bravely. His plan was not without risk. He could have been executed for approaching the Persian king uninvited. But there was no other way Nehemiah could see his beloved city restored.

What was going through Nehemiah's mind when the king recognized his sadness and asked about it? Nehemiah saw it as an invitation to bring his petition before the king, and he moved forward boldly. The king might have pointed out that the Israelites had gotten what they deserved when they were carried into exile. He might have imprisoned Nehemiah for his impertinence in asking special favors.

But that isn't how it turned out. Miraculously, the king asked what Nehemiah wanted. This was another decisive moment. Nehemiah prayed that he might get it right and that the king might agree. The king did agree, and Nehemiah was sent to rebuild Jerusalem.

Moments of opportunity can be terrifying. But those situations, like sharing or defending our faith, are often essential to God's plan. Let us face them as Nehemiah did, with confidence and urgent prayer.

THE LAW OF GOD AND THE LIVES OF HIS PEOPLE

On the first day of the seventh month, Ezra the priest brought the law before the assembly of men, women, and all who could listen with understanding. While he was facing the square in front of the Water Gate, he read out of it from daybreak until noon before the men, the women, and those who could understand. All the people listened attentively to the book of the law. . . .

Ezra opened the book in full view of all the people, since he was elevated above everyone. As he opened it, all the people stood up. Ezra blessed the LORD, the great God, and with their hands uplifted all the people said, "Amen, Amen!" Then they bowed down and worshiped the LORD with their faces to the ground.

Nehemiah 8:2–3, 5–6 HCSB

When Moses first received the law of God, he read it to the people. He read it to them again when they arrived at the Promised Land. And after Joshua had conquered it, he had the law read to them too.

When the people returned from exile, Ezra read the law again. The men, women, and all the children old enough to understand came and listened attentively. Ezra blessed the Lord for giving the law and taking care of his people, and the people responded with worship and praise. Then the Levites explained the law—preaching the Word—so that the people might understand even more.

What better way could there be to mark the momentous events in the life of a nation? The Lord was to be the center and focus of all his people did. His law was to instruct and guide them how to live. Reading the law set the expectations for what was to become the next phase of their lives.

Are you facing changes and transitions in your life? Do you want a renewed relationship with the Lord? Rereading his Word is a great way to mark transitions and get a new focus.

An Unlikely Deliverance?

The king again asked, "Queen Esther, what is your petition? It will be given you. What is your request? Even up to half the kingdom, it will be granted."

Then Queen Esther answered, "If I have found favor with you, O king, and if it pleases your majesty, grant me my life—this is my petition. And spare my people—this is my request. For I and my people have been sold for destruction and slaughter and annihilation." . . .

King Xerxes asked Queen Esther, "Who is he? Where is the man who has dared to do such a thing?"

Esther said, "The adversary and enemy is this vile Haman." Then Haman was terrified before the king and queen. . . .

They hanged Haman on the gallows he had prepared for Mordecai. Then the king's fury subsided.

Esther 7:2–6, 10 NIV

Haman hated Mordecai. He hated him because he was a Jew. He hated him because Mordecai wouldn't kowtow to him. He hated him and wanted him dead.

But Mordecai was uncle to the queen and had saved the king's life. Of course, the king didn't know either of these things until Haman had already arranged for the deaths not only of Mordecai but also of all the Jews in the empire.

The story of Haman and Mordecai parallels the ongoing story of God's people. There are always those who seem to hate God's children with an unnatural spite and fight to see them destroyed. But God often raises up an unlikely hero like Esther, an orphan girl who replaced the first queen when she fell out of favor. And he grants favor to his people through powerful worldly rulers.

We may have enemies and adversaries, human and spiritual. But we also have an unlikely champion, a lowly born carpenter who just happened to be the Son of God. God delivers us from sin and death in Christ, and will save us from worldly perils too.

KNOWING WHAT'S GOOD FOR US

The LORD has spoken: "I have nourished and brought up children, and they have rebelled against Me; the ox knows its owner and the donkey its master's crib; but Israel does not know, my people do not consider."

Alas, sinful nation, a people laden with iniquity, a brood of evildoers, children who are corrupters! They have forsaken the LORD, they have provoked to anger the Holy One of Israel, they have turned away backward.

Why should you be stricken again? You will revolt more and more. The whole head is sick, and the whole heart faints. From the sole of the foot even to the head, there is no soundness in it.

Isaiah 1:2–6 NKJV

Sometimes when people are especially sinful we speak of them as behaving like animals. Isaiah said, in effect, "I wish I could say Israel was acting like animals." At least animals have the instincts to do what is best for themselves. But sin causes human beings to act against their own best interests—even when they're trying to be selfish!

The people of Israel were God's chosen ones, his children. He cared and provided for them and protected them. Most important, he loved them. But they were like ungrateful children, rebellious against his authority, as well as his commands to maintain a just society and to worship only him.

The Lord does not accept ignorance as an excuse. Even ignorant animals knew better than God's people. Their ignorant rebellion hurt them.

Later in his prophecy, Isaiah warned of judgment, and then he promised deliverance, including the coming of Christ. But first, he made a case for the seriousness of sin and for how hurtful it is. We should listen too; we're just as sinful as the Israelites, and we still need a Savior.

LET'S TALK ABOUT IT

[The LORD says,] "Your hands are full of blood. Wash yourselves and make yourselves clean. Stop doing the evil things I see you do. Stop doing wrong. Learn to do good. Seek justice. Punish those who hurt others. Help the orphans. Stand up for the rights of widows."

The LORD says, "Come, let us talk about these things. Though your sins are like scarlet, they can be as white as snow. Though your sins are deep red, they can be white like wool. If you become willing and obey me, you will eat good crops from the land. But if you refuse to obey and if you turn against me, you will be destroyed by your enemies' swords."

Isaiah 1:15–20 NCV

Isaiah's readers had a serious problem—a guilt problem. They had blood on their hands. Even those who hadn't hurt anyone directly had stood by while others hurt the weak. They failed to punish crime. They let the powerful oppress the helpless. For sins of commission and sins of omission, Isaiah's response was simple: "Stop it!"

The command to stop was paired with an invitation. "Come, let's talk about these things," God said. The people's deepest stain could be made clean again. Notice that in the first part of the passage, the verbs are active: *Stop. Learn. Seek. Punish. Help. Stand up.* God is demanding things of his people. But in the latter part of the passage, God does the work. All the people had to do was believe and turn to him, and then they would be as white as snow, as white as wool. The Lord himself would do the cleaning.

God calls us to stop, to learn, to punish, to stand up. But he also calls us to believe and to see what he can do in our lives.

ANSWERING THE CALL

In the year that King Uzziah died, I had a vision of the LORD. He was on his throne high above, and his robe filled the temple. Flaming creatures with six wings each were flying over him. . . . They shouted, "Holy, holy, holy, LORD All-Powerful! The earth is filled with your glory." . . .

I cried out, "I'm doomed! Everything I say is sinful, and so are the words of everyone around me. Yet I have seen the King, the LORD All-Powerful."

One of the flaming creatures flew over to me with a burning coal. . . . It touched my lips with the hot coal and said, "This has touched your lips. Your sins are forgiven, and you are no longer guilty."

After this, I heard the LORD ask, "Is there anyone I can send? Will someone go for us?"

"I'll go," I answered. "Send me!"

Isaiah 6:1–3, 5–8 CEV

Isaiah saw God, and it was amazing! He was regal. He was glorious. There were angels flying around praising him, saying, "Holy, holy, holy."

Isaiah's response was not to pump his fist in the air and shout as we might for a human celebrity. He was completely overwhelmed by his own sin in the presence of God's holiness. His first thought was simple: *I'm doomed!*

Isaiah wasn't just being humble. His was an inevitable response. Throughout the Bible, people who encounter God's holiness are overwhelmed.

But God didn't show himself to Isaiah in order to annihilate him. He had a job that needed doing. Once Isaiah understood his unworthiness, God purified him and forgave his sins. And immediately, Isaiah became a willing servant. God asked for someone to be his messenger, and this time Isaiah did shout, "I'll go! Send me!"

What a beautiful picture of the gospel. Aware of God's holiness, we are convicted of our sins. But when we humble ourselves, he forgives us. The inevitable response, then, is grateful willingness to serve.

GOD WITH US

The Lord Himself will give you a sign: Behold, a virgin will be with child and bear a son, and she will call His name Immanuel. . . .

You shall multiply the nation, You shall increase their gladness; they will be glad in Your presence. . . . For You shall break the yoke of their burden. . . .

For a child will be born to us, a son will be given to us; and the government will rest on His shoulders; and His name will be called Wonderful Counselor, Mighty God, Eternal Father, Prince of Peace.

There will be no end to the increase of His government or of peace, on the throne of David and over his kingdom, to establish it and to uphold it with justice and righteousness from then on and forevermore. The zeal of the LORD of hosts will accomplish this.

Isaiah 7:14; 9:3–4, 6–7 NASB

If the history of the Jewish nation proved anything, it was that people resist God's authority. In the modern age, we don't do any better.

But God, in his grace, still loved Judah and still wanted to save his people. And he wants to save us. The problem was not just the Israelites, but the human heart. The problem is universal. It affects people, families, communities, and nations. And God would save them all.

His solution, though, began in the most surprising way. He didn't appear directly from heaven in all of his glory. He did not send a god-king to reign and whip us into shape. His plan to save the world was to send a baby.

He was no ordinary baby. He was a miracle child, born to a mother, but without a human father. God's plan to restore peace and justice to all nations and society and government began with one perfect, miraculous child. A risky plan, maybe, but the Christ child has changed human history. And he isn't done yet. He is still transforming cultures, and he is coming again to reign.

THE LION, THE LAMB, AND THE LITTLE CHILD

The wolf shall dwell with the lamb, and the leopard shall lie down with the young goat, and the calf and the lion and the fattened calf together; and a little child shall lead them. . . .

The nursing child shall play over the hole of the cobra, and the weaned child shall put his hand on the adder's den. They shall not hurt or destroy in all my holy mountain; for the earth shall be full of the knowledge of the LORD as the waters cover the sea.

In that day the root of Jesse, who shall stand as a signal for the peoples—of him shall the nations inquire, and his resting place shall be glorious.

Isaiah 11:6, 8–10 ESV

It's hard for us to imagine life without danger. But Isaiah describes a world where domestic animals don't fear wild ones. Even among humans there will be no fear. The youngest, most vulnerable child will not need to fear the most dangerous of poisonous snakes.

Knowledge of the Lord will bring about this kind of change in the natural order of things. Knowing him with our hearts, not just our heads, changes everything. In the world to come this knowledge will be as universal as water on the sea. And because of it, there will be no hurt or destruction. There will be peace.

A little child shall be the leader of this new world. The child is Christ Jesus, the root of David's father, Jesse, and descendant of David and heir of his throne.

There are still dangers in this life. But Christ's reign has begun, and one day all nations will know him and the peace he brings. Even now, that gives us a great comfort and makes us want to know him more.

Prepare for Comfort

Comfort, comfort my people, says your God. Speak tenderly to Jerusalem, and cry to her that her warfare is ended, that her iniquity is pardoned, that she has received from the LORD's hand double for all her sins.

A voice cries: "In the wilderness prepare the way of the LORD; make straight in the desert a highway for our God. Every valley shall be lifted up, and every mountain and hill be made low; the uneven ground shall become level, and the rough places a plain.

"And the glory of the LORD shall be revealed, and all flesh shall see it together, for the mouth of the LORD has spoken."

Isaiah 40:1–5 ESV

The prophecy of Isaiah is often divided into two parts: the book of judgment and the book of comfort. This passage begins the book of comfort. And the comfort more than surpasses the judgment. Israel can be at peace; she has received from the Lord's hand double for all her sins. That word *double* doesn't mean God punishes twice as much as our sins deserve. The punishment is the match, the double for the sin.

Once our sins are dealt with, everything that follows is blessing. Isaiah calls Israel to get ready to receive it, to prepare the way, to remove every obstacle to the revelation of the glory of the Lord. That's an amazing thing to think about: if we are in Christ, our sins are gone, and the rest is blessing, whatever happens. Hardships aren't punishment; rather, they are blessings that build our character. Suffering only serves to make us more like Jesus.

The gospel doesn't make sin and judgment irrelevant. The gospel says that it's all been dealt with. Those are the truest words of comfort for the weary soul. Prepare your heart to receive the blessings that follow.

LEARNING TO FLY . . . AND WAIT

Why do you say, O Jacob, . . . "My way is hidden from the LORD, and my just claim is passed over by my God"?

Have you not known? Have you not heard? The everlasting God, the LORD, the Creator of the ends of the earth, neither faints nor is weary. His understanding is unsearchable. He gives power to the weak, and to those who have no might He increases strength. Even the youths shall faint and be weary, and the young men shall utterly fall, but those who wait on the LORD shall renew their strength; they shall mount up with wings like eagles, they shall run and not be weary, they shall walk and not faint.

Isaiah 40:27–31 NKJV

It is easy for us to protest when we feel we are being ignored. Our troubles and complaints seem so big to us that we can't imagine there is any way to deal with them other than immediately. And if they are not addressed immediately, it must mean that they are being ignored altogether. We wonder if nobody sees us struggling along the path.

Isaiah showed us two things, though, about our God. First, God does care about us and about our troubles. Second, his timing is different from ours.

The Lord gives strength to the weak and encouragement to the weary. But the Lord does not function on our timetable. And that is frustrating. The Lord God created the ends of the earth (and the beginning and the middle too). He knows what is what and how things work. And sometimes he doesn't help us out just when we think he should. It's not because he likes to watch us suffer, but because he wants to grow our faith in him. Waiting is a kind of faith, and the rewards are rich. They soar like eagles.

MISSION ACCOMPLISHED

[God said,] "I don't think the way you think. The way you work isn't the way I work. For as the sky soars high above earth, so the way I work surpasses the way you work, and the way I think is beyond the way you think.

"Just as rain and snow descend from the skies and don't go back until they've watered the earth, doing their work of making things grow and blossom, producing seed for farmers and food for the hungry, so will the words that come out of my mouth not come back empty-handed. They'll do the work I sent them to do, they'll complete the assignment I gave them. So you'll go out in joy, you'll be led into a whole and complete life."

Isaiah 55:8–12 MSG

God is not like us. That's very good news. His ways are as high above us as the sky is above the earth. He can do things we cannot even imagine. He can save us when we cannot save ourselves. He can give us peace and joy when the world gives us grief and our own efforts yield only frustration.

In fact, the Lord accomplishes his will so effortlessly he doesn't have to *do* anything. His words do the work. He speaks, and things happen. At Creation, God said, "Let there be," and there was everything. But not just at Creation. Even now when God speaks, he makes reality.

In the Bible God speaks realities into being: He says, "I delight in you," and we are delightful. He says, "I gave my Son so you might have eternal life," and we have eternal life. He doesn't speak without his words' doing the work he meant for them to accomplish. That's as true as it ever was. Take comfort. Have hope. God is still speaking realities that are as high above our meager imaginations as the sky is above the earth.

COME BACK!

Jeremiah, shout toward the north: Israel, I am your LORD—come back to me! You were unfaithful and made me furious, but I am merciful, and so I will forgive you. Just admit that you rebelled and worshiped foreign gods under large trees everywhere. You are unfaithful children, but you belong to me. Come home! I'll take one or two of you from each town and clan and bring you to Zion. Then I'll appoint wise rulers who will obey me, and they will care for you like shepherds. . . .

The whole city of Jerusalem will be my throne. All nations will come here to worship me, and they will no longer follow their stubborn, evil hearts.

Jeremiah 3:12–17 CEV

The northern kingdom had been destroyed nearly a hundred years. Judah, the southern kingdom was limping along, going from one idolatry to the next, trying out every kind of worship the ancient Near East had to offer. But still God called out to Judah like the parent of a rebellious child: "Come back!"

He didn't order the people to come back. He begged them. "You made me furious," he said, "but I am merciful."

It is a hard thing to return to a parent whose heart you've broken. But as any parent knows, no matter how rebellious a child is, no matter how shamefully he has treated his parents, a parent is still a parent, and he still loves that child. He would welcome him back with joy if only the child would come back.

Some parents are hard-hearted enough to reject a child who comes home and says, "I am sorry. I want to be a part of this family again." But God is not one of those parents.

God is merciful. It is never too late. Is it time you came home?

SUFFERING FOR OBEDIENCE

As soon as Jeremiah finished telling all the people everything the LORD had commanded him to say, the priests, the prophets and all the people seized him and said, "You must die! Why do you prophesy in the LORD's name that this house will be like Shiloh and this city will be desolate and deserted?" And all the people crowded around Jeremiah in the house of the LORD.

When the officials of Judah heard about these things, they went up from the royal palace to the house of the LORD and took their places at the entrance of the New Gate of the LORD's house. Then the priests and the prophets said to the officials and all the people, "This man should be sentenced to death because he has prophesied against this city. You have heard it with your own ears!"

Jeremiah 26:8–11 NIV

Jeremiah had a terrible job. He was constantly speaking hard truths to his neighbors, and they hated him for it. But he couldn't help but speak. When he didn't, it felt like fire shut up in his bones, burning its way out. It was a simple message he was called on to proclaim: repent, or see Jerusalem destroyed.

The people of Judah found their national identity not in the Lord but in the city of Jerusalem. The idea of offending God didn't seem to bother them much; they lived, but offending God wasn't a big deal to them. But speaking threats against the great city of Jerusalem was another thing altogether. That was high treason to their ears. They were enraged at the prophet; they wanted to kill him.

The things that make us angry are a clue to where we really place our trust and our identity. Is there some truth that really makes you mad? Examine that anger. It might be completely appropriate anger. Or, as in the case of the Jerusalemites who wanted to murder Jeremiah, it might be the tip-end of a hidden idol.

LIFE GOES ON

This is what the Lord Almighty, the God of Israel, says to all those I carried into exile from Jerusalem to Babylon: "Build houses and settle down. . . . Marry and have sons and daughters; find wives for your sons and give your daughters in marriage. . . . Increase in number there; do not decrease. Also, seek the peace and prosperity of the city to which I have carried you into exile. Pray to the Lord for it, because if it prospers, you too will prosper. . . .

"When seventy years are completed for Babylon, I will come to you and fulfill my gracious promise to bring you back to this place. For I know the plans I have for you," declares the Lord, "plans to prosper you and not to harm you, plans to give you hope and a future."

Jeremiah 29:4–7, 10–11 NIV

The people of Israel were crushed. They had been carried out of their homeland and into exile in Babylon. Since Abraham, God had promised to give his people the land of Canaan. It was a land flowing with milk and honey. It was the land of David's glory and Solomon's temple. It was the Jewish homeland for centuries. When God evicted them, they lost more than their national sovereignty; they lost their identity.

God instructed Jeremiah to send a letter to the leaders of the Jews in exile. The letter had a straightforward message: Get on with your life. You're not in Canaan anymore; you're in Babylon. So live in Babylon. Build houses. Get married. And here's the real shocker: pray for the peace and prosperity of Babylon!

The end of the world isn't necessarily the end of the world. God is faithful, even in what seem to be the worst possible circumstances. We mourn our losses. We grieve. Then we get on with our lives. There's no sense growing bitter: You're in Babylon? Then do what you can to make Babylon the kind of place you'd like to live.

THE WIDOWED CITY

Jerusalem once was full of people, but now the city is empty. Jerusalem once was a great city among the nations, but now she is like a widow. . . .

She cries loudly at night, and tears are on her cheeks. There is no one to comfort her; all who loved her are gone. All her friends have turned against her and are now her enemies. Judah has gone into captivity where she suffers and works hard. She lives among other nations, but she has found no rest. Those who chased her caught her when she was in trouble. The roads to Jerusalem are sad, because no one comes for the feasts. No one passes through her gates.

Lamentations 1:1–4 NCV

It was the Holy City, the City of David. It was home to the temple, where God had said, "There shall my Name be" (2 Kings 23:27 NIV). Now it was in smoking ruins, for Jerusalem had also been the site of a great turning from God to wickedness and idolatry. It was a place where all of the other advantages were rejected, along with the God who had given them.

Jeremiah described Jerusalem as a widow. That personification of the city shows that what happened to Jerusalem happened not to a city made of stone, but to the people who had lived there. And it didn't just happen to the people; it happened because of the people. The whole thing was as sad as a death in the family.

It broke God's heart to destroy Jerusalem. But he loved the people of Jerusalem far more than he loved the buildings on a hill. God took extreme measures so that the people might reject their idols and turn to him as the one true God.

A Weeping Prophet, a Message of Hope

Remember my affliction and my wanderings, the wormwood and the gall! My soul continually remembers it and is bowed down within me. But this I call to mind, and therefore I have hope: The steadfast love of the LORD never ceases; his mercies never come to an end; they are new every morning; great is your faithfulness.

"The LORD is my portion," says my soul, "therefore I will hope in him." The LORD is good to those who wait for him, to the soul who seeks him. It is good that one should wait quietly for the salvation of the LORD. It is good for a man that he bear the yoke in his youth.

Lamentations 3:19–27 ESV

Jeremiah, the author of Lamentations, is sometimes called "the Weeping Prophet." He could be a downer sometimes. He prophesied about the destruction of Jerusalem, and then he mourned and wept when it happened.

But in the end, Jeremiah wasn't a pessimist. In the midst of all the tragedy, God entrusted Jeremiah with some of the most beautiful and profound promises of hope in all of Scripture. Jeremiah was afflicted, and his soul was bowed down, but he also knew that "the steadfast love of the LORD never ceases; his mercies never come to an end; they are new every morning."

When Jeremiah awoke each new morning, Jerusalem was still in ruins. But he knew too that God was still good. At a time when it appeared that the dream of Israel was over, never to return, Jeremiah announced that the Babylonian Exile would last a finite amount of time—seventy years—and that the people of Israel would return.

Jeremiah was a man true to his times. His words were harsh and tragic when that was God's message for his people. But because God is merciful, Jeremiah ultimately had a message of hope.

A Terrifying, Welcome Vision

It came to pass in the thirtieth year, in the fourth month, on the fifth day of the month, as I was among the captives by the River Chebar, that the heavens were opened and I saw visions of God. On the fifth day of the month, which was in the fifth year of King Jehoiachin's captivity, the word of the Lord came expressly to Ezekiel the priest, the son of Buzi, in the land of the Chaldeans by the River Chebar; and the hand of the Lord was upon him there.

Then I looked, and behold, a whirlwind was coming out of the north, a great cloud with raging fire engulfing itself; and brightness was all around it and radiating out of its midst like the color of amber, out of the midst of the fire.

Ezekiel 1:1–4 NKJV

Ezekiel was among the first of the exiles, carried off to Babylon more than ten years before the final siege and fall of Jerusalem. He had been taken away with the king, the royal family, and the leading men of the land. They were alive and with their compatriots, and they maintained some status. But they were captives in a foreign land.

What a joy and relief it must have been to Ezekiel to see a vision from God. As a priest, he would have been spiritually sensitive to the reasons the Jews had been exiled. He would have understood that their punishment was a direct result of God's anger with them. As far as Ezekiel knew, God might never talk to them again. But then came Ezekiel's vision. God appeared in awesome power, with a whirlwind, a raging fire, and brightness radiating.

We all go through spiritual valleys and dark places, sometimes because of our sin, sometimes for reasons we do not understand. Sometimes we seem far from God. But he is there, even when we don't see him, and every now and then, he gives us a little glimpse.

New Hearts for Old

"This is what the Sovereign LORD says: Although I sent them far away among the nations and scattered them among the countries, yet for a little while I have been a sanctuary for them in the countries where they have gone. . . . I will gather you from the nations and bring you back from the countries where you have been scattered, and I will give you back the land of Israel again."

They will return to it and remove all its vile images and detestable idols. I will give them an undivided heart and put a new spirit in them; I will remove from them their heart of stone and give them a heart of flesh. Then they will follow my decrees and be careful to keep my laws. They will be my people, and I will be their God.

Ezekiel 11:16–20 NIV

The people of Israel had a long history of rejecting the Lord. He sent judges and prophets to warn them and foreign kings to punish them. And they reformed . . . for a while. When the threat was gone, they always fell back into their old patterns.

Now in exile, the people finally understood what they had done. But could they ever get back? Could they reform themselves enough that God would have them again?

The answer, of course, was no. Sinful people cannot improve or clean themselves up well enough to be received by God. But as Ezekiel pointed out, it doesn't start with us. Even when his people were under punishment, God was a sanctuary for them. Then he gathered up the scattered and brought them home again. Most important, he changed them from the inside. He gave them undivided hearts of flesh to replace their cold, dead hearts of stone.

We can't reform ourselves either. We don't have to. God gives us new hearts in Christ, calls us his children, and brings us home.

WHOM DO YOU TRUST?

The word of the LORD came to me: "Son of man, prophesy against the prophets of Israel who are now prophesying. Say to those who prophesy out of their own imagination: 'Hear the word of the LORD! This is what the Sovereign LORD says: Woe to the foolish prophets who follow their own spirit and have seen nothing! Your prophets, O Israel, are like jackals among ruins. . . .

"'Their visions are false and their divinations a lie. They say, "The LORD declares," when the LORD has not sent them; yet they expect their words to be fulfilled. . . .

"'They lead my people astray, saying, "Peace," when there is no peace, and because, when a flimsy wall is built, they cover it with whitewash. . . . When the wall collapses, will people not ask you, "Where is the whitewash you covered it with?"'"

Ezekiel 13:1–6, 10–12 NIV

From his vantage point in Babylon, after King Nebuchadnezzar's first attack on Judah and the final destruction of Jerusalem, Ezekiel could see that everything was decidedly not all right.

But there were so-called prophets back in Judah who kept telling the people everything was going to be okay. Things were going to get better. There would be peace instead of war. Ezekiel knew better; the Lord told him greater judgment was coming. The prophets' message didn't square with what the Lord had already said, that the people would be punished for their rebellion against him. The people hadn't repented, so why should things change?

It's easy to say, "Thus says the Lord." It's even easy to convince yourself that something is truth when you've just wished it or made it up. Ezekiel marveled at the prophets who prophesied out of their own imagination and then expected their words to be fulfilled. It isn't just false prophets who paint over flimsy walls with whitewash and hope they'll pass inspection. But in the end, the Word of God is the only reliable basis for what is true and what is not.

THE GOOD SHEPHERD

This is what the Sovereign LORD says: I myself will search and find my sheep. I will be like a shepherd looking for his scattered flock. . . . I will bring them back home to their own land of Israel from among the peoples and nations. I will feed them on the mountains of Israel and by the rivers and in all the places where people live. Yes, I will give them good pastureland on the high hills of Israel. There they will lie down in pleasant places and feed in the lush pastures of the hills. . . .

I will search for my lost ones who strayed away, and I will bring them safely home again. I will bandage the injured and strengthen the weak. But I will destroy those who are fat and powerful. I will feed them, yes—feed them justice!

Ezekiel 34:11–16 NLT

It's always hurtful when religious leaders let us down. It happens all the time. And it's nothing new. The Bible is full of religious leaders who didn't take care of their flocks, from Eli and his sons to the Pharisees of Jesus' time. Ezekiel offered up a special message to religious charlatans—and to the people who have been hurt by them.

Israel's shepherd had failed them. The priests had not kept them from disaster, but had spurred them toward it. Some corrupted their worship with idolatry. Others served only for a paycheck, and looked for opportunities to cheat the people.

God promised to destroy the "fat and powerful"—to feed them justice. But the other side of that promise was a promise to the sheep who had been left to fend for themselves. God promised to be their Good Shepherd: he would seek out those who had been scattered for want of a shepherd's care.

Ultimately, God is our Shepherd, not our human leaders. Our hope is that our leaders will serve us well, but whether they do or they don't, God is our Good Shepherd who lays down his life for his sheep.

DRY BONES

The hand of the LORD came upon me and brought me out in the Spirit of the LORD, and set me down in the midst of the valley; and it was full of bones. . . .

And He said to me, "Son of man, can these bones live?"

So I answered, "O Lord GOD, You know."

Again He said to me, "Prophesy to these bones, and say to them, 'O dry bones, hear the word of the LORD! Thus says the Lord GOD to these bones: "Surely I will cause breath to enter into you, and you shall live. I will put sinews on you and bring flesh upon you, cover you with skin and put breath in you; and you shall live. Then you shall know that I am the LORD."'"

Ezekiel 37:1, 3–6 NKJV

In one of the creepier Bible stories, Ezekiel found himself in a valley of dry bones. It was a vision, but the effect is still chilling. It's a picture of just how far gone the people of Israel were. They weren't spiritually slow or sick or sleepy. They were spiritually dead. Without God, it's true of all of us.

But the dead can live.

Ezekiel preached to the bones, and the bones began to rattle. They connected one to another into whole skeletons. Then tendons and flesh appeared, and skin. Then the bones began to breathe, and then they stood upon their feet—a vast army of living, breathing soldiers where once there had been only dried-up bones.

The dead can live. It happens all the time. Someone speaks the truth, and a spirit as dead as a pile of dried-up bones comes to life. Life out of death. Beauty out of ashes. Abundance out of emptiness. That's the gospel. And it has the power to transform every aspect of our lives.

EATING RIGHT

The king ordered Ashpenaz, his chief of staff, to bring to the palace some of the young men of Judah's royal family and other noble families. . . .

"Select only strong, healthy, and good-looking young men," he said. "Make sure they are well versed in every branch of learning, are gifted with knowledge and good judgment, and are suited to serve in the royal palace. Train these young men in the language and literature of Babylon." The king assigned them a daily ration of food and wine from his own kitchens. They were to be trained for three years, and then they would enter the royal service. . . .

But Daniel was determined not to defile himself by eating the food and wine given to them by the king. He asked the chief of staff for permission not to eat these unacceptable foods.

Daniel 1:3–5, 8 NLT

Daniel had hit the jackpot. He may not have been in his homeland, but he was living in a king's palace. He was given every advantage—good food, a great education, everything he needed. He was in a position to thrive and prosper, to take a position of leadership in the community in which he now found himself.

The Babylonians' strategy was to take advantage of the best and the brightest from throughout the empire, helping them to assimilate and, in so doing, diluting the national identity of captive peoples. It was a way of preventing rebellions. But Daniel knew that mixing with the people of Babylon would lead to his spiritual corruption too.

It came down to something as simple as food. The Jews had a special diet given them by Moses, and it didn't include food that had been sacrificed to Babylonian idols. Daniel said, "Thanks, but no thanks," to the sumptuous diet with which the Babylonians bribed him. He took a stand on something simple because it had greater implications. There are times when we have to let go of pleasures and even privileges to keep our faith pure.

CONSIDER THE SOURCE

Daniel went to Arioch, whom the king had appointed to execute the wise men of Babylon, and said to him, "Do not execute the wise men of Babylon. Take me to the king, and I will interpret his dream for him."

Arioch took Daniel to the king at once and said, "I have found a man among the exiles from Judah who can tell the king what his dream means."

The king asked Daniel (also called Belteshazzar), "Are you able to tell me what I saw in my dream and interpret it?"

Daniel replied, "No wise man, enchanter, magician or diviner can explain to the king the mystery he has asked about, but there is a God in heaven who reveals mysteries. He has shown King Nebuchadnezzar what will happen in days to come."

Daniel 2:24–28 NIV

Nebuchadnezzar had a terrifying dream and couldn't figure out what it meant. He was sure his own magicians and wise men didn't know either. Nebuchadnezzar angrily ordered the execution of all the wise men in the land, including Daniel.

Daniel himself did not know the answer, but he didn't want to die or see the other wise men killed, so he prayed to the Lord and asked his friends to pray.

God gave Daniel the answer. Daniel, in turn, made it very clear to the king that the answer had come from God and not from him. Nebuchadnezzar knew that he might be the greatest ruler on earth, but there was a God in heaven who ruled over all, and that God was Daniel's God.

We are sometimes threatened or intimidated by people with power and authority over us. Sometimes we feel we are asked to do the impossible. But nothing is impossible for God. We can't solve the impossible alone, but with prayer and humility, God will show us what we need to do.

DOING THE RIGHT THING

[Shadrach, Meshach, and Abednego] replied, "Your Majesty, we don't need to defend ourselves. The God we worship can save us from you and your flaming furnace. But even if he doesn't, we still won't worship your gods and the gold statue you have set up." . . .

So the soldiers tied up Shadrach, Meshach, and Abednego and threw them into the flaming furnace with all of their clothes still on, including their turbans. The fire was so hot that flames leaped out and killed the soldiers.

Suddenly the king jumped up and shouted, "Weren't only three men tied up and thrown into the fire?"

"Yes, Your Majesty," the people answered.

"But I see four men walking around in the fire," the king replied. "None of them is tied up or harmed, and the fourth one looks like a god."

Daniel 3:16–18, 21–25 CEV

It was a remarkable statement of faith: "God can save us, but even if he doesn't, we still won't worship your gods." Shadrach, Meshach, and Abednego worshipped God because he was God, not simply because of what he could do for them. To put it another way, they didn't view their service to God as a quid pro quo. They knew that God could deliver them. He could do anything he pleased. But that was the point. Whether it was God's pleasure to deliver them or to let them burn, they wouldn't bow down to any other gods.

Shadrach, Meshach, and Abednego showed incredible self-possession. To bow down to Nebuchadnezzar's idols may have saved their skin, but it would have cost them their dignity. They couldn't separate themselves from the true worship that motivated their lives.

As it turned out, God did deliver the three young men. He went in the furnace with them; Nebuchadnezzar himself couldn't deny that the insolent-sounding Jewish men were right all along.

God is faithful. He can deliver us from every earthly difficulty. He very often does; but sometimes he doesn't. Even then, he is worthy of our worship.

THE WRITING ON THE WALL

King Belshazzar gave a great banquet for a thousand of his nobles and drank wine with them. While Belshazzar was drinking his wine, he gave orders to bring in the gold and silver goblets that Nebuchadnezzar his father had taken from the temple in Jerusalem, so that the king and his nobles, his wives and his concubines might drink from them. So they brought in the gold goblets that had been taken from the temple of God in Jerusalem. . . .

As they drank the wine, they praised the gods of gold and silver, of bronze, iron, wood and stone.

Suddenly the fingers of a human hand appeared and wrote on the plaster of the wall, near the lampstand in the royal palace. The king watched the hand as it wrote. His face turned pale and he was so frightened that his knees knocked together and his legs gave way.

Daniel 5:1–6 NIV

It was an elaborate display of worldly wealth and power—a thousand people eating and drinking. But when Belshazzar pulled out the goblets that had been looted from Solomon's temple and he raised a toast to Babylon's false gods, otherworldly power crashed the party. God showed up.

Belshazzar was terrified at the sight of a disembodied hand writing on the wall. Just a few minutes before, he was making a spectacle of his power; now, knees knocking, he was downright clownish in his fear.

God clearly had a message for Belshazzar. And he wasn't ready to hear it. He was proud, and trusted in his position for his security. He was frivolous and recklessly indulged in short-term pleasures.

Daniel was called in to read the handwriting on the wall. The message was scarier than the spectacle itself: "God has numbered the days of your reign and brought it to an end. . . . You have been weighed on the scales and found wanting" (Dan. 5:26–27 NIV).

The party was over in more ways than one. We may ignore the spiritual world as much as we like, but ultimately the spiritual is always brought to bear on the life we live.

Who's in Charge?

The king gave the command, and they brought Daniel and cast him into the den of lions. But the king spoke, saying to Daniel, "Your God, whom you serve continually, He will deliver you." . . .

Then the king arose very early in the morning and went in haste to the den of lions. And when he came to the den, he cried out with a lamenting voice to Daniel. The king spoke, saying to Daniel, "Daniel, servant of the living God, has your God, whom you serve continually, been able to deliver you from the lions?"

Then Daniel said to the king, "O king, live forever! My God sent His angel and shut the lions' mouths, so that they have not hurt me, because I was found innocent before Him."

Daniel 6:16, 19–22 NKJV

King Darius did not intend to persecute Daniel. He was tricked by those who resented Daniel's preferred status. They attacked Daniel's faithfulness to God, portraying it as disloyalty to the king.

The king loved and trusted Daniel, but he was bound by the law. It grieved him to sentence Daniel to death, and he blessed Daniel as he was thrown to the lions. After a sleepless night, he ran to the lions' den at first light, hoping aloud that God had saved him.

Daniel was fine. He blessed the king, praised God for saving him, and proclaimed again his innocence.

Even powerful and influential people cannot always stand against the plans of the evil to harm God's people. There are spiritual struggles that take advantage of ruthless ambition apart from the ordinary power politics of human rulers.

But Daniel and the king were both vindicated. God saved Daniel and spared Darius the guilt of a great injustice. David's integrity in his prayers, his loyalty to the king, and the king's confidence in the power of Daniel's God were greater than the schemes of those who opposed all three.

CHEATING HEARTS

When the Lord began speaking through Hosea, the Lord said to him, "Go, and marry an unfaithful woman and have unfaithful children, because the people in this country have been completely unfaithful to the Lord." So Hosea married Gomer daughter of Diblaim. . . .

"You are to call your brothers, 'my people,' and your sisters, 'you have been shown pity.'

"Plead with your mother. Accuse her, because she is no longer my wife, and I am no longer her husband. Tell her to stop acting like a prostitute, to stop behaving like an unfaithful wife. If she refuses, I will strip her naked and leave her bare like the day she was born. I will make her dry like a desert, like a land without water, and I will kill her with thirst."

Hosea 1:2–3; 2:1–3 NCV

It is easy to feel sorry for Hosea as he goes into a marriage knowing that his wife will be unfaithful, knowing that he will have to raise their children alone while she runs around on him.

But this is God's story more than Hosea's. God understood the cheating human heart from the very beginning, but he called Israel to be his people anyway. When she strayed—as he knew she would—he earnestly called for her to return to him, even though he knew what her reply would be.

The Lord had plans for his people. As the God who had created and redeemed them, he wanted a loving, intimate, faithful relationship, like a marriage. But the nation of Israel rejected the Lord. She wanted to see other people.

It is easy to relate to Hosea's plight. But Hosea doesn't represent us in this story. Gomer represents us. Gomer is the character to whom we ought to relate. Like Hosea, God is always wooing us, always loving us when we are at our worst.

THE HATEFUL PROPHET

The sea was getting rougher and rougher. So [the sailors] asked [Jonah], "What should we do to you to make the sea calm down for us?"

"Pick me up and throw me into the sea," he replied, "and it will become calm." . . .

Instead, the men did their best to row back to land. But they could not, for the sea grew even wilder than before. Then they cried to the LORD, "O LORD, please do not let us die for tak-ing this man's life." . . . Then they took Jonah and threw him overboard, and the raging sea grew calm. At this the men greatly feared the LORD, and they offered a sacrifice to the LORD and made vows to him.

But the LORD provided a great fish to swallow Jonah, and Jonah was inside the fish three days and three nights.

Jonah 1:11–17 NIV

God told Jonah to preach to Ninevah, the capital of Assyria. Jonah wasn't afraid of failure; he was afraid he would succeed. He was afraid that his hated enemies might repent and be spared. So Jonah boarded a ship heading the opposite direction.

The Lord intervened. When the terrified sailors asked what they should do in the storm Jonah caused, Jonah could have said, "Turn the ship around." Instead, he chose to die. But he didn't offer to jump into the ocean. He told the sailors to throw him in, so they would be guilty of his death.

The pagan sailors were more pious than Jonah, the prophet of God. They did not want to be judged for sin. And, unlike Jonah, the sailors worshipped God when they saw his anger appeased.

Jonah typified the people of ancient Israel who were so focused on their national identity that they wanted to see their neighbors destroyed—never mind that God wanted to spare them. May this never be our attitude. May our prejudices never cause us to sit in judgment of who should be saved and who should be destroyed.

A Change from the Inside—of a Fish

Jonah prayed to the Lord his God from the stomach of the fish, and he said, "I called out of my distress to the Lord, and He answered me. I cried for help from the depth of Sheol; You heard my voice.

"For You had cast me into the deep, into the heart of the seas, and the current engulfed me. All Your breakers and billows passed over me.

"So I said, 'I have been expelled from Your sight.' . . .

"Those who regard vain idols forsake their faithfulness, but I will sacrifice to You with the voice of thanksgiving. That which I have vowed I will pay. Salvation is from the Lord."

Jonah 2:1–4, 8–9 NASB

Throughout the Bible, the sea is used as a metaphor for chaos, for ruin. It was in the heart of the sea and the belly of the fish that Jonah realized just how chaotic he had let his life become. It was in the belly of the fish that Jonah was finally ready to call out to God. And as always, God answered.

"Salvation is from the Lord," Jonah said. Once he realized that he needed God's salvation, he realized that he had no business trying to withhold salvation from the Ninevites who so desperately needed it. He no longer saw himself as so very different from the Ninevites. Their wickedness may have been more spectacular, but it didn't go any deeper than his wickedness. The Ninevites' idols may have been more tangible, but Jonah worshipped a few false gods himself—his own moral superiority, for one.

Need and trouble cause us to cry out to God. When we truly feel our need—when we recognize that we bring no more to God than anybody else does—it is very hard to be judgmental about other people.

AN ASTONISHING TURNAROUND

The people of Nineveh listened, and trusted God. They proclaimed a citywide fast and dressed in burlap to show their repentance. . . .

When the message reached the king of Nineveh, he got up off his throne, threw down his royal robes, dressed in burlap, and sat down in the dirt. Then he issued a public proclamation throughout Nineveh, authorized by him and his leaders: ". . . Everyone must turn around, turn back from an evil life and the violent ways that stain their hands. Who knows? Maybe God will turn around and change his mind about us, quit being angry with us and let us live!"

God saw what they had done, that they had turned away from their evil lives. He *did* change his mind about them. What he said he would do to them he didn't do.

Jonah 3:5–10 MSG

There were many reasons the Ninevites wouldn't be expected to pay any attention to a prophet of God. For one thing, they were famously wicked. As God told Jonah, "Their wickedness has come up before me" (Jonah 1:2 NKJV). They were wicked enough, in fact, that God was ready to wipe them off the face of the earth. For another thing, Nineveh was a great and wealthy city, the center of the Assyrian Empire. They wouldn't seem to need any advice from a small-time prophet from a tiny nation they had defeated more than once. For Jonah to preach on the streets of Nineveh would be about as odd as a Paraguayan preacher calling Paris to repentance; he just wouldn't quite seem relevant.

But God moved. He changed the hearts of the Ninevites, and, miraculously, they repented. The destruction God threatened through Jonah was delayed.

God does as he pleases. He rescues whomever he wants to rescue, and he doesn't ask our advice about it. In truth, we're all Ninevites. A change in an Assyrian heart may be surprising from where we sit, but it's really no more miraculous than any other heart change.

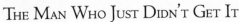

The Man Who Just Didn't Get It

The LORD God provided a vine and made it grow up over Jonah to give shade for his head to ease his discomfort, and Jonah was very happy about the vine. But at dawn the next day God provided a worm, which chewed the vine so that it withered. When the sun rose, God provided a scorching east wind, and the sun blazed on Jonah's head so that he grew faint. He wanted to die, and said, "It would be better for me to die than to live."

But God said to Jonah, "Do you have a right to be angry about the vine? . . . You have been concerned about this vine, though you did not tend it or make it grow. It sprang up overnight and died overnight. But Nineveh has more than a hundred and twenty thousand people. . . . Should I not be concerned about that great city?"

Jonah 4:6–11 NIV

A whole city repented—and a famously wicked city at that! But in the letdown after that success, Jonah's old petulance found a foothold again. He didn't praise God for the work he had done in Nineveh. He didn't even congratulate himself for his effective preaching. He said, "God, I knew you were going to do this! I knew you were going to save our enemies. That's why I didn't want to come here."

He was so angry he asked God to kill him. He sat down and waited to die. But instead of bringing death, God brought a vine to shade and comfort him. The next day, while Jonah was still enjoying the shade, God sent a worm to kill the vine and wither Jonah's shade.

Jonah was furious. In his fury, God revealed his heart. We get it in our heads that we deserve certain things—comfort, security, plenty. We come to take those things very seriously. Sometimes we take them even more seriously than we take the people in our lives. It helps to take a step back and see things from God's perspective: every person is important.

ROBBING GOD

"Will a man rob God? Yet you are robbing Me! But you say, 'How have we robbed You?' In tithes and offerings.

"You are cursed with a curse, for you are robbing Me, the whole nation of you!

"Bring the whole tithe into the storehouse, so that there may be food in My house, and test Me now in this," says the LORD of hosts, "if I will not open for you the windows of heaven and pour out for you a blessing until it overflows.

"Then I will rebuke the devourer for you, so that it will not destroy the fruits of the ground; nor will your vine in the field cast its grapes," says the LORD of hosts.

"All the nations will call you blessed, for you shall be a delightful land," says the LORD of hosts.

Malachi 3:8–12 NASB

There are several ways to justify a failure to give back to God. We say we'll get around to it next week. We say it's been a rough month. We say God doesn't need our money anyway. God says it's robbery.

It's true that God doesn't need our money. He's going to be okay. When we rob God, we're really robbing ourselves of the opportunity to see God work. "Test me in this," God says. The call to tithe often feels like a test for us: Are we going to be faithful or not? God turns that idea around completely. God is being put to the test when we give. Will God come through or won't he?

By giving to God, we give new meaning to the stuff we give away. We say, "This isn't just money or time or talent; it's God's money, God's time, God's talent." God promises to come through with abundance—not just to give us what we need, but to keep giving until it overflows. It's the sort of thing he delights in doing—overturning the world's economy and bringing plenty out of lack.

HEALING JUDGMENT

Behold, the day is coming, burning like an oven, when all the arrogant and all evildoers will be stubble. The day that is coming shall set them ablaze, says the LORD of hosts, so that it will leave them neither root nor branch. But for you who fear my name, the sun of righteousness shall rise with healing in its wings. You shall go out leaping like calves from the stall. And you shall tread down the wicked, for they will be ashes under the soles of your feet, on the day when I act, says the LORD of hosts. . . .

Behold, I will send you Elijah the prophet before the great and awesome day of the LORD comes. And he will turn the hearts of fathers to their children and the hearts of children to their fathers.

Malachi 4:1–3, 5–6 ESV

The coming judgment. The very words are scary, the sound of doom. But for those who fear God, judgment is something to look forward to. Those who oppress, harm, and frighten today will be put to flight. The wicked seem as solid as oak trees now, but when judgment comes, they'll all be gone—root and branch alike.

For those who fear God, judgment means a new freedom, a new start. It's not a sunset leading into darkness; it is a new dawn. "The sun of righteousness shall rise with healing in its wings." All the brokenness that haunts every action and every interaction will be bound up and healed.

There's no clearer picture of this world's brokenness than the brokenness of families—absent fathers, rebellious children. But on the Day of Judgment, that which has been torn apart will be put back together. Fathers' hearts will turn back toward their children; children's hearts will be turned toward their fathers. Judgment isn't simply a matter of destruction; it's a burning-away that allows good things to flourish.

Interlude

The Bible is full of songs and poems. You see the hearts of the people in whom God is working: their joys, fears, hopes, sorrows—sometimes their anger, bitterness, and doubts. They aren't always pretty, these outpourings of the heart, but they are true, and they offer an intimate glimpse of what happens when a person brings his or her whole self to God.

God, examine me and know my heart; test me and know my anxious thoughts. See if there is any bad thing in me. Lead me on the road to everlasting life.

Psalm 139:23–24 NCV

The Challenge

One day, when the angels had gathered around the LORD, and Satan was there with them, the LORD asked, "Satan, where have you been?" Satan replied, "I have been going all over the earth."

Then the LORD asked, "What do you think of my servant Job? No one on earth is like him—he is a truly good person, who respects me and refuses to do evil."

"Why shouldn't he respect you?" Satan remarked. "You are like a wall protecting not only him, but his entire family and all his property. You make him successful in whatever he does, and his flocks and herds are everywhere. Try taking away everything he owns, and he will curse you to your face."

The LORD replied, "All right, Satan, do what you want with anything that belongs to him, but don't harm Job."

Job 1:6–12 CEV

One day God and the angels were in a celestial huddle. Satan, an angelic being with a destructive twist, was included. God asked about Satan's latest travels and bragged on one-of-a-kind Job from the ancient land of Uz. Job was considered an astute businessman—the most affluent man in the region and a true worshipper of God.

Satan challenged God to a duel over what would make wealthy Job buckle and curse his Creator. He contended that Job's faith was shallow and dependent upon his success from God's hand. The challenge went forward, and ultimately Job's faith endured. Job's experience provides a blueprint for us in difficult times.

As he did with Job, Satan challenges your faith each day, often through contrary and painful circumstances. Like Job, you may be wondering why God allows these things to happen. Like Job, you may be confused and discouraged, wondering if God has abandoned you.

Know this. Satan has only what power God permits. As you press on in turbulent times, the challenger must fall back and ultimately retreat. And like Job, your faith in God will become stronger, even in the most daring of tests.

BIG ENOUGH

The LORD answered Job out of the storm. He said: "Who is this that darkens my counsel with words without knowledge? Brace yourself like a man; I will question you, and you shall answer me.

"Where were you when I laid the earth's foundation? Tell me, if you understand. Who marked off its dimensions? Surely you know! . . . Have you ever given orders to the morning, or shown the dawn its place, that it might take the earth by the edges and shake the wicked out of it? . . . Can you raise your voice to the clouds and cover yourself with a flood of water? Do you send the lightning bolts on their way?"

Job 38:1–5, 12–13, 34–35 NIV

To some, the book of Job reads like an epic tragedy. In calamity after calamity, the righteous man Job loses his ten children and his vast servants and possessions, and then he encounters terrible physical suffering. Job's wife and close friends offer little comfort. God feels silent and distant. Finally, God speaks directly to Job, giving the beleaguered man the communication he demanded.

God does not review his creation résumé to intimidate Job or ridicule his faith. Instead, Job is nudged toward a richer view of God's executive power. He is reminded in no uncertain terms that as the overseer of the earth's establishment, God will have no problem handling anything that enters Job's life . . . or yours.

Job's epic tragedy is in reality a magnificent lesson in faith. It's important for us to acknowledge that God is all-knowing and all-powerful. He reversed Job's fortune and restored to him twice what he had lost, and he can reach you where you are today—no matter how hopeless your situation might seem, no matter how deep your despair. That truth is Job's joyful legacy.

STARTING FRESH

Job replied to the LORD: "I know that you can do anything, and no one can stop you. You asked, 'Who is this that questions my wisdom with such ignorance?' It is I—and I was talking about things I knew nothing about, things far too wonderful for me. You said, 'Listen and I will speak! I have some questions for you, and you must answer them.' I had only heard about you before, but now I have seen you with my own eyes. I take back everything I said, and I sit in dust and ashes to show my repentance." . . .

So the LORD blessed Job in the second half of his life even more than in the beginning.

Job 42:1–6, 12 NLT

Enduring immense grief and pain, Job shared his honest struggle with God over suffering when innocent. But Job was never informed of Satan's behind-the-scenes plot to test him and discredit God. God never explained the mystery of the respected entrepreneur's relentless trials.

Yet in this final chapter of Job, one message is clear: Job concluded he was ignorant of God's marvelous ways. Job respectfully confessed that God is God and no one can come close to his power and majesty.

Sometimes, like Job, it's hard to humble ourselves and admit our limitations and mistakes, particularly when we need to "take back everything" we say. Sometimes it's hard to own up to the fact that we may not know God as we think we do.

Job longed for an answer to his adversity, and yet by the end of the book, he longed even more to know God intimately. Job's loss of prosperity, and eventually his pride, opened his eyes to a vibrant view of God. While still wrestling with his obstacles, Job committed to starting fresh in his faith. Every day, no matter what we are facing, we also have an invitation to start fresh with God.

DIG DEEP

How blessed is the man who does not walk in the counsel of the wicked, nor stand in the path of sinners, nor sit in the seat of scoffers! But his delight is in the law of the LORD, and in His law he meditates day and night. He will be like a tree firmly planted by streams of water, which yields its fruit in its season and its leaf does not wither; and in whatever he does, he prospers.

The wicked are not so, but they are like chaff which the wind drives away. Therefore the wicked will not stand in the judgment, nor sinners in the assembly of the righteous.

Psalm 1:1–5 NASB

Contrasts emphasize differences. Sweet vs. sour. Sunshine vs. rain. Country vs. city. The book of Psalms opens with the contrast between happy and satisfied people who do what is right and those who follow the unfulfilling ways of the world's wisdom. The world's wisdom shouts for us to seek insights from those greedily pursuing whatever they please, whenever they please. The world's wisdom taunts us to backbite and mock others.

But God's wisdom has no need to scream or scratch its way into your life. God's wisdom speaks calmly and clearly from the Bible. People who practice the ways of God and lean into the truths of his words are firmly grounded. The deeper you dig your roots into the nourishment of "the law of the LORD," the greater your inner contentment like a fruit tree gaining sustenance along a lively stream.

In contrast, those who sow their own selfish ways and ignore God's guidelines are tossed about like chaff in the wind. Every day you can choose to be like a luxurious tree or a windblown seed covering. You can choose to dig deep and stay green.

REAL HELP

GOD! Look! Enemies past counting! Enemies sprouting like mushrooms, mobs of them all around me, roaring their mockery: "Hah! No help for *him* from God!" But you, GOD, shield me on all sides; you ground my feet, you lift my head high; with all my might I shout up to GOD, his answers thunder from the holy mountain.

I stretch myself out. I sleep. Then I'm up again—rested, tall and steady, fearless before the enemy mobs coming at me from all sides.

Up, GOD! My God, help me! Slap their faces, first this cheek, then the other, your fist hard in their teeth!

Real help comes from GOD. Your blessing clothes your people!

Psalm 3:1–8 MSG

Israel's legendary King David is heralded for both his military bravery and his tender heart toward God. While politically earning his people's respect, David's personal life crumbled. Violence and dissent rumbled among his children. Absalom, the third of David's six sons, was angered that his father did little when brother Amnon raped Absalom and Amnon's half sister. After years of seething, Absalom conspired to overthrow David, and the mighty king had to flee Jerusalem with a band of his loyal followers.

On the run from rebellious Absalom and tens of thousands of disaffected citizens, David wrote Psalm 3. Tempted to wallow in despondency, the hurting king cried out to God. Instead of ordering armies to save him, the commander in chief turned to his true Deliverer. Instead of relying on his wealth and position to buy his way out of trouble, the prominent ruler placed his life in the capable hands of God.

Stripped of earthly prestige, David turned to his heavenly power. The man who once killed behemoth Goliath with a single small stone understood the limits of his own strength and cunning strategies. Instead, King David humbly prayed and confidently declared that "real help comes from GOD."

Telling God Everything

O Lord, rebuke me not in your anger, nor discipline me in your wrath. Be gracious to me, O Lord, for I am languishing; heal me, O Lord, for my bones are troubled. My soul also is greatly troubled. But you, O Lord—how long?

Turn, O Lord, deliver my life; save me for the sake of your steadfast love. For in death there is no remembrance of you; in Sheol who will give you praise?

I am weary with my moaning; every night I flood my bed with tears; I drench my couch with my weeping. . . .

The Lord has heard my plea; the Lord accepts my prayer. All my enemies shall be ashamed and greatly troubled; they shall turn back and be put to shame in a moment.

Psalm 6:1–6, 9–10 ESV

The book of Psalms is a collection of poems, prayers, and songs that were typically set to music for the Jewish people to sing in their temple worship. King David penned almost half of the 150 psalms, and in this psalm of lament, he pleaded for relief. Israel's leader was burdened by some physical illness that sank David into despair. An accomplished musician who once played the lyre to lift King Saul's melancholy moods, David knew sweet melodies would not ultimately cure his own ailing body.

The prevailing warrior was drained physically and emotionally and shared that his agony had forced him to sob every night. The world leader was not afraid to admit his struggle and tears. Perhaps you're facing a similar heaviness of body and soul. Maybe life is pressing too heavily upon you or those you love. As David modeled, be honest with God. Pour out your pain and angst. Tell God everything, and then, as David did, rest assured that God hears your plea and accepts your prayer. God is listening, and his help is on the way.

SEEING YOUR WORTH

O LORD, our Lord, your majestic name fills the earth! Your glory is higher than the heavens.

You have taught children and infants to tell of your strength. . . .

When I look at the night sky and see the work of your fingers—the moon and the stars you set in place—what are people that you should think about them, mere mortals that you should care for them? Yet you made them only a little lower than God and crowned them with glory and honor. You gave them charge of everything you made, putting all things under their authority—the flocks and the herds and all the wild animals.

Psalm 8:1–7 NLT

One gaze into the night sky and you see God's incomparable handiwork. The colossal stars and moon beam with God's creative flair. Astrophysicists have no way of counting exactly how many stars dot the universe, but many estimate the count at thousands of trillions. Yet God knows exactly how many stars scatter across the skies, and he has individually named each one!

If God pays that much attention to twinkly balls of gas light-years away from earth, think about how much he cares for us. In considering the vast and magnificent cosmos, the psalmist asked the poignant question: Who am I that God would think about and care for me? Understanding our significance in God's grand creative scheme is crucial to our valuing our purpose in everyday life.

Psalm 8 is the ideal image booster. To realize that we humans were designed "only a little lower than God," crowned with honor, and put in charge of helping rule the earth, elevates us to a proper perspective of our worth. As a one-of-a-kind work of God's fingers, every individual is immensely valued even more than the trillions of celestial lights all together.

WATCHING AND WAITING

The fool has said in his heart, "There is no God." They are corrupt, they have done abominable works, there is none who does good.

The LORD looks down from heaven upon the children of men, to see if there are any who understand, who seek God. They have all turned aside, they have together become corrupt; there is none who does good, no, not one.

Have all the workers of iniquity no knowledge, who eat up my people as they eat bread, and do not call on the LORD? There they are in great fear, for God is with the generation of the righteous. You shame the counsel of the poor, but the LORD is his refuge.

Psalm 14:1–6 NKJV

The psalmist minced no words in pitting atheists against God-followers. David described those who deny the existence of God as fools. Calling someone a fool is essentially saying the person lacks wisdom and judgment, a weak-minded individual who meanders after silly notions. David's words challenged some people in ancient times just as they challenge some individuals today. No one appreciates being labeled a "fool."

The Israelite king issued a warning and a promise in these verses. He sounded the alarm that rejecting God leads to corruption and no good. Refusing to believe that God exists and that he's actively involved in the affairs of humankind is a dead-end street. David explained that God looks down on earth searching for those who understand and seek after him. God is watching. God is waiting.

The promise comes for the righteous who do acknowledge God's existence even if they cannot see him face-to-face. God rewards those individuals with his comforting presence, a continual refuge at all times. God is watching, and God is waiting to uplift those who turn aside from foolish thinking and foolish actions.

BE GOD'S GUEST

LORD, who may abide in Your tabernacle? Who may dwell in Your holy hill?

He who walks uprightly, and works righteousness, and speaks the truth in his heart; he who does not backbite with his tongue, nor does he do evil to his neighbor, nor does he take up a reproach against his friend; in whose eyes a vile person is despised, but he honors those who fear the LORD; he who swears to his own hurt and does not change; he who does not put out his money at usury, nor does he take a bribe against the innocent.

He who does these things shall never be moved.

Psalm 15:1–5 NKJV

The biblical psalms are classified in common groupings such as lament, thanksgiving, pilgrimage, and wisdom psalms. Psalm 15 is considered a wisdom psalm because it imparts sound counsel often found in the wisdom literature of Proverbs and Ecclesiastes. Wisdom psalms typically contrast the lifestyles of those who embrace God's guidance and those who reject it.

The writer in Psalm 15 described the people who are welcomed guests in God's tabernacle or his place of worship. Did a person need to be without fault to worship in God's presence? No. If that were the case, no human could ever draw near his Maker. Only God is perfect and with a spotless record. God is not demanding we live without blunders or regrettable mistakes before he will associate with us, but our personal integrity and how we treat God and others still matter.

This psalm encourages us to walk honorably before our friends, neighbors, and even strangers. We are reminded to speak truth, avoid slander, and guard our financial dealings. Right living does have a payoff—stability and confidence that only God can offer.

Breaking Out in Song

Protect me, God, because I trust in you. I said to the LORD, "You are my Lord. Every good thing I have comes from you." As for the godly people in the world, they are the wonderful ones I enjoy. But those who turn to idols will have much pain. I will not offer blood to those idols or even speak their names.

No, the LORD is all I need. He takes care of me. My share in life has been pleasant; my part has been beautiful.

I praise the LORD because he advises me. Even at night, I feel his leading. I keep the LORD before me always. Because he is close by my side, I will not be hurt.

Psalm 16:1–8 NCV

From their earliest days, the Jewish people regarded poetry and music as an essential part of their lives. After the Israelites successfully escaped Egypt, Moses broke out in song. Hannah sang a prayer of gratitude when she dedicated her son, Samuel, to God's service. The book of Psalms was considered the hymnbook of the Hebrew people, but a book truly intended for readers of any ethnicity. In the Hebrew language, *psalms* actually means "songs of praise."

As the praise-writer of Psalm 16, David proclaimed his delight in God's continual provision. You can sense the upbeat tempo of this musical poem. David reaffirmed his trust in God and credited his Creator for "every good thing." David extolled God for his care and advice. The appreciative poet affirmed God's protective presence. The secret to David's joy and contentment is found in verse 8: "I keep the LORD before me always." Despite his fluctuating circumstances and emotions—including his rise from forgotten sheepherder to triumphant royalty—David knew to keep God at the forefront of daily life. There's much wisdom in seeking God first and recounting his generous nurturing and leadership.

TIMELY SUPPORT

He reached down from on high and took hold of me; he drew me out of deep waters. He rescued me from my powerful enemy, from my foes, who were too strong for me. They confronted me in the day of my disaster, but the LORD was my support. He brought me out into a spacious place; he rescued me because he delighted in me.

The LORD has dealt with me according to my righteousness; according to the cleanness of my hands he has rewarded me. For I have kept the ways of the LORD; I have not done evil by turning from my God. All his laws are before me; I have not turned away from his decrees.

Psalm 18:16–22 NIV

David accumulated his share of enemies. The Philistines were not happy when the shepherd boy killed their fiercest warrior. After Israel's king Saul disobeyed God, God appointed David as Saul's eventual successor to the throne. On one hand Saul invited David to live in the royal palace; on the other Saul grew increasingly jealous of David's rising popularity. Saul's resentment of David festered into hatred to the point that the insecure king ordered a hit on David's life.

David fled and remained a fugitive on the run for years. King Saul eventually died in battle, but David still faced opposition to his ascent to the throne and in his presidential dealings. Some enemies just never seem content to desist.

Our modern-day enemies are often disguised as a storied past, a bossy coworker, a meddling family member—even a warring within ourselves. In Psalm 18, David celebrated his victories over his enemies. He gave God credit for his numerous rescues and declared that even though jeered and jostled to the point of near death, "the LORD was my support." No enemy, whether a person or a trial, can overcome the timely support of God.

DUMPED BY GOD?

God, God . . . my God! Why did you dump me miles from nowhere? Doubled up with pain, I call to God all the day long. No answer. Nothing. I keep at it all night, tossing and turning.

And you! Are you indifferent, above it all, leaning back on the cushions of Israel's praise? . . . Everyone pokes fun at me; they make faces at me, they shake their heads: "Let's see how GOD handles this one; since God likes him so much, let *him* help him!" . . .

From the four corners of the earth people are coming to their senses, are running back to GOD. Long-lost families are falling on their faces before him. GOD has taken charge; from now on he has the last word.

Psalm 22:1–3, 7–8, 27–28 MSG

David opened this psalm feeling abandoned by God, as if deserted in a faraway wasteland. Centuries after David penned his lament, Jesus spoke David's words in Aramaic as he was dying on the cross: "My God, My God, why have You forsaken Me?" (Matt. 27:46 NKJV). Scholars disagree over the parallels between David's cries in Psalm 22 and Jesus' passionate pleas during his own suffering, but one can't miss David's view that God turned his back.

Everyone encounters times when God seems distant and indifferent. Often those dark struggles stem from feeling misunderstood or rejected by others, just as David bemoaned, "Everyone pokes fun at me." When we feel that life has kicked us while we are down, it's easy to transfer this angst to God. We lose confidence in God when he does not seem to answer us. Fortunately, David shared the secret to reconnecting with God and trusting him despite our jumbled feelings. David's psalms are always a fervent mix of complaint and praise. After expressing his aloneness and dejection, David eventually came back to the assurance that God is still in charge. What comfort it is to know that God is nearby after all.

Your Personal Shepherd

The LORD is my shepherd; I shall not want. He makes me lie down in green pastures. He leads me beside still waters. He restores my soul. He leads me in paths of righteousness for his name's sake. Even though I walk through the valley of the shadow of death, I will fear no evil, for you are with me; your rod and your staff, they comfort me.

You prepare a table before me in the presence of my enemies; you anoint my head with oil; my cup overflows. Surely goodness and mercy shall follow me all the days of my life, and I shall dwell in the house of the LORD forever.

Psalm 23 ESV

As the youngest of eight sons, David cared for the family's sheep. The skilled herdsman gently nurtured his flock and guarded them from harm. Fighting off wild animals in the pasturelands, David learned to depend upon God as his own watchful Shepherd.

It is believed David wrote this most famous of his psalms near the end of his life after years of trusting God's protection. Both Jews and Christians sing this beloved psalm as a hymn and often read it at funerals because verse 4 speaks of God's comfort when facing death.

The psalm can be divided into two distinct sections: God shepherding his sheep and God hosting a grand banquet for his followers. Throughout this uplifting psalm, we are drawn to meditate upon rest and revival instead of stress and strain. Why sweat anything when you have a personal Shepherd leading your daily journey? David reminded us that peace and security are ours when we settle into God presence and let him fully refresh us. The invitation is ours to enjoy the rewards of steadily following God's guiding hand as each day unfolds.

A Clean Celebration

The earth is the LORD's and the fullness thereof, the world and those who dwell therein, for he has founded it upon the seas and established it upon the rivers.

Who shall ascend the hill of the LORD? And who shall stand in his holy place? He who has clean hands and a pure heart, who does not lift up his soul to what is false and does not swear deceitfully. . . .

Lift up your heads, O gates! And be lifted up, O ancient doors, that the King of glory may come in. Who is this King of glory? The LORD, strong and mighty, the LORD, mighty in battle!

Psalm 24:1–4, 7–8 ESV

Psalm 24 is considered one of the most majestic hymns in the book of Psalms. This triumphant hymn was most likely sung when the ark of the covenant, the ornate box that contained the Jews' most sacred artifacts and served as a divine symbol of God's presence among his people, was transferred to Jerusalem. Jewish king David led a procession that carried the ark to the hill of Zion, and as groups approached Jerusalem on a number of other occasions, they most likely broke out in song with this psalm.

David's words celebrate God as the supreme Owner of the earth and everything in it. As king of the Jews, David honored the One deserving of all praise—the King of glory. In adoring his Creator, David defined that those who long to worship God are to do so with purity of hands and heart. The psalmist directed us to right living, free of falsehood and deceit. People can see our actions through the works of our hands. Only God can look inside our hearts. Only he can declare us truly forgiven and clean.

Above All Else

Though an army besiege me, my heart will not fear; though war break out against me, even then will I be confident.

One thing I ask of the LORD, this is what I seek: that I may dwell in the house of the LORD all the days of my life, to gaze upon the beauty of the LORD and to seek him in his temple. For in the day of trouble he will keep me safe in his dwelling; he will hide me in the shelter of his tabernacle and set me high upon a rock. Then my head will be exalted above the enemies who surround me; at his tabernacle will I sacrifice with shouts of joy.

Psalm 27:3–6 NIV

Sovereign over ancient Israel, King David exuded confidence under extreme pressure. Time and time again, the valiant warrior faced off with his enemies, from his solo slingshot victory over the Philistines to his army-driven conquests over neighboring nations. Yet in all his courageous successes of both war and diplomacy, David did not trust in his own military or leadership prowess. His outward calm was a reflection of his inward assurance. David's faith in God centered and settled him.

In this passage, we discover the undergirding to David's political and personal poise. Above all things he could desire from God—including deliverance from his enraged foes and a prosperous life—David chose one thing. Israel's most revered king thirsted after enjoying God's presence. David longed for daily close communion with God.

Even though David was not chosen to a build a physical temple for worship, the king knew that by his own prayer and praise he could always make himself at home with God. In our own lives, it's tempting to make our relationships, our work, our goals, and our comfort a consuming priority. Psalm 27 reminds us that nothing is more vital than purposely seeking God.

GOD, HEAR ME

Don't turn a deaf ear when I call you, GOD. If all I get from you is deafening silence, I'd be better off in the Black Hole.

I'm letting you know what I need, calling out for help and lifting my arms toward your inner sanctum.

Don't shove me into the same jail cell with those crooks, with those who are full-time employees of evil. They talk a good line of "peace," then moonlight for the Devil. Pay them back for what they've done, for how bad they've been. Pay them back for their long hours in the Devil's workshop; then cap it with a huge bonus.

Psalm 28:1–4 MSG

God, hear me" has echoed from the lips of humankind since the beginning of time. From Adam and Abraham to Zebulun and Zechariah, the Bible is replete with individuals who cry out for God to hear and answer their prayers. The words *hear* and *listen* are expressed almost seven hundred times throughout the Scriptures. Being heard and understood is a weighty deal to both humans and God.

Throughout Psalms, passionate King David scribes some of his most honest pleas for his Maker to listen. David began this psalm boldly, directing God to open his ears. Israel's leader seemed urgently troubled and perhaps pressed for his own safety. In his immediacy, David was candid with God: "I'm letting you know what I need."

Too often, we try to handle life challenges on our own and approach God only when we've exhausted other reasonable options. Sometimes we're afraid to be honest with God about our real needs. Maybe we just don't quite trust him to pull through for us.

David's prayer can nudge us toward the practice of telling God everything. Our fears. Our burdens. Even our desire for payback and justice.

Forgiveness Brings Joy

Blessed is he whose transgression is forgiven, whose sin is covered. Blessed is the man to whom the LORD does not impute iniquity, and in whose spirit there is no deceit. When I kept silent, my bones grew old through my groaning all the day long. For day and night Your hand was heavy upon me; my vitality was turned into the drought of summer. Selah

I acknowledged my sin to You, and my iniquity I have not hidden. I said, "I will confess my transgressions to the LORD," and You forgave the iniquity of my sin. Selah

For this cause everyone who is godly shall pray to You in a time when You may be found.

Psalm 32:1–6 NKJV

David fesses up in this second of seven psalms of confession (Pss. 6; 32; 38; 51; 102; 130; and 143), or penitential psalms as Saint Augustine of Hippo called them in the fifth century. Some biblical scholars attribute David's Psalm 32 confession to his dalliance with Bathsheba and the cover-up killing of her solider husband, Uriah. Whatever misdeed was tormenting David and draining his vitality, the Jewish emperor turned to God's embrace of forgiveness.

David needed his guilty conscience expunged. His silence over his offense was eating him alive. The favored leader went straight to the only One who could truly set him free from his failings. Notice that David penned *iniquity* three times in his confessional. *Iniquity* describes a moral twistedness, a flagrant violation of what is right. David didn't sugarcoat what he had done.

Note also the double use of *Selah*, which is commonly considered a Hebrew word for a musical pause or special emphasis on the preceding words. David was enlivened by the joy of forgiveness, and he exclaimed over his newfound freedom. He ended with a declaration for us too to keep a clean slate with God. *Selah*.

TEST GOD'S GOODNESS

I will praise the LORD at all times; his praise is always on my lips. My whole being praises the LORD. The poor will hear and be glad. Glorify the LORD with me, and let us praise his name together. I asked the LORD for help, and he answered me. He saved me from all that I feared. . . .

Examine and see how good the LORD is. Happy is the person who trusts him. You who belong to the LORD, fear him!

Those who fear him will have everything they need. Even lions may get weak and hungry, but those who look to the LORD will have every good thing.

Psalm 34:1–4, 8–10 NCV

David escaped death at the hand of King Saul by fleeing to the nearby city of Gath. David feigned madness before the king of Gath, who then sent away the "crazed" Hebrew. Refugee David hid out in a cave in Adullam, where he wrote this song thanking God for his deliverance. One of David's greatest classic thanksgiving psalms, Psalm 34 is also a song of invitation.

Fresh off his capture and release, the psalmist shared his joyful heart in praising God continually, regardless of life's challenges. David's nearly fatal experiences before two enemy kings fueled his call to God-followers to lift up God's name. The future king of Israel invited everyone to check out God's track record and see for themselves his goodness and trustworthiness.

We are challenged to examine who God is and make our faith personal. We can't live off the exuberance of this ancient man of distinction to bolster our own pilgrimage with God. But we can take David up on his request that we put God to the test in our own lives. When we do, we are promised a lightened heart and plenty of good things to enjoy.

WORTH THE WAIT

I waited patiently for the LORD, and He turned to me and heard my cry for help.

He brought me up from a desolate pit, out of the muddy clay, and set my feet on a rock, making my steps secure.

He put a new song in my mouth, a hymn of praise to our God. Many will see and fear, and put their trust in the LORD.

How happy is the man who has put his trust in the LORD and has not turned to the proud or to those who run after lies! LORD my God, You have done many things—Your wonderful works and Your plans for us; none can compare with You. If I were to report and speak [of them], they are more than can be told.

Psalm 40:1–5 HCSB

Waiting is not our favorite pastime. Everyone struggles at times with life's delays and postponements. In the two psalms leading up to this one, David felt he was stuck in a celestial gridlock. God was not yet rescuing David from his prickly circumstances and his troubled emotions. But finally, after patient endurance, Israel's chief musician recorded this song of gratefulness to God for pulling him out of the pit.

What comfort and joy to know that no matter how low we sink in life or how far away God feels, he is eager to grab hold of us and secure our steps. As David proclaimed, our ultimate Deliverer can always be trusted. God is unfailingly worthy of our belief in him. God is always a sure thing and deserving of our confidence and devotion. Even if we tried to recount the myriad ways God proves himself faithful to us day after day, we couldn't begin to record them all. We are to settle our trust in God not just because of the wonderful blessings he gives to us but simply because of his reliable character. Trustworthy God is always worth the wait.

DIVINE THIRST

As the deer pants for streams of water, so my soul pants for you, O God. My soul thirsts for God, for the living God. When can I go and meet with God? My tears have been my food day and night, while men say to me all day long, "Where is your God?" These things I remember as I pour out my soul: how I used to go with the multitude, leading the procession to the house of God, with shouts of joy and thanksgiving. . . .

Put your hope in God, for I will yet praise him, my Savior and my God.

Psalm 42:1–5 NIV

Living in spiritually desolate times makes one parched for refreshment of the soul. The writer of this psalm apparently lived in an arid land distant from Jerusalem and deeply missed the revitalizing temple worship services. His innermost being craved intimacy with God. He quenched after more than just external religious practices; he eagerly desired communion with the living God.

Many sources list the author of this psalm as the sons of Korah, a family of temple singers associated with David. Psalm 42 is considered one of thirteen *maskil* psalms, which means it lends rich insight or is accompanied by special music. The essence of this poem blends both longing and hope.

In all of Scripture, these verses remind us of our insatiable need to connect with God. We can attend church services, read books, pray, and talk to others about God, but our faith must individually rest in our own pursuit of God and his satisfying closeness. Even in the dry days of spiritual listlessness, we are called to look to God as our hope and true soul thirst-quencher.

Always Strong, Always There

God is our refuge and strength, a very present help in trouble. Therefore we will not fear, though the earth should change and though the mountains slip into the heart of the sea; though its waters roar and foam, though the mountains quake at its swelling pride. Selah.

There is a river whose streams make glad the city of God, the holy dwelling places of the Most High. God is in the midst of her, she will not be moved; God will help her when morning dawns. The nations made an uproar, the kingdoms tottered; He raised His voice, the earth melted. The Lord of hosts is with us; the God of Jacob is our stronghold.

Psalm 46:1–7 NASB

Although which human author penned this psalm is in question, the song's clarity of meaning leaves no doubt about God—he is our always-strong, ever-present help in trouble. Even if we face earth-shattering news of accidents, tragedies, and deaths, God is vigilantly on duty to rescue us. And on routine days without any great upheavals, God is still our steady support.

God is our place to flee if we simply need a time to collect our harried thoughts or a solace to unleash our wearisome tears. Psalm 46 was the inspiration for German Reformer Martin Luther's most well-known hymn, "A Mighty Fortress Is Our God." God is our strong fort and safe tower. We can run, walk, limp, or crawl to him, and he will secure us in his all-powerful arms. As the psalmist described, even if the mountains tremble and world powers wobble, God will not falter, he will be our rock and refuge. He will be around to protect and sustain us no matter what life brings us. Who needs to worry or fear with this kind of always-there strength on our side?

CLEAN HEART, CLEAN START

Have mercy on me, O God, according to your steadfast love; according to your abundant mercy blot out my transgressions. Wash me thoroughly from my iniquity, and cleanse me from my sin! For I know my transgressions, and my sin is ever before me. Against you, you only, have I sinned and done what is evil in your sight, so that you may be justified in your words. . . .

Create in me a clean heart, O God, and renew a right spirit within me. Cast me not away from your presence, and take not your Holy Spirit from me. Restore to me the joy of your salvation, and uphold me with a willing spirit.

Psalm 51:1–4, 10–12 ESV

When the prophet Nathan confronted King David about his affair with Bathsheba and his order to move her military husband into the heat of battle so he'd die, David at first did not express sorrow for his actions. He later wrote this psalm of confession and brokenness. As the presidential authority over the nation of Israel, David's adultery and murder conspiracy were not just a private matter; his indiscretions affected the public he led. The weight of his wrongdoing finally sank in, and David pleaded for God's mercy.

Remorseful David wanted to be restored to God's favor. The mighty king humbly admitted his moral failings were actually an offense against God. David begged God not to just forgive his bad behavior but to fully cleanse him from any stain of wrongdoing. David wanted his misconduct blotted out and erased. He knew that only God could expunge his record. Sensing the agony of feeling separated from God, David sought a do-over, a clean start to prove he could please God with better life choices. Then the repentant leader boldly asked for a freshly laundered heart and spirit intent on doing right.

Longing for God

O God, You are my God; early will I seek You; my soul thirsts for You; my flesh longs for You in a dry and thirsty land where there is no water. So I have looked for You in the sanctuary, to see Your power and Your glory. Because Your lovingkindness is better than life, my lips shall praise You. Thus I will bless You while I live; I will lift up my hands in Your name. My soul shall be satisfied as with marrow and fatness, and my mouth shall praise You with joyful lips. . . .

The king shall rejoice in God; everyone who swears by Him shall glory; but the mouth of those who speak lies shall be stopped.

Psalm 63:1–5, 11 NKJV

King David's turmoil in his family life spewed into a civil war within Israel, pitting David against his son Absalom. Absalom demanded the throne and at one point forced his aging father to flee Jerusalem. On his escape route, David passed through the wilderness of Judah where he penned this psalm.

Exiled from the public worship center in Jerusalem, David knew he could still meet with God. This "morning song" expressed David's intense longing for personal communion with his Creator. The psalmist tasted the strength and majesty of God and yearned to reconnect with that satisfying experience. David used the picture of insatiable thirst to describe his eagerness to be refreshed in God's presence.

Daily distractions and responsibilities often crowd out thoughts of God. As a man on the run, David faced pressing problems, yet he still paused to meditate upon God's being near. David refused to let his circumstances interfere with his celebrating God's lovingkindness. Even in his desperate banishment from his palace and prosperity, the king deeply desired to pay tribute to God. Instead of railing, David chose to rejoice.

SOS FROM THE PIT

My soul is full of troubles, and my life draws near to the grave. I am counted with those who go down to the pit; . . . but to You I have cried out, O LORD, and in the morning my prayer comes before You.

LORD, why do You cast off my soul? Why do You hide Your face from me? I have been afflicted and ready to die from my youth; I suffer Your terrors; I am distraught.

Your fierce wrath has gone over me; Your terrors have cut me off. They came around me all day long like water; they engulfed me altogether. Loved one and friend You have put far from me, and my acquaintances into darkness.

Psalm 88:3–4, 13–18 NKJV

This gloomiest of all the psalms is credited to Heman, one of the sons of Korah and part of Israel's temple choir. Those singing sons were descendants of the revered Levi tribe. Perhaps the melody to this sad song sounded like a funeral march. It's not clear whether Heman was writing from his personal life or simply expressing despondency that any person would encounter.

With fervent emotional honesty, Psalm 88 reads like a private journal entry of suffering and sadness. The afflicted psalmist felt God was hiding and had actually dumped the miserable man in the pit. "Pit" in the originating Hebrew language is *Sheol*, typically considered an underworld place where the dead were abandoned by God. Beaten up by life, the writer felt he'd already joined the dead.

Although the passage does not reveal God's answering this man's prayers, there is a glimmer of hope in verse 13: "In the morning my prayer comes before You." Even though he felt forsaken, the psalmist continued to send his SOS heavenward. Troubled times were no time to stop approaching God. God does hear and will answer, even if his timing appears delayed.

PROTECTIVE PRESENCE

The one who lives under the protection of the Most High dwells in the shadow of the Almighty. I will say to the LORD, "My refuge and my fortress, my God, in whom I trust." . . .

You will not fear the terror of the night, the arrow that flies by day, the plague that stalks in darkness, or the pestilence that ravages at noon. . . .

Because you have made the LORD—my refuge, the Most High—your dwelling place, no harm will come to you; no plague will come near your tent. For He will give His angels orders concerning you, to protect you in all your ways. They will support you with their hands so that you will not strike your foot against a stone.

Psalm 91:1–2, 5–6, 9–12 HCSB

The unidentified author of this psalm was descriptive in listing things to fear. *Terror*, *plague*, and *pestilence* were not reassuring words. The psalmist pointed out the worrisome and dreadful scenarios, but confidently spoke of God's protective power as the antidote to those frightful conditions.

While he is the divine Shield and Defender, God is much more than a superhero waiting to save the day. He can easily defeat any menacing terror, plague, or pestilence. Yet it is important to note that no one on this earth is immune from harm. Illnesses still strike. Floods still ravage. Relationships still turn sour. The promise in these verses is not protection *from* trouble but protection *in* trouble. With God and his angels on patrol, we need not fear, no matter how doubtful our path.

God is a reliable refuge at all times. As a secure haven, God wants us to move under his supportive shadow. Each new day is our call to trust him to go before us, stay right beside, or sometimes send divine guardians to watch over us in all our ways.

Worthy of Praise

Sing to the Lord a new song; sing to the Lord, all the earth. Sing to the Lord, bless His name; proclaim good tidings of His salvation from day to day. Tell of His glory among the nations, His wonderful deeds among all the peoples. For great is the Lord and greatly to be praised; He is to be feared above all gods. For all the gods of the peoples are idols, but the Lord made the heavens. Splendor and majesty are before Him, strength and beauty are in His sanctuary. . . .

Ascribe to the Lord the glory of His name; bring an offering and come into His courts. Worship the Lord in holy attire; tremble before Him, all the earth.

Psalm 96:1–6, 8–9 NASB

Many things in life are deserving of awe and praise. The Seven Wonders of the Ancient World. A cuddly newborn. Olympic athletes. Medical cures. The Israelites of early Bible times admired beauty and achievements too, but many of them followed their neighbors in adoring idols often crafted as metal figures or stone pillars.

Humans have always possessed a bent toward esteeming something they've made or something they can control. People's idols today are often more subtle than a massive carved statue. For some it's money, and for others it's possessions. Sometimes individuals idolize another person or a charismatic religious leader. God warned throughout the Bible not to trust in or revere any god but him. Psalm 96 urges full adoration and praise of God and God alone.

The songwriter directed everyone among the nations to break out in song and worship to "the Lord" (which is a personal name for God or Jehovah and appears seven times in this passage). The Lord who made the heavens and earth was to be praised with great fervor. The strong and majestic Lord deserved top respect and attention, not some inanimate icon, flashy gadget, or winsome person.

Count Your Blessings

O my soul, bless GOD. From head to toe, I'll bless his holy name! O my soul, bless God, don't forget a single blessing! He forgives your sins—every one. He heals your diseases—every one. He redeems you from hell—saves your life! He crowns you with love and mercy—a paradise crown. He wraps you in goodness—beauty eternal. He renews your youth—you're always young in his presence. . . .

As high as heaven is over the earth, so strong is his love to those who fear him. And as far as sunrise is from sunset, he has separated us from our sins. As parents feel for their children, GOD feels for those who fear him.

Psalm 103:1–5, 11–13 MSG

One of the weaknesses of human beings is our tendency at times to forget. We forget birthdays, bill payments, and where we placed our car keys, but forgetting the blessings and good things in our lives is another story. Many Bible students believe King David wrote this psalm when he was elderly. Looking back over his eventful and heroic life, David did not want to pass over the true credit for his accomplishments and fame.

David encouraged thankfulness and counseled, "Don't forget a single blessing!" In case our memory fails us somewhere in our pressure-packed days, David provided a specific list of reasons to speak highly of God. Included in God's résumé are forgiving sins, healing diseases, rescuing people from hell, and giving vitality to the aging. The Jewish king could have penned countless more examples of God's showering his children with benefits and advantages—the pleasant gifts in daily life that sometimes drift to the back of one's mind.

If we lose track of God's caring intervention in our personal lives, Psalm 103 is an inspiring reminder to focus on the innumerable ways we are blessed bit by bit each day.

ENDLESS MERCY

Oh, give thanks to the Lord, for He is good! For His mercy endures forever. Who can utter the mighty acts of the Lord? Who can declare all His praise? Blessed are those who keep justice, and he who does righteousness at all times! . . .

We have sinned with our fathers, we have committed iniquity, we have done wickedly. Our fathers in Egypt did not understand Your wonders; they did not remember the multitude of Your mercies, but rebelled by the sea—the Red Sea. Nevertheless He saved them for His name's sake, that He might make His mighty power known. He rebuked the Red Sea also, and it dried up.

Psalm 106:1–3, 6–9 NKJV

Sometimes "forever" is a marvelous measure of time. This poem by an unknown author thanks God for his mercy that is ceaselessly everlasting. Considered both a hymn and a confession of collective wrongdoing, Psalm 106 starts with gratefulness for God's character. The psalmist recognized God's qualities that reflect his loyalty and kindness to the Jewish people, who continually proved unworthy of his patient responses to their waywardness.

The passage established up front that God extends unfailing favor, and then the writing admitted the Israelites' failure to follow God fully. Despite the people's misdeeds and forgetfulness of God's innumerable sympathies, he continued to extend compassionate care. Fortunately, God's enduring nature did not end with Israel's escape from Egypt via the Red Sea or during the time this psalm was written. God tirelessly rescued his people as part of modeling his consistent, long-suffering reputation.

"Forever" means God's mercy will not run dry when our attitudes or behaviors run amiss. Repeatedly when we test his best design for our lives, God offers no punitive judgment or harm. No wonder this song is considered a thanksgiving psalm.

TRUE DEVOTION

Not to us, LORD, not to us, but to Your name give glory because of Your faithful love, because of Your truth. Why should the nations say, "Where is their God?" Our God is in heaven and does whatever He pleases.

Their idols are silver and gold, made by human hands. They have mouths, but cannot speak, eyes, but cannot see. They have ears, but cannot hear, noses, but cannot smell. They have hands, but cannot feel, feet, but cannot walk. They cannot make a sound with their throats. Those who make them are just like them, as are all who trust in them.

Psalm 115:1–8 HCSB

Peer pressure is millenniums old. In ancient Israel, the surrounding cultures pressed the Jews to stop believing in a God they couldn't see and turn their eyes and hearts to something they could view— the handcrafted silver and gold gods and goddesses, the statues and temples erected in the name of deities based in nature. Even the Israelites let those false religions creep into their belief system.

The psalmist came back at the idol-followers with fighting words that they gave homage to lifeless images and dead gods. The writer opened with profound counsel: no human and no idol should receive adoration and glory; only the one true God deserves this honor.

How easy it is today to let people such as superstars in sports, music, and film receive our devoted attention. How innocent it can be to credit popular leaders with triumphant accolades. All the while, the One who is deserving of all respect and glory is nudged to the outer edge of the spotlight. While the Israelites of old were lured to esteem gold and silver idols, we may be tempted to esteem idols who own a lot of gold and silver.

GOD TAKING SIDES

I love GOD because he listened to me, listened as I begged for mercy. He listened so intently as I laid out my case before him. . . .

Up against it, I didn't know which way to turn; then I called out to GOD for help: "Please, GOD!" I cried out. "Save my life!" GOD is gracious—it is he who makes things right, our most compassionate God. GOD takes the side of the helpless; when I was at the end of my rope, he saved me. I said to myself, "Relax and rest. GOD has showered you with blessings. Soul, you've been rescued from death; Eye, you've been rescued from tears; and you, Foot, were kept from stumbling."

Psalm 116:1, 3–8 MSG

What a tremendous relief and comfort to know that God "takes the side of the helpless." When the Egyptians held the Israelites as slaves, God took Israel's side and allowed the Jews to escape via the Red Sea. Part of celebrating this grand rescue includes a festive meal and singing of Psalms 113–118, known as the Egyptian Hallel or Act of Praise.

The unknown writer of Psalm 116 was ecstatic over God's rescuing the psalmist from death. We don't know if the writer was gravely ill or threatened by enemies or waiting execution in prison, but we do know that he cried out for God's deliverance. And God heard this man's pleas. God listened intently.

God not only listened, but he acted. He graciously freed the psalmist from his life-and-death struggle. God compassionately took the vulnerable man's side. We don't have to wait until we get to the end of our rope to call upon God. He takes our side long before troubles overwhelm us and we feel we are sinking into despair.

EXERCISING THE HEART

How can a young man keep his way pure? By living according to your word. I seek you with all my heart; do not let me stray from your commands. I have hidden your word in my heart that I might not sin against you. Praise be to you, O LORD; teach me your decrees. . . .

I delight in your decrees; I will not neglect your word.

Do good to your servant, and I will live; I will obey your word. Open my eyes that I may see wonderful things in your law. I am a stranger on earth; do not hide your commands from me.

Psalm 119:9–12, 16–19 NIV

The longest of all the psalms and the longest chapter in the entire Bible, this poem is an acrostic, presenting eight verses for each of the twenty-two letters of the Hebrew alphabet. The alphabetic style helped the Israelites memorize and recite the life lessons in this instructive psalm.

The unidentified Jewish writer focused this passage on a key to wise living—letting God's word infiltrate the heart and affect one's actions. *Heart* here means the inner life or character, as well as the center of thoughts, emotions, and the will. To live out wholesome choices, the psalmist advised seeking God and his directives. Not only are we to desire God's Word, but we are also to tuck away his counsel in our minds and let his truths permeate our inner being and personality.

One way to do this is to read and meditate on the Bible. Another is to memorize verses as the Israelites did. Ultimately, as Psalm 199 explains, the way to a joyful, prosperous life is to obey the guidelines God sets out for us. Or, in other words, spiritually exercise our hearts.

WATCHFUL PROTECTOR

I will lift up my eyes to the hills—from whence comes my help? My help comes from the LORD, who made heaven and earth. He will not allow your foot to be moved; He who keeps you will not slumber. Behold, He who keeps Israel shall neither slumber nor sleep.

The LORD is your keeper; the LORD is your shade at your right hand. The sun shall not strike you by day, nor the moon by night. The LORD shall preserve you from all evil; He shall preserve your soul. The LORD shall preserve your going out and your coming in from this time forth, and even forevermore.

Psalm 121:1–8 NKJV

You've no doubt heard the phrase "Am I my brother's keeper?" Essentially the question asks about responsibility for keeping an eye on another person's every action. Cain snapped back at God with those words after the world's first child grew up and killed his brother, Abel. Cain didn't appreciate that his Creator saw everything.

Even if you prefer to hide some things from God or even escape talking to him, you are never out of God's sight. Your always-watching God never takes a nap, never collapses in sleep. He's continually on duty, looking out for your best interests and protecting you day and night. He is intent on preserving your body and soul.

This upbeat psalm reassures that no matter what you encounter in life, God is your watchful keeper. It's widely believed that the Jewish people sang Psalms 120–134 during their travels to Jerusalem for ceremonial festivals and feasts. These Songs of Ascents, or pilgrimage songs, inspired the Israelites along life's journey. Psalm 121 reminded the sojourners that God was guarding their every step. He's overseeing yours too.

Peace Be with You

I rejoiced with those who said to me, "Let us go to the house of the Lord." Our feet are standing within your gates, Jerusalem—Jerusalem, built as a city . . . solidly joined together, where the tribes, the tribes of the Lord, go up to give thanks to the name of the Lord. (This is an ordinance for Israel.) There, thrones for judgment are placed, thrones of the house of David.

Pray for the peace of Jerusalem: "May those who love you prosper; may there be peace within your walls, prosperity within your fortresses." Because of my brothers and friends, I will say, "Peace be with you." Because of the house of the Lord our God, I will seek your good.

Psalm 122 HCSB

Considered one of the most famous cities on earth, Jerusalem during the writing of this psalm was the capital of the united kingdom of Israel towering in the hills of Judah. Centuries later, this enduring city is still considered sacred by Jews and by Christians and Muslims as well.

In ancient times, God set aside Jerusalem as a physical place to represent God's living among his people. The psalmist recorded his delight in making the pilgrimage to stand before God in Jerusalem. Today biblical scholars often regard Jerusalem as the symbolic picture of Christ-followers on earth and heaven as the New Jerusalem. To pray for the peace of Jerusalem can mean to pray for the blessing of protection and prosperity on God's visible gathering of followers. Peace is more than an absence of war; it is the security of resting in God's care.

We don't need to travel to Jerusalem to meet with God, but he does desire that his people this side of heaven thrive and reflect his love and goodness. Praying for God to bring peace on earth is one prayer always worth praying.

SEEKING GOD'S FAVOR

It seemed like a dream when the LORD brought us back to the city of Zion. We celebrated with laughter and joyful songs. In foreign nations it was said, "The LORD has worked miracles for his people." And so we celebrated because the LORD had indeed worked miracles for us.

Our LORD, we ask you to bless our people again, and let us be like streams in the Southern Desert. We cried as we went out to plant our seeds. Now let us celebrate as we bring in the crops. We cried on the way to plant our seeds, but we will celebrate and shout as we bring in the crops.

Psalm 126 CEV

The 1962 movie *The Miracle Worker* tells the true story of Annie Sullivan, who broke through myriad obstacles to teach blind, deaf, and mute Helen Keller to communicate. This song of ascents describes an even greater miracle worker: the God who set Israel free from captivity to foreign nations. For seventy years, the Israelites languished in bondage to the Babylonians. Most likely, this psalm referred to the Jews' celebratory return to Zion, also known as Jerusalem.

The writer was grateful to be released from oppression, and yet he didn't rest on God's provisions from the past. Instead, he asked for God's favor in the present and in the days ahead. With confidence, the psalmist implored God to allow his people to flourish. When we feel like parched ground where no seed can grow, this passage encourages us to ask God to reverse our fortunes. God is the ultimate miracle worker who longs for us to depend on him in both dreary and vibrant times. Our job is to remain expectant of more good things to come and to keep the party hats ready.

PROPER CREDIT

Unless the LORD builds the house, they labor in vain who build it; unless the LORD guards the city, the watchman keeps awake in vain. It is vain for you to rise up early, to retire late, to eat the bread of painful labors; for He gives to His beloved even in his sleep.

Behold, children are a gift of the LORD, the fruit of the womb is a reward. Like arrows in the hand of a warrior, so are the children of one's youth. How blessed is the man whose quiver is full of them; they will not be ashamed when they speak with their enemies in the gate.

Psalm 127 NASB

The Jews who made pilgrimages to Jerusalem considered this popular psalm a type of folk song or ballad. The words penned by Solomon, who became Israel's king after his father, David, resonated in the people's hearts and in their culture. Applicable both to the Israelites and to us today, Psalm 127 is a reminder that nothing we attempt to accomplish or take credit for in life is truly of our own doing.

God is the One who builds houses, protects cities, and creates families. Even those who work diligently and go nonstop from early morning to late at night will find no enjoyable reward for their labors. Being out of control with self-effort is painful!

Instead of depending on us to rule our worlds, God has a better option. He wants us to shift our focus to see him as the Giver of success and satisfaction. He refreshes us in our sleep. He creates children in the womb and delights families with those precious gifts. He gives strength and patience to parents. He watches over our every human endeavor and deserves the credit where credit is due.

Expectant Waiting

From the depths of despair, O Lord, I call for your help. Hear my cry, O Lord.

Pay attention to my prayer. Lord, if you kept a record of our sins, who, O Lord, could ever survive? But you offer forgiveness, that we might learn to fear you.

I am counting on the Lord; yes, I am counting on him. I have put my hope in his word. I long for the Lord more than sentries long for the dawn, yes, more than sentries long for the dawn.

O Israel, hope in the Lord; for with the Lord there is unfailing love. His redemption overflows. He himself will redeem Israel from every kind of sin.

Psalm 130 NLT

Desperation can be an attention getter. The author of this song of ascents pleaded for God to notice his prayers of repentance. At first, the psalmist longed for God's forgiveness, and then he longed for God's unfaltering love to blanket his life. Whether he was feeling the need for personal forgiveness or was calling his countrymen to embrace God's restorative powers, the writer decided to settle down in expectant hope. He determined to wait for God.

To some in our instant-gratification culture, waiting is viewed as passive resignation or idleness. But in this psalm, we read of a man anything but lackadaisical about waiting. He boldly penned that he was counting on God to show up. He's aligned his confidence in God's promises. He deeply desired to be close with God like a security guard pulling the graveyard shift and eager for morning to arrive. The psalmist's keen expectancy for God's love and forgiveness is evident.

Oh, to be passionate about a pursuit of God. What a wonder to "long for the Lord" and to be at peace with him each day.

PRAISEWORTHY NAME

Hallelujah! Praise the name of GOD, praise the works of GOD. All you priests on duty in GOD's temple, serving in the sacred halls of our God, shout "Hallelujah!" because GOD's so good, sing anthems to his beautiful name. And why? Because GOD chose Jacob, embraced Israel as a prize possession.

I too give witness to the greatness of GOD, our Lord, high above all other gods. He does just as he pleases—however, wherever, whenever. He makes the weather—clouds and thunder, lightning and rain, wind pouring out of the north. He struck down the Egyptian firstborn, both human and animal firstborn. He made Egypt sit up and take notice, confronted Pharaoh and his servants with miracles.

Psalm 135:1–9 MSG

Composer George Frideric Handel wrote the oratorio *Messiah* with its now famous "Hallelujah" chorus. A chorus of Jewish people in Bible times performing Psalm 135 must have sounded equally magnificent. In the original Hebrew language, *hallelujah* means "praise ye Yah." *Yah* was the shortened form of God's special Hebrew name *Yahweh*.

Repeatedly the psalmist called for everyone to praise or agree that God is incredibly great. And why? Because God has an impeccable track record. He set aside Israel as a choice people and patiently guided them and rescued them from slavery in Egypt. We praise God today because he has an impeccable record of accomplishment. He reigns supreme over any other gods—even those with fancy temples. He commands the weather with a supreme touch. And he never loses sight of a single detail in each of our lives.

There's no need to wait until Christmas to sing a "Hallelujah." Every day is a day to speak well of God and sing in honor of his most excellent name.

AUGUST 6

UNFORGETTABLE LOVE SONG

Give thanks to the Lord of lords, for his steadfast love endures forever; to him who alone does great wonders, for his steadfast love endures forever; to him who by understanding made the heavens, for his steadfast love endures forever; to him who spread out the earth above the waters, for his steadfast love endures forever; . . . to him who struck down the firstborn of Egypt, for his steadfast love endures forever; and brought Israel out from among them, for his steadfast love endures forever. . . .

It is he who remembered us in our low estate, for his steadfast love endures forever; . . . and rescued us from our foes, for his steadfast love endures forever.

Psalm 136:3–6, 10–11, 23–24
ESV

History is replete with unforgettable love songs. Elvis's "Love Me Tender" and Celine Dion's "My Heart Will Go On" are just a couple, but Psalm 136 is a golden oldie that describes *hesed*, or God's kind love. The Jews revered this psalm as "the Great Hallel" or greatest song of praise. The leader of worshippers or Israelite choir would sing one verse, and the people would repeat the chorus, celebrating God's unceasing love.

The beloved song calls for thankfulness not simply because God does great wonders, but because of his steady character of relentless love. What good would God ultimately be if he did tremendous things for us but his heart was far from us? We humans try to equate God's consistent love with the deepest love we experience on earth, but no love outside of God's love is richly perfect and guaranteed to endure into infinity and beyond.

No word in the English language matches *hesed*, Hebrew's unique word for God's constantly pursuing love. Words literally fail to describe God's ever-faithful love. While Air Supply may be "All Out of Love," God will never be.

WHEN THE MUSIC FADES

By the rivers of Babylon we sat and wept when we remembered Zion. There on the poplars we hung our harps, for there our captors asked us for songs, our tormentors demanded songs of joy; they said, "Sing us one of the songs of Zion!"

How can we sing the songs of the LORD while in a foreign land? If I forget you, O Jerusalem, may my right hand forget its skill. May my tongue cling to the roof of my mouth if I do not remember you, if I do not consider Jerusalem my highest joy.

Remember, O LORD, what the Edomites did on the day Jerusalem fell.

Psalm 137:1–7 NIV

Sometimes life steals the songs from our hearts. When we are burdened by grief or despair, the last thing we want to do is sing. The Jewish people held in captivity in the nation of Babylon from 586 BC to 518 BC didn't feel like singing either, not even when chided by their captors. The downcast Israelites couldn't muster a note, particularly a grand song about Zion, Jerusalem's majestic hill.

The forlorn Jews missed their homeland, and they would gather along the banks of Babylon's rivers to console one another. In misery, the hostage Israelites didn't stop only their singing, but they also stopped playing their harps and hung them on the branches of the riverbanks' poplar trees. Once so accustomed to singing and playing instruments to celebrate God and their proud nation, the saddened Jews could lift no tune at all. Even we face times when the music ceases in our lives. Death, divorce, job loss, illness, and a host of other struggles can keep us from an upbeat tempo. Yet as the psalmist reminded us, even if a melody in our hearts fades at times, we are still to remember God.

Contagious Gratitude

Thank you! Everything in me says "Thank you!" Angels listen as I sing my thanks. I kneel in worship facing your holy temple and say it again: "Thank you!" Thank you for your love, thank you for your faithfulness; most holy is your name, most holy is your Word.

The moment I called out, you stepped in; you made my life large with strength. When they hear what you have to say, GOD, all earth's kings will say "Thank you." They'll sing of what you've done: "How great the glory of GOD!" And here's why: GOD, high above, sees far below; no matter the distance, he knows everything about us.

Psalm 138:1–6 MSG

Thankfulness is not an attitude simply reserved for Thanksgiving Day. In our self-focused world where people's rudeness is often mixed with an air of entitlement, being thankful can slip to a low priority. In this psalm, David showed proper etiquette in expressing gratitude—especially gratitude to God.

No fewer than five times in six verses, David exclaimed, "Thank you!" Perhaps David's mother taught the Judean boy well and he never forgot to show appreciation. David proclaimed that even the angels are listening, so he didn't hold back in respecting the hand that directed his life. The mighty king physically presented a humble posture on his knees as a sign of his inwardly bowed heart.

David gave specific thanks for God's love, his faithfulness, his word, and his strengthening protection. Then David stressed that once world leaders recognized God's incredible ways, they too would break out in a round of "thank yous."

Genuine gratitude is contagious. Perhaps we could sharpen our thankfulness skills on not just the big things like healed diseases or solid finances, but on the everyday privileges of the air we breathe, the food we eat, and the people we love.

The Ultimate Know-It-All

Lord, you have examined me and know all about me. You know when I sit down and when I get up. You know my thoughts before I think them. You know where I go and where I lie down. You know everything I do. Lord, even before I say a word, you already know it. . . .

Where can I go to get away from your Spirit? Where can I run from you? If I go up to the heavens, you are there. If I lie down in the grave, you are there. If I rise with the sun in the east and settle in the west beyond the sea, even there you would guide me. With your right hand you would hold me.

Psalm 139:1–4, 7–10 NCV

As humans, we can feel uneasy about letting someone know what we're *really* thinking or feeling. We may hesitate to let others see our true selves with all our quirks and flaws. What a relief to know that no matter how imperfect we are, God knows us intimately and longs to remain faithfully by our side.

The psalmist declares that God knows everything about us, from our every thought to our whereabouts every second of the day. Just think about it—every nanosecond of every minute he knows how we feel about work, what words we'll speak, and what snacks we'll munch. If we catch a power nap at the desk or on the sofa, he'll be on watchful duty.

But God doesn't work like some mystical Global Positioning System, continually tracking our reasoning and moves. He stays aware of our entire lives because of his unending love and concern. There is not one thought we can contemplate or one action we can take that will surprise God. No matter where we journey in life, God knows what we're *really* thinking and feeling, and he loves us just the same.

GIVING GOD ATTABOYS

Great is the LORD, and greatly to be praised; and His greatness is unsearchable. One generation shall praise Your works to another, and shall declare Your mighty acts. I will meditate on the glorious splendor of Your majesty, and on Your wondrous works. Men shall speak of the might of Your awesome acts, and I will declare Your greatness. They shall utter the memory of Your great goodness, and shall sing of Your righteousness.

The LORD is gracious and full of compassion, slow to anger and great in mercy. The LORD is good to all, and His tender mercies are over all His works. All Your works shall praise You, O LORD, and Your saints shall bless You.

Psalm 145:3–10 NKJV

If King David had a top-five playlist, Psalm 145 would be a number one favorite. Some scholars think that David especially enjoyed this psalm and sang it often. He wrote of God's greatness over and over again. It's as if David was giving God a series of "fantastic," "excellent," and "terrific" attaboys. It's hard not to applaud God when you consider, as did David, all God's splendor, his mighty works, and his amazing goodness. Add in his righteousness, his gracious compassion, his patience, and his tender mercies, and God deserves an unending standing ovation.

The problem is, we sometimes forget about God's limitless greatness when our circumstances don't feel so great. When our lives are clouded by pain, postponements, and predicaments, it's a challenge to brag on God's wonderful acts. Yet perhaps speaking well of God is the very thing that will turn the tide on our struggles. Maybe a focus on God's incomparable character and his extension of grace when we feel grouchy and a focus on his compassion when we feel critical is just what we need. Maybe his tolerance when we feel ticked and his mercy when we feel mean will make our top playlist.

Voice Lessons

Wisdom calls aloud in the street, she raises her voice in the public squares; at the head of the noisy streets she cries out, in the gateways of the city she makes her speech: "How long will you simple ones love your simple ways? . . .

"Since they would not accept my advice and spurned my rebuke, they will eat the fruit of their ways and be filled with the fruit of their schemes. For the waywardness of the simple will kill them, and the complacency of fools will destroy them; but whoever listens to me will live in safety and be at ease, without fear of harm."

Proverbs 1:20–22, 30–33 NIV

Solomon was a true wise guy. As Israel's king after his father, David, Solomon asked God for wisdom to lead the people. He didn't ask for fame or riches, but God endowed him generously with those gifts nevertheless. Solomon was not only keen of mind but also sharp with the written word. Most of the book of Proverbs, including the first twenty-one chapters, is credited to Solomon's authorship.

In the Hebrew language, *wisdom* is a feminine noun. And in this opening chapter, wisdom is seen as a female prophet or street preacher urging people to take a hard look at their lives. Wisdom here can be defined as living life skillfully, which was no easy assignment in Solomon's day or in ours. Lady Wisdom gave a warning to avoid the waywardness of fools. She contrasted those who listened to the voice of rebellion with those who listened to the voice of reason. One group ends in destruction, and the other ends in safety and serenity.

Every day we face the same voices. Our culture shouts for us to pursue our selfish interests and unruly passions while God whispers to us to seek better choices.

SMART MOVE

Trust GOD from the bottom of your heart; don't try to figure out everything on your own. Listen for GOD's voice in everything you do, everywhere you go; he's the one who will keep you on track. Don't assume that you know it all.

Run to GOD! Run from evil! Your body will glow with health, your very bones will vibrate with life! Honor GOD with everything you own; give him the first and the best. Your barns will burst, your wine vats will brim over.

But don't, dear friend, resent GOD's discipline; don't sulk under his loving correction. It's the child he loves that GOD corrects; a father's delight is behind all this.

Proverbs 3:5–12 MSG

It's believed that Solomon amassed a collection of wisdom literature, and the Bible's book of 1 Kings credits Solomon with writing 3,000 proverbs and 1,005 songs himself. Solomon lacked no access to human counsel and knowledge. But the astute king understood that he needed to rely on an even higher source for decision making.

During Solomon's early time in office, God appeared to Solomon in a dream and asked the king what he'd like. Solomon asked for a wise, perceptive heart to direct his people with good and right decisions. Instead of trying to figure out everything on his own, Solomon yearned to look to and trust God's guidance.

It's our human nature to rely chiefly upon ourselves—to make our own decisions and carve our own destinies. We thrive on self-determination. Independence can be beneficial, but not to the point of excluding God. Instead, Solomon advised us to listen up and realize that we really don't know everything. The wisdom writer also directed us to rest our faith completely in God's intellect, but not with just a halfhearted devotion or casual compliance. Trusting God above ourselves is always a smart move.

IDLE CHARACTER

A wise son makes a father glad, but a foolish son is a grief to his mother. Ill-gotten gains do not profit, but righteousness delivers from death. The LORD will not allow the righteous to hunger, but He will reject the craving of the wicked. Poor is he who works with a negligent hand, but the hand of the diligent makes rich. He who gathers in summer is a son who acts wisely, but he who sleeps in harvest is a son who acts shamefully.

Blessings are on the head of the righteous, but the mouth of the wicked conceals violence. The memory of the righteous is blessed, but the name of the wicked will rot.

Proverbs 10:1–7 NASB

During his forty-year reign, Solomon accomplished extensive building projects and political and commercial alliances that propelled Israel to its highest splendor in history. Solomon oversaw the construction of Jerusalem's temple, a royal palace, a citywide water system, and fortifications for the capital. Solomon modeled both purpose and prosperity.

It's no wonder Solomon spoke against the idleness of character that leads to ineffective choices. In this passage, Solomon addressed the contrast between wise and right living and foolish and deceitful living. The noble person works with dedication whether engineering architectural wonders or serving as a refuse engineer. Perseverance is not about profitable paychecks. Solomon was not preaching that diligence guarantees dollars. He approached the broader richness of a satisfied life and right standing with God and others. Solomon warned about laziness of mind and spirit—essentially, emotional and spiritual apathy. Any life left unchecked would lead to a poverty of the soul, which can foster a poverty of relationships and material resources.

The remedy for idle character is to move toward the principles of God. Step-by-step, make goals and plan ahead. Work hard. Make your loved ones and God proud.

Nothing to Envy

Do not be envious of evil men, nor desire to be with them; for their heart devises violence, and their lips talk of troublemaking. . . .

A wise man is strong, yes, a man of knowledge increases strength; for by wise counsel you will wage your own war, and in a multitude of counselors there is safety. . . .

Do not lie in wait, O wicked man, against the dwelling of the righteous; do not plunder his resting place; for a righteous man may fall seven times and rise again. . . .

Do not fret because of evildoers, nor be envious of the wicked; for there will be no prospect for the evil man.

Proverbs 24:1–2, 5–6, 15–16, 19–20 NKJV

Envy distracts and often does so subtly. For instance, we pause to read of celebrity glamour and glitz in checkout lines. We watch televised stars parading their opulence and fame. We go to the gym to work out and are mesmerized by the toned and tanned people. Proverbs 24 takes things up a notch in its description of troublemakers who seem to get away with wanton actions. That type of envy destroys.

Plenty of rulers in the ancient Near East had reason to envy Solomon's riches and wise leadership. But until the final years, Solomon remained resolutely grounded in a strength that focused on God. Solomon saw how jealousy, greed, and resentment could eat away at an individual and a nation. Solomon saw through an envious woman's plan to claim another woman's infant. The king threatened to divide the child in half, thus prompting the real mother to cry out for her son's protection.

Solomon knew that right-living people may trip up in life but will eventually regain their footing. Those who could trip over their own egos are never on sure ground, and they certainly don't merit envy.

Putting Out Fires

Don't answer the foolish arguments of fools, or you will become as foolish as they are. . . .

Interfering in someone else's argument is as foolish as yanking a dog's ears. Just as damaging as a madman shooting a deadly weapon is someone who lies to a friend and then says, "I was only joking." Fire goes out without wood, and quarrels disappear when gossip stops. A quarrelsome person starts fights as easily as hot embers light charcoal or fire lights wood. Rumors are dainty morsels that sink deep into one's heart. Smooth words may hide a wicked heart, just as a pretty glaze covers a clay pot.

Proverbs 26:4, 17–23 NLT

We've all known busybodies and perhaps on occasion have fallen into their divisive style ourselves. A busybody meddles in the affairs of others and typically spreads gossip and rumors. King Solomon didn't mince words regarding the destructive force of busybodies and people who stir up trouble by feeding the fire of contention.

Sometimes it takes only a single word to set aflame another person's reputation. *Liar. Jerk. Moron. Slut. Swindler.* Those are just a few words that can spark quarrels and tensions among family members, friends, coworkers, neighbors, and fellow citizens. One initial harsh word can flicker an onslaught that demoralizes and devastates another person, particularly when the other party is innocent. Whole families and whole countries have collapsed because of verbal firebombs. As David and Bathsheba's first living child after their affair, Solomon was born into slanderous times.

Gratefully, Solomon offered the retardant that could squelch sizzling conversations and heated quarrels: Remove the wood from the fire. Stop passing on the gossip. Refuse to spread the rumors. Do not answer foolish arguments. Stick to the truth and guard your lips. Decline to join the "Society of Busybodies."

Captivatingly Beautiful

An excellent wife who can find? She is far more precious than jewels. The heart of her husband trusts in her, and he will have no lack of gain. She does him good, and not harm, all the days of her life. . . .

Strength and dignity are her clothing, and she laughs at the time to come. She opens her mouth with wisdom, and the teaching of kindness is on her tongue. She looks well to the ways of her household and does not eat the bread of idleness. Her children rise up and call her blessed; her husband also. . . .

Charm is deceitful, and beauty is vain, but a woman who fears the LORD is to be praised.

Proverbs 31:10–12, 25–28, 30 ESV

Where does beauty come from? Do you know? Does it come from a diet, or a makeup kit? Is it the result of winning the genetic lottery? Is it the property of the few, while every other woman must stand before the mirror and find herself wanting?

In this passage, God weighs in on beauty and where he finds it. Make no mistake; God is on the lookout for beauty, and he finds it in you. Every time you keep a promise, every time you speak a kind word, every time a fragile person is safe with you . . . God takes note and smiles.

This isn't the flashy, strutting-down-the-runway supermodel kind of appeal. Rather, this appeal is a quiet loveliness that grows with the years, a radiance that can no longer be hidden, that God puts on display. Your children will rise up and call you blessed. This appeal isn't meant only for the wife and mother. This appeal is for every woman who invests herself in others. Your sacrifice of love will not go unnoticed. Your choices make you captivating.

SUCCESS OR SIGNIFICANCE?

What has been is what will be, and what has been done is what will be done; there is nothing new under the sun. Can one say about anything, "Look, this is new"? It has already existed in the ages before us. There is no memory of those who came before; and of those who will come after there will also be no memory among those who follow [them]. . . .

I have seen all the things that are done under the sun and have found everything to be futile, a pursuit of the wind. What is crooked cannot be straightened; what is lacking cannot be counted.

Ecclesiastes 1:9–11, 14–15
HCSB

Where do we look for significance? Most of the achievements of men and women have been erased from our collective memory, just as their very names are fading from their gravestones. Can you remember the names of your great-great-grandparents—or tell what they accomplished in their day? So too, your name will soon be forgotten, vanishing in but a few short generations.

Success, fame, and wealth—may you have all three—but know this: with the getting, you will not get significance. Your achievements may be many, but they will not buy you what we all long for, a place in eternity.

Is everything futile? It all depends. If we race around "under the sun" hoping that more and more will make us into something, then we will find ourselves on a circular track, ending where we started. But if we find our places in God's heart, our chairs at his table, and our roles in his kingdom, then our successes as well as our setbacks become part of the great adventure with him. We don't need those successes to *become* who we are; we enjoy them *because of* who we are.

SAVORING EACH MOMENT

There is a time for everything, and a season for every activity under heaven: a time to be born and a time to die, a time to plant and a time to uproot, a time to kill and a time to heal, a time to tear down and a time to build, a time to weep and a time to laugh, a time to mourn and a time to dance . . . a time to search and a time to give up, a time to keep and a time to throw away . . . a time to tear and a time to mend, a time to be silent and a time to speak.

Ecclesiastes 3:1–4, 6–7 NIV

This orderly view of time is wonderful news for those of us who are surrounded by unfinished projects, who have to-do lists that keep getting longer no matter how many items we check off. It's important for us to know there really is time for everything. God is not stingy. He has given us time for everything we need.

Within the abundance of time God has put in our hands, certain actions are appropriate at certain times and totally out of place on other occasions. For example, as a rule we don't dance at funerals, sleep at work, or shout in the library.

But there is an even greater message in this passage. In all the planting and uprooting, mourning and dancing, silence and speech, God is there. The same God who made all those things appropriate at certain times is not hiding inside a church building, waiting for his appointed hour on Sunday. Rather, he is with us on our journeys from birth to death, savoring each moment, crying when we cry, and laughing when we laugh.

SEEING WITH NEW EYES

Crying is better than laughing. It blotches the face but it scours the heart. . . .

Endings are better than beginnings. Sticking to it is better than standing out. Don't be quick to fly off the handle. Anger boomerangs. You can spot a fool by the lumps on his head. Don't always be asking, "Where are the good old days?" Wise folks don't ask questions like that. . . .

Take a good look at God's work. Who could simplify and reduce Creation's curves and angles to a plain straight line? On a good day, enjoy yourself; on a bad day, examine your conscience. God arranges for both kinds of days so that we won't take anything for granted.

Ecclesiastes 7:3, 8–10, 13–14
MSG

We would all like to think that following God leads to a carefree life. But it doesn't work that way. We need to know that sometimes tears will flow, many tears. Some events in our lives will make no sense. We will look heavenward in bewilderment, not understanding how a loving God could be aloof and seemingly uncaring when we are hurting.

Go the distance. Don't shortchange yourself or try to escape the path of tears. There's no substitute for experience. If you let your troubles do their God-given work, they will present you with gifts that money can never buy. As your tears dry, you will see with new eyes what is important and what is not. You will gain endurance, the strength to finish what you start. You will grow patient. From bad drivers to incompetent waiters to irksome family members, they just won't bother you anymore because in your time of trouble you'll find the presence of God. Annoying people simply cannot take away the abundance that you now possess. You will look around with wonder, letting God and people be as beautifully complex as they are, savoring each today, living in the now.

RACING TO BE WITH YOU

Ah, I hear my lover coming! He is leaping over the mountains, bounding over the hills. My lover is like a swift gazelle or a young stag. . . .

My lover said to me, "Rise up, my darling! Come away with me, my fair one!

"Look, the winter is past, and the rains are over and gone. The flowers are springing up, the season of singing birds has come, and the cooing of turtledoves fills the air. The fig trees are forming young fruit, and the fragrant grapevines are blossoming. Rise up, my darling! Come away with me, my fair one!"

Song of Songs 2:8–13 NLT

Isn't spring wonderful? We wake up one morning and the birds are singing again. The gray winter sky is replaced with bright, hopeful sunshine. The blanket of snow is melting, and green grass is poking through. The naked trees clothe themselves with new leaves. God has opened his hand, and life returns to the earth.

There are many important lessons in the seasons, and here is a lesson of spring: drudgery isn't meant to last forever. We all go through dreary seasons, but they end. The One who loves us makes all things new.

Did you know that while you are studying God, he is studying you? Did you know that right now he is shopping in the store of his unlimited imagination for the gifts with which to fill your eternity? He looks at you and is filled with delight. He doesn't see the blemishes you see. He focuses not on your faults, but on the delight you and he share when you step away with him.

What's the message? Look up. He's racing to be with you, and what he has in store cannot be measured with human words.

The Promised One

This is the climax of the story of the Bible. God promised a Deliverer as far back as the Garden of Eden. Jesus, at long last, was that Deliverer. He was a new kind of King; the people he came to rescue usually didn't know what to do with him. But Jesus pressed on, showing earth dwellers how things work in heaven.

He was in the world, and the world was made through Him, and the world did not know Him. He came to His own, and His own did not receive Him. But as many as received Him, to them He gave the right to become children of God, to those who believe in His name.

John 1:10–12 NKJV

GOD WILL FIND A WAY

The angel said to her, "Do not be afraid, Mary, for you have found favor with God. And behold, you will conceive in your womb and bear a son, and you shall call his name Jesus. He will be great and will be called the Son of the Most High. And the Lord God will give to him the throne of his father David, and he will reign over the house of Jacob forever, and of his kingdom there will be no end."

And Mary said to the angel, "How will this be, since I am a virgin?"

And the angel answered her, "The Holy Spirit will come upon you, and the power of the Most High will overshadow you; therefore the child to be born will be called holy—the Son of God."

Luke 1:30–35 ESV

Picture yourself standing in Nazareth five minutes before this, the greatest announcement in history. So much had been lost. The once great nation of Israel was now a poor Roman colony. At any moment, Rome could demand from you taxes you couldn't pay, service you couldn't perform. God's great design for us—a perfect earth filled with his presence—was a discarded memory. In its place were deception, corruption, hardship, and turmoil.

In that soil, God planted his seed.

To the forgotten, to the unknown, and to the powerless, God sent his angel, to Mary, a young, pure virgin. How would God take on the ruthless Roman Empire? How would God bring life from the dead? How would God reverse our rebellion against him?

God's solution wasn't a great army or dazzling fireworks. Rather it was a tiny, fragile, vulnerable baby conceived in an unexpected way. God entered our universe, and he made his home with us.

Today God stands ready to enter your world. What problems are you facing? Where have you given up hope? Expect the unexpected. God will find a way.

Seeing beyond the Present

Mary said: "My soul magnifies the Lord, and my spirit has rejoiced in God my Savior. For He has regarded the lowly state of His maidservant; for behold, henceforth all generations will call me blessed. For He who is mighty has done great things for me, and holy is His name. And His mercy is on those who fear Him from generation to generation. . . .

"He has put down the mighty from their thrones, and exalted the lowly. He has filled the hungry with good things, and the rich He has sent away empty. He has helped His servant Israel, in remembrance of His mercy, as He spoke to our fathers, to Abraham and to his seed forever."

Luke 1:46–50, 52–55 NKJV

The presence of God opens our eyes to see that things are not as they appear. What had changed for Mary? On the outside, not much had changed. What little standing she had as a female member of an oppressed minority was about to be torn away from her when the people of her village discovered that she was pregnant out of wedlock. From that place, at the bottom of the totem pole, her eyes were opened, and she was given the power to see beyond the present into the eternal plan of God.

The eternal plan of God is that no matter how poor, how misunderstood, how forgotten, or how insignificant you may feel, God will come looking for you. He will remember you. The order of things will be overthrown. The arrogant will not stand in the presence of God. Those who gain wealth and power by oppression will lose their place, while those who serve with humility will find favor.

The gift of faith is open eyes to see and an open heart to celebrate the triumph of God's goodness, even when it seems like nothing—absolutely nothing—has changed at all.

Beneath the Radar

Augustus Caesar sent an order that all people in the countries under Roman rule must list their names in a register. This was the first registration; it was taken while Quirinius was governor of Syria. And all went to their own towns to be registered.

So Joseph left Nazareth, a town in Galilee, and went to the town of Bethlehem in Judea, known as the town of David. Joseph went there because he was from the family of David. Joseph registered with Mary, to whom he was engaged and who was now pregnant. While they were in Bethlehem, the time came for Mary to have the baby, and she gave birth to her first son. Because there were no rooms left in the inn, she wrapped the baby with pieces of cloth and laid him in a feeding trough.

Luke 2:1–7 NCV

What did Augustus Caesar hope to discover by getting a list of everybody in a register? Besides the obvious—a poll tax—what was he trying to gain? Would he read the register and find the names of Joseph, Mary, and Jesus on the Bethlehem list? Would he realize that somewhere in his empire, a baby was born before whom he would someday bow? Almost certainly not. Augustus Caesar probably didn't even know that Bethlehem existed.

Caesar could not have predicted that a feeding trough—the manger—would become more important in human history than he was. He could not have known that school kids would remember his name for a test and then promptly forget it but that no one would forget the trek of Joseph and Mary to Bethlehem.

In the same way, we cannot predict the consequences of our actions or the unfolding of our circumstances. But we can understand that the work of God often flies under the radar. In so doing, we can make room for the presence of God by welcoming the unexpected, embracing the humble, and showing compassion to people in need.

GOOD NEWS OF GREAT JOY

In the same region, shepherds were staying out in the fields and keeping watch at night over their flock. Then an angel of the Lord stood before them, and the glory of the Lord shone around them, and they were terrified. But the angel said to them, "Don't be afraid, for look, I proclaim to you good news of great joy that will be for all the people: today a Savior, who is Messiah the Lord, was born for you in the city of David. This will be the sign for you: you will find a baby wrapped snugly in cloth and lying in a feeding trough."

Suddenly there was a multitude of the heavenly host with the angel, praising God and saying: "Glory to God in the highest heaven, and peace on earth to people He favors!"

Luke 2:8–14 HCSB

The "good news of great joy" was that heaven had entered earth. God the Son put on skin and wrapped himself in the body of a newborn. God had returned to reclaim what was stolen from him, his precious people. God was opening a door into his presence. God was showing us—in a baby, in a child, in a teenager, in a man—who he is. God was inviting us back to the table, bringing us back into the family.

The invitation is for all of us. That's the reason for the shepherds and the baby lying in a manger. Any of us can come to look with wonder at the new life. While we stand there at the manger, gazing on this sleeping baby, something happens inside us. At first, we may not understand. But then it will become clear. God became fragile in our presence, and our hurts would soon be his hurts. Everything that went wrong with humanity would fall upon that precious child.

We wish we could protect him, but we cannot. He will carry our hurts. Then he will open the door and say, "Welcome home."

Wanting the Very Best

There was a man in Jerusalem called Simeon, who was righteous and devout. He was waiting for the consolation of Israel, and the Holy Spirit was upon him. It had been revealed to him by the Holy Spirit that he would not die before he had seen the Lord's Christ. Moved by the Spirit, he went into the temple courts.

When the parents brought in the child Jesus . . . Simeon took him in his arms and praised God, saying: "Sovereign Lord, as you have promised, you now dismiss your servant in peace. For my eyes have seen your salvation, which you have prepared in the sight of all people, a light for revelation to the Gentiles and for glory to your people Israel."

Luke 2:25–32 NIV

What are you watching for? What hope are you holding on to?

God gave Simeon the gift of holding in his hands the Lord's Christ. What gift does he have for you? What do you want most of all? What will make life worth living? What do you need to receive in order to say, "I'm satisfied. My life is now complete"?

Depending on our circumstances and stage in life, we might answer those questions many different ways—a spouse, perhaps; or seeing our children happily married, successful, and serving the Lord; freedom from anxiety or addiction; financial security; freedom from pain.

Simeon most likely wanted those things. Yet something overshadowed all the God-given desires and rose to the top for him. He wanted the very, very best. God didn't rebuke him for wanting the best of the best. Rather, he was pleased to grant it for his servant.

Let Simeon's life inspire you. Aim high with God. Find the best he has for you, and go for it.

What the Wise Men Saw

Herod secretly called in the wise men and asked them when they had first seen the star. He told them, "Go to Bethlehem and search carefully for the child. As soon as you find him, let me know. I want to go and worship him too."

The wise men listened to what the king said and then left. And the star they had seen in the east went on ahead of them until it stopped over the place where the child was. They were thrilled and excited to see the star.

When the men went into the house and saw the child with Mary, his mother, they knelt down and worshiped him. They took out their gifts of gold, frankincense, and myrrh and gave them to him. Later they were warned in a dream not to return to Herod.

Matthew 2:7–12 CEV

What do we do when someone else is exalted? In this passage, we see two paths. Ruthless King Herod plotted to murder the Messiah. The wise men, also called Magi, came to celebrate the Christ.

Although the account of the wise men is often connected to the Christmas story, more than likely Jesus was no longer a newborn, but a child of one to two years in age, living in a house somewhere in Bethlehem. The wise men had studied and followed the star for many months. Their studies led them to conclude that something pivotal was taking place, and they wanted to be right in the middle of the momentous event.

But Herod was trapped by his own narrow mind. He couldn't make room for the reality that Jesus wasn't after his throne, that Jesus was after him. The Messiah didn't come to take away. He came to give.

Learning to rejoice at the other person's success comes about when we finally get that there are no shortages in God's kingdom. We are all rich beyond our wildest imaginations.

SEEING WITH OUR HEARTS

John came, baptizing in the desert region and preaching a baptism of repentance for the forgiveness of sins. . . .

John wore clothing made of camel's hair, with a leather belt around his waist, and he ate locusts and wild honey. And this was his message: "After me will come one more powerful than I, the thongs of whose sandals I am not worthy to stoop down and untie. I baptize you with water, but he will baptize you with the Holy Spirit."

At that time Jesus came from Nazareth in Galilee and was baptized by John in the Jordan. As Jesus was coming up out of the water, he saw heaven being torn open and the Spirit descending on him like a dove. And a voice came from heaven: "You are my Son, whom I love; with you I am well pleased."

Mark 1:4, 6–11 NIV

How do you spot the person who pleases God? Can you tell by the clothes they wear, the house they live in, the food they eat?

In this passage, we catch up with Jesus at about age thirty. Years earlier, warned by God, Joseph and Mary fled with Jesus from Bethlehem to Egypt to escape the wrath of Herod. Later they returned to Nazareth, where Jesus grew up and probably worked as a carpenter until he was baptized by John. And John, a popular preacher in his day, had one main job—to get a nation ready to welcome God's man.

John correctly understood that we don't see the important things with our eyes. We see them with our hearts. That's why he preached "a baptism of repentance for the forgiveness of sins." Heaven can be torn open and the Spirit can descend, but we will never notice if our hearts aren't in the right place. We must repent. We must accept God's mind-set and head off in a new direction, looking at things from God's point of view. Then, and only then, do we see clearly.

UNCHARTED TERRITORY

Jesus, walking by the Sea of Galilee, saw two brothers, Simon called Peter, and Andrew his brother, casting a net into the sea; for they were fishermen. Then He said to them, "Follow Me, and I will make you fishers of men." They immediately left their nets and followed Him.

Going on from there, He saw two other brothers, James the son of Zebedee, and John his brother, in the boat with Zebedee their father, mending their nets. He called them, and immediately they left the boat and their father, and followed Him.

And Jesus went about all Galilee, teaching in their synagogues, preaching the gospel of the kingdom, and healing all kinds of sickness and all kinds of disease among the people. Then His fame went throughout all Syria.

Matthew 4:18–24 NKJV

To follow Jesus, we must make a choice. We will always need to leave something behind. In the case of Peter, Andrew, James, and John, it was their livelihood, their identity as fishermen. Jesus chose those men and others to be his disciples—learners and companions through whom the early Christian faith spread and eventually covered the world. But it all started with a choice. Keep the familiar, or launch out into uncharted territory with the One who can be trusted.

Peter, Andrew, James, and John chose to launch out. They stepped outside their comfort zone and joined Jesus Christ. But look what they received in return. It started with a new identity—"fishers of men." Then they received a front-row seat to the supernatural. They were given access to the only Teacher who knew all the answers. They were the first to hear the good news about God's unfolding kingdom. And they watched as sickness and disease lost its power to terrorize families and communities.

What does God have for you? There's only one guarantee. It will be far greater and far better than anything you leave behind.

The Reason behind the Miracle

[Jesus' first miracle—the wedding at Cana:]

Nearby stood six stone water jars, the kind used by the Jews for ceremonial washing, each holding from twenty to thirty gallons.

Jesus said to the servants, "Fill the jars with water"; so they filled them to the brim.

Then he told them, "Now draw some out and take it to the master of the banquet."

They did so, and the master of the banquet tasted the water that had been turned into wine. He did not realize where it had come from. . . . Then he called the bridegroom aside and said, "Everyone brings out the choice wine first and then the cheaper wine after the guests have had too much to drink; but you have saved the best till now."

This, the first of his miraculous signs, Jesus performed in Cana in Galilee.

John 2:6–11 NIV

Every time there's a miracle, look for the reason behind it. God doesn't need to show off; there's always a reason why he suspends the laws of nature and does the impossible. In this case, Jesus launched his miracle ministry at a wedding. The reception was on, and the family was embarrassed. They ran out of wine. Either they didn't plan for the crowd that showed up, or they didn't have the resources to deal with those who answered their invitations. In either case, a joyous event and a family's reputation were about to become tainted.

Family members were looking around frantically, trying to come up with a strategy for damage control. But Jesus went beyond damage control. Quietly, in the background, he turned the water into wine.

Why does God show up and do the supernatural in our lives? In this case, it was to salvage a reputation, protect from shame, preserve a happy memory, and give yet another reason to celebrate.

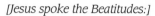

He Knows Us

[Jesus spoke the Beatitudes:]

Blessed are the poor in spirit, for theirs is the kingdom of heaven. Blessed are those who mourn, for they will be comforted. Blessed are the meek, for they will inherit the earth. Blessed are those who hunger and thirst for righteousness, for they will be filled. Blessed are the merciful, for they will be shown mercy. Blessed are the pure in heart, for they will see God. Blessed are the peacemakers, for they will be called sons of God. Blessed are those who are persecuted because of righteousness, for theirs is the kingdom of heaven.

"Blessed are you when people insult you, persecute you and falsely say all kinds of evil against you because of me."

Matthew 5:3–11 NIV

With a few short words, Jesus sliced through centuries of confusion. Who is God? What is he really looking for? What is he like? Who does he care about? What are people to do with a world that makes no sense?

We discover that God is on the side of the hurting and the oppressed. We find out that God cares more about what's in our hearts than how well we observe the religious to-do list. Slowly it dawns on us that God has really seen us. He knows what we've suffered. He knows the quiet hurts that we have carried. He remembers, and he has promised to make it right.

In his address, Jesus invited the people to join God in making things right by being merciful, peacemakers, pure in heart. It wouldn't be easy. People would be misunderstood and would face opposition. But none of those things would shake their—or our—eternal destiny as sons and daughters of God. We will find mercy. We will inherit the earth. And our eyes will be opened to see what we have always longed to see, the face of God.

How Things Really Work

When you pray, do not heap up empty phrases as the Gentiles do, for they think that they will be heard for their many words. Do not be like them, for your Father knows what you need before you ask him. Pray then like this:

"Our Father in heaven, hallowed be your name. Your kingdom come, your will be done. on earth as it is in heaven. Give us this day our daily bread, and forgive us our debts, as we also have forgiven our debtors. And lead us not into temptation, but deliver us from evil. For if you forgive others their trespasses, your heavenly Father will also forgive you, but if you do not forgive others their trespasses, neither will your Father forgive your trespasses."

Matthew 6:7–15 ESV

In this passage, Jesus taught not only how to pray but also how things really work. Everything starts with connection to God, "our Father. . . ." Everything flows out of that relationship. Then Jesus used a marketing principle. Major corporations pay millions of dollars to marketing firms because they want to influence the position their product has in our heads. If we think that their soap is the only soap that will get us clean, then it will be the only soap we buy. In the same way, if God's name is hallowed in our hearts, that is, if deep inside we really believe he is who he says he is, then every good thing that comes with his rule will be ours.

One of the best things about the rule of God in our lives is this—we don't need to carry around the damage that comes from a world gone mad. When others hurt us, and they surely will, we can release them and free ourselves from the poison of bitterness. From that place of freedom, all our needs will be met.

A Different Mind-Set

Don't hoard treasure down here where it gets eaten by moths and corroded by rust or—worse!—stolen by burglars. Stockpile treasure in heaven, where it's safe from moth and rust and burglars. It's obvious, isn't it? The place where your treasure is, is the place you will most want to be, and end up being.

Your eyes are windows into your body. If you open your eyes wide in wonder and belief, your body fills up with light. If you live squinty-eyed in greed and distrust, your body is a dank cellar. If you pull the blinds on your windows, what a dark life you will have!

You can't worship two gods at once. Loving one god, you'll end up hating the other. Adoration of one feeds contempt for the other. You can't worship God and Money both.

Matthew 6:19–24 MSG

If you called together a meeting of investors, how many poor people would show up? Not too many, right? The poor can barely scrape together enough money to pay the bills, much less to invest. Yet the rich know that investment is the key to wealth. They have a different mind-set.

Jesus told the crowds that he was calling them into a world of wealth. In that world, money would snap to attention when they walked into the room, rather than the other way around. In that world, money served the purposes of God, which would be unleashed in them.

What does it mean to stockpile treasures in heaven? It may mean dropping part of your earnings into the offering plate as an affirmation of your financial freedom. But it also may mean that you are operating from a position of immense wealth. No longer scraping about for your own survival, you are now a kingdom investor. Everything you are and everything you do would be held openhanded up to God as an offering to him and an investment in eternity.

Escaping the Trap of Worry

Look at the birds. They don't plant or harvest or store food in barns, for your heavenly Father feeds them. And aren't you far more valuable to him than they are? Can all your worries add a single moment to your life?

And why worry about your clothing? Look at the lilies of the field and how they grow. They don't work or make their clothing, yet Solomon in all his glory was not dressed as beautifully as they are. . . .

So don't worry about these things, saying, "What will we eat? What will we drink? What will we wear?" . . .

Seek the Kingdom of God above all else, and live righteously, and he will give you everything you need. So don't worry about tomorrow, for tomorrow will bring its own worries. Today's trouble is enough for today.

Matthew 6:26–29, 31, 33–34
NLT

On what does our provision ultimately rest? Yes, we should work hard and work smart. Yes, we should be wise managers of the resources God has given us. Ultimately, however, we face the future with complete confidence because we are God's children. If God feeds his pets, he will feed his children. If God clothes his garden, he will clothe his sons and daughters.

How do we escape the trap of worry? We take our fears to God, because our anxieties represent our misunderstandings about God and our relationship to him. Does God want to punish us? Has he forgotten us? Does he not care about us? Will he not defend us? We need to know the answers to these questions, and he has the answers. Ask him. He will find a way to answer you. We must learn the truth because the truth sets us free. That doesn't mean the truth will set us free from trouble. Rather, it means the truth will set us free from the power trouble has to bully us with worry.

GOOD GIFTS

Ask, and it will be given to you; seek, and you will find; knock, and it will be opened to you. For everyone who asks receives, and he who seeks finds, and to him who knocks it will be opened. Or what man is there among you who, when his son asks for a loaf, will give him a stone? Or if he asks for a fish, he will not give him a snake, will he?

If you then, being evil, know how to give good gifts to your children, how much more will your Father who is in heaven give what is good to those who ask Him! In everything, therefore, treat people the same way you want them to treat you, for this is the Law and the Prophets.

Matthew 7:7–12 NASB

Jesus invited us to put the same value on others that we put on ourselves. Something will happen as we begin to treat others the way we want to be treated. Loving others will transform us and change our values. Parents understand this. Parents want only the things that will enrich their children and make their lives better.

A good gift is something that empowers us to love other people.

Life with Jesus is not a boot camp. It's a dance. He has a part; we have a part. Throughout life, God will come to you and ask you, "What do you want?" He expects you to tell him. And he will place the same value on your request that you do, as evidenced by how you ask, how you seek, and how you knock.

This is how it works: We value others. We recognize good gifts. We go after them in God's presence. And he is delighted to award them.

Each Little Decision You Make

A centurion came forward to [Jesus], appealing to him, "Lord, my servant is lying paralyzed at home, suffering terribly."

And he said to him, "I will come and heal him."

But the centurion replied, "Lord, I am not worthy to have you come under my roof, but only say the word, and my servant will be healed. For I too am a man under authority, with soldiers under me. And I say to one, 'Go,' and he goes, and to another, 'Come,' and he comes, and to my servant, 'Do this,' and he does it."

When Jesus heard this, he marveled and said to those who followed him, "Truly, I tell you, with no one in Israel have I found such faith." . . . And to the centurion Jesus said, "Go; let it be done for you as you have believed."

Matthew 8:5–10, 13 ESV

In his ministry, Jesus found the people of God and led them into the next step in God's plan. For the most part, that community of faith was confined to the Jewish nation. But the centurion was an exception. He was a non-Jew, a Roman officer. He was a man who used his power not to oppress the people in his district, but to serve them. He even used his resources to build the local Jewish synagogue.

In that culture, servants were part of everyday life. This centurion had servants, but again, he stepped outside the norm. The centurion valued his servant "highly." The Roman officer could have shown contempt for Jesus, a traveling rabbi. But instead, he held him in high honor. In that context, he made his great pronouncement of faith: "Lord . . . only say the word."

The time will come when you too may make your great pronouncement of faith. But it won't come in a vacuum. It will flow out of the strength of your life, built up every day by each little decision you make.

Hidden Things

[Jesus said,] "I thank You, Father, Lord of heaven and earth, that You have hidden these things from the wise and prudent and have revealed them to babes. Even so, Father, for so it seemed good in Your sight. All things have been delivered to Me by My Father, and no one knows the Son except the Father. Nor does anyone know the Father except the Son, and the one to whom the Son wills to reveal Him.

"Come to Me, all you who labor and are heavy laden, and I will give you rest. Take My yoke upon you and learn from Me, for I am gentle and lowly in heart, and you will find rest for your souls. For My yoke is easy and My burden is light."

Matthew 11:25–30 NKJV

Jesus rejoiced because the truth was hidden from some and revealed to others. Why would he do that?

Let's start here. If you want to draw a circle around God, you are going to need a lot of ink! In other words, God is too big to fit inside our own understanding. We cannot reduce God to a theology lesson, a book, or a sermon. We may say things that are true about God, not because we figured him out, but because he revealed himself.

God reveals himself to his family and to his friends. In other words, if God is for you just an object of study, then he will forever escape your grasp. However, if you honor God as your Father and if you love to spend time with him, then your study of him will be rewarded because God loves sharing things with his children. True understanding flows from a relationship. For some, knowledge is power. Knowledge is an opportunity to boast. But for those who love God, the things God reveals bring comfort and give rest.

TEACHABLE MOMENTS

The disciples came up and asked, "Why do you tell stories?"

He replied, "You've been given insight into God's kingdom. You know how it works. Not everybody has this gift, this insight; it hasn't been given to them. Whenever someone has a ready heart for this, the insights and understandings flow freely. But if there is no readiness, any trace of receptivity soon disappears. That's why I tell stories: to create readiness, to nudge the people toward receptive insight. In their present state they can stare till doomsday and not see it, listen till they're blue in the face and not get it. . . .

"But you have God-blessed eyes—eyes that see! And God-blessed ears—ears that hear! A lot of people, prophets and humble believers among them, would have given anything to see what you are seeing."

Matthew 13:10–13, 16–17
MSG

Parents of teenagers understand that teens have a tremendous capacity to tune them out. Parents may have all kinds of wisdom to share with teens, but that wisdom will be ignored and even resented if they don't wait for a teachable moment.

Jesus often told stories or parables to illustrate insights that he wanted to share with his followers. Why? Why not just put the truth straight out there? Jesus may have had many reasons, but here's one: he was waiting for a teachable moment. His stories would hang in the minds of his listeners. They would be repeated, remembered, and recorded, even if the lessons behind them were lost. But at some point, we would want to know more. At some point, we would care enough about Jesus to want to know what was behind those stories. When our hearts are ready, the understanding becomes clear.

How do we know if our hearts are ready? How much do we want what Jesus has for us? If we long to experience the presence of Christ and everything that goes with it, understanding comes easily.

STEPPING OUT OF THE BOAT

Jesus went out to them, walking on the lake. When the disciples saw him walking on the lake, they were terrified. "It's a ghost," they said, and cried out in fear.

But Jesus immediately said to them: "Take courage! It is I. Don't be afraid."

"Lord, if it's you," Peter replied, "tell me to come to you on the water."

"Come," he said.

Then Peter got down out of the boat, walked on the water and came toward Jesus. But when he saw the wind, he was afraid and, beginning to sink, cried out, "Lord, save me!"

Immediately Jesus reached out his hand and caught him. "You of little faith," he said, "why did you doubt?"

And when they climbed into the boat, the wind died down. Then those who were in the boat worshiped him.

Matthew 14:25–33 NIV

Why did Jesus walk on the water? Was it merely a way to get to his disciples when he had no boat? Was it to teach a lesson about faith—that looking at the wind and the waves instead of Jesus causes us to sink?

Could it be that the real reason had to do with Peter's stepping out of the boat? Peter was a professional fisherman on a stormy sea who knew that his safety depended on his staying inside that boat, and yet he stepped way outside his comfort zone, took a risk, and put his foot on the surface of the water. In that one single action, he set aside everything that experience had taught him. He trusted in Someone greater than his experience.

The real miracle was that Peter walked on the water. Yes, he sank. But even then, there is a lesson for us. We take a risk. We do what we believe God is calling us to do. If we fail, Jesus is still there. He won't abandon us. His own hand will pull us to safety.

THE ONE QUESTION WE ALL MUST ANSWER

When Jesus arrived in the villages of Caesarea Philippi, he asked his disciples, "What are people saying about who the Son of Man is?"

They replied, "Some think he is John the Baptizer, some say Elijah, some Jeremiah or one of the other prophets."

He pressed them, "And how about you? Who do you say I am?"

Simon Peter said, "You're the Christ, the Messiah, the Son of the living God."

Jesus came back, "God bless you, Simon, son of Jonah! You didn't get that answer out of books or from teachers. My Father in heaven, God himself, let you in on this secret of who I really am. And now I'm going to tell you who you are, *really* are. You are Peter, a rock. This is the rock on which I will put together my church."

Matthew 16:13–18 MSG

Everything hinges on getting the answer to this question right: Who is Jesus Christ?

The crowds knew Jesus was unusual, but nobody could figure out why. Their best explanation—he was a rerun of one of their heroes—fell short of the truth.

It matters because if Jesus is just the latest in a long line, then we'll always be waiting for someone else to come along and upstage him. His relevance would diminish over time, and his importance would fade. But since Jesus is the One and Only, we cannot afford to make any mistakes in our relationship with him.

Peter got it right, not because he studied the question, but because he was connected with the One who has all the answers. God the Father showed Peter the truth. Jesus, the foundation of the church, made it clear that Peter and his affirmation would be instrumental in transforming the world. Peter was there at the beginning, getting the church started, because he knew the truth. The Man who rose from the dead was God's Son and Israel's Messiah.

Only God Understands

Jesus began to point out to His disciples that He must go to Jerusalem and suffer many things from the elders, chief priests, and scribes, be killed, and be raised the third day. Then Peter took Him aside and began to rebuke Him, "Oh no, Lord! This will never happen to You!"

But He turned and told Peter, "Get behind Me, Satan! You are an offense to Me because you're not thinking about God's concerns, but man's."

Then Jesus said to His disciples, "If anyone wants to come with Me, he must deny himself, take up his cross, and follow Me. For whoever wants to save his life will lose it, but whoever loses his life because of Me will find it. What will it benefit a man if he gains the whole world yet loses his life?"

Matthew 16:21–26 HCSB

What do we do when the plan of God makes no sense? Like many of us, Peter tried to stuff God back into the box of his own narrow thinking. But God doesn't belong in little boxes.

It was inconceivable to Peter that mere humans could murder the Author of Life. But God saw a bigger picture. Before the Cross, who could measure the love of God? Gifts from a billionaire mean little, but the sacrifice of one's very life means everything.

The disciples did not yet understand how Jesus could embrace suffering. It was outside anything they could imagine. But in time, each one followed Jesus. All except two of the original twelve disciples were put to death for their faith. Since then, another one hundred million believers have perished simply because they chose Christ. Many martyred believers left behind loved ones who tried to understand.

Only God could answer that question for them. Only he can see far enough into the future to know that someday each could say, "I wouldn't have had it any other way." Only he understands what we will gain.

Open Hands

[Jesus said to His disciples,] "It is easier for a camel to go through the eye of a needle, than for a rich man to enter the kingdom of God."

When the disciples heard this, they were very astonished and said, "Then who can be saved?"

And looking at them Jesus said to them, "With people this is impossible, but with God all things are possible."

Then Peter said to Him, "Behold, we have left everything and followed You; what then will there be for us?"

[Jesus said,] "Everyone who has left houses or brothers or sisters or father or mother or children or farms for My name's sake, will receive many times as much, and will inherit eternal life.

"But many who are first will be last; and the last, first."

Matthew 19:24–27, 29–30
NASB

Those who are willing to give up everything can be saved. The gates of heaven are too narrow to permit anything but our dependence on Jesus to pass through. Our accomplishments—religious and otherwise—don't carry us to heaven. Instead, Christ's accomplishments open heaven's door.

The disciples were amazed that those who had made it in this life hadn't necessarily made it in the next. The ability to acquire wealth and the ability to acquire eternal riches are two different things. There's a big difference between self-reliance and God reliance.

Not everyone is called to give up material wealth in order to follow Jesus. But everyone is called to open his hands in the presence of God. Those who stop clinging to whatever is holding them back suddenly find themselves surrounded by much more than they let go.

This is how the bank of heaven works. In the words of Jim Elliott, "He is no fool who gives up what he cannot keep to gain what he cannot lose."

COME OUT OF HIDING

A leper came to Jesus, beseeching Him and falling on his knees before Him, and saying, "If You are willing, You can make me clean."

Moved with compassion, Jesus stretched out His hand and touched him, and said to him, "I am willing; be cleansed."

Immediately the leprosy left him and he was cleansed.

And He sternly warned him and immediately sent him away, and He said to him, "See that you say nothing to anyone; but go, show yourself to the priest and offer for your cleansing what Moses commanded, as a testimony to them."

But he went out and began to proclaim it freely and to spread the news around, to such an extent that Jesus could no longer publicly enter a city, but stayed out in unpopulated areas; and they were coming to Him from everywhere.

Mark 1:40–45 NASB

With a single touch, Jesus turned everything we thought we knew about religion upside down. For centuries, the people of God were taught that whatever a leper touched became unclean. Lepers were required to live apart from other people, to cover their faces, and to shout, "Unclean! Unclean!" wherever they went. But Jesus, by the power of his presence, undid not only a disease, but also an entire culture of hurt. He touched the leper, and the leper became clean.

This is a lesson for today. We also believe that what we touch makes us unclean. For example, if we touch pornography, our minds become soiled. If we touch drugs, our lives are tainted. And so on. But here is a greater truth. We take our uncleanness to Jesus, hopeless as it is, and let him touch us. We come out of hiding and give Jesus access to the real persons we are deep inside. What Jesus touches becomes clean. Inviting Jesus in makes us stronger than trying to keep evil out.

No wonder the leper couldn't keep silent!

AN INVITATION FOR EVERYONE

All the crowd was coming to him, and he was teaching them. And as he passed by, he saw Levi the son of Alphaeus sitting at the tax booth, and he said to him, "Follow me." And he rose and followed him.

And as he reclined at table in his house, many tax collectors and sinners were reclining with Jesus and his disciples, for there were many who followed him. And the scribes of the Pharisees, when they saw that he was eating with sinners and tax collectors, said to his disciples, "Why does he eat with tax collectors and sinners?" And when Jesus heard it, he said to them, "Those who are well have no need of a physician, but those who are sick. I came not to call the righteous, but sinners."

Mark 2:13–17 ESV

Huge differences in social standing exist in every culture. In the West, a millionaire in a chauffeur-driven limousine will be treated differently than a homeless man who hasn't showered in two weeks. In Jesus' day, tax collectors were despised. It was bad enough, in the Jewish mind, that they betrayed their own people and represented the interests of Rome. On top of that, many of them made themselves rich by extorting money from people beyond the taxes owed.

Why would Jesus hang out with someone like that? First, he could reach across the lines that separate us because he didn't need the comfort of a clique. Second, he could go to the most broken person and make him whole because Jesus' very presence was and is transforming. Finally, he came to open all the doors that had been closed. There is a way back.

Everybody needs Jesus. We get to everybody by starting with the outcasts; find the people no one wants. The world will then understand that Christianity isn't a club for the snobbish; it is an invitation for everyone.

LESSONS FROM THE GARDEN

He taught them by telling many stories in the form of parables, such as this one: "Listen! A farmer went out to plant some seed. As he scattered it across his field, some of the seed fell on a footpath, and the birds came and ate it. Other seed fell on shallow soil with underlying rock. The seed sprouted quickly because the soil was shallow. But the plant soon wilted under the hot sun, and since it didn't have deep roots, it died. Other seed fell among thorns that grew up and choked out the tender plants so they produced no grain. Still other seeds fell on fertile soil, and they sprouted, grew, and produced a crop that was thirty, sixty, and even a hundred times as much as had been planted!"

Mark 4:2–8 NLT

Why does the gospel take root and flourish in some people while it never gets a foothold in others? How is it that two people can hear the same message, but respond in different ways?

Jesus told a simple story to a group of farmers and gardeners. Same seed, different results. Why? The answer was familiar to them: it depended on where the seed landed.

Jesus later interpreted his story. The seed is God's word. Some people are easily distracted by the devil, and they quickly abandon God's word. Some never develop the roots needed to withstand the storms that come to challenge our Christian faith. Others are so entangled in this world that they can't let go. But the fertile soil stands for what God intended, noble and good hearts that receive God's word and produce a harvest.

We can trust God enough to give up everything else. We can care enough to listen when he speaks. We can cling to him when the storms come, when nothing makes sense anymore. If we want success with God, we must understand this.

LESSONS FROM THE STORM

When they had left the multitude, they took Him along in the boat as He was. And other little boats were also with Him. And a great windstorm arose, and the waves beat into the boat, so that it was already filling. But He was in the stern, asleep on a pillow. And they awoke Him and said to Him, "Teacher, do You not care that we are perishing?"

Then He arose and rebuked the wind, and said to the sea, "Peace, be still!" And the wind ceased and there was a great calm. But He said to them, "Why are you so fearful? How is it that you have no faith?"

And they feared exceedingly, and said to one another, "Who can this be, that even the wind and the sea obey Him!"

Mark 4:36–41 NKJV

You will never learn some things in a church building or in a theology class. Jesus needs to take each one of us out into the storm to teach us lessons that cannot be learned in the safety of the shore.

If you had surveyed the disciples before they got on the boat and asked them what they believed about Jesus, you probably would have received some of these answers: "He's God's man." "When we are with him, we are in the exact center of God's will." "We're safe with him."

Hidden behind those fine statements, however, are different sets of beliefs, and it took a storm to bring those beliefs to the surface: "God doesn't care." "I'm not safe with Jesus." "Jesus can't or won't do anything about the mess I'm in."

If this doesn't sound familiar, your storm may be coming. But take heart. Jesus isn't asleep. When Jesus finishes speaking into our storms, in the place of fear will be peace, wonder, and awe.

The Cure for Hidden Hurts

In the crowd was a woman who had been bleeding for twelve years. . . .

The woman had heard about Jesus, so she came up behind him in the crowd and barely touched his clothes. She had said to herself, "If I can just touch his clothes, I will get well." As soon as she touched them, her bleeding stopped, and she knew she was well.

At that moment Jesus felt power go out from him. He turned to the crowd and asked,

"Who touched my clothes?" . . .

The woman knew what had happened to her. She came shaking with fear and knelt down in front of Jesus. Then she told him the whole story.

Jesus said to the woman, "You are now well because of your faith. May God give you peace! You are healed, and you will no longer be in pain."

Mark 5:25, 27–30, 33–34 CEV

Why did Jesus stop? Why did he demand to know who touched him? Why did he pull this woman out of the shadows and make her the center of attention? Jesus was hurrying to reach the home of a dying girl. He should not be delayed. But he stopped anyway.

There is a message in his actions: "I see you. I notice you. You matter to me. You will never be swept under the rug of insignificance. You have a place."

We are told elsewhere that this woman went from doctor to doctor hoping for a cure, but instead of a cure, their treatments only intensified her suffering. In addition, her condition made her "unclean," which excluded her from religious life and community. In the same way, all of us have problems we cannot solve and deeply hidden hurts that distance us from others. As we bounce from "solution" to "solution," our hopes may fade. But we can take hope. Jesus will notice us. Jesus cares about our secret needs. Deep inside we will find comfort.

CLOSER THAN WE THINK

"All of you listen," he said, "and try to understand. It's not what goes into your body that defiles you; you are defiled by what comes from your heart."

Then Jesus went into a house to get away from the crowd, and his disciples asked him what he meant by the parable he had just used.

"Don't you understand either?" he asked. "Can't you see that the food you put into your body cannot defile you? Food doesn't go into your heart, but only passes through the stomach and then goes into the sewer. . . .

"It is what comes from inside that defiles you. For from within, out of a person's heart, come evil thoughts, sexual immorality, theft, murder, adultery, greed, wickedness, deceit, lustful desires, envy, slander, pride, and foolishness. All these vile things come from within; they are what defile you."

Mark 7:14–23 NLT

We have met the enemy and he is us." Walt Kelly's famous line in the *Pogo* comic strip pretty much sums up the condition of humanity apart from Jesus Christ. It's easy to blame food, spouses, siblings, jobs, health, or any of a thousand other things for our outbursts, bitterness, lusts, and collection of vices. But Jesus goes past our excuses and holds up a mirror. The problem is closer than we think. The problem is within.

For fifteen hundred years, the people of God had understood holiness in terms of diet and ceremonial regulations. But Jesus said it was time to grow up in our understanding. God is more interested in what's in our hearts than what's in our stomachs.

How do we clean up our acts? We don't change our diets. We don't change our spouses. We can't reengineer our hearts by changing our circumstances. Instead, surgery is needed. The presence of Christ is needed deep inside of us. If we make a practice of opening the door, we will find that the darkness in our hearts cannot cope with the light of Jesus Christ.

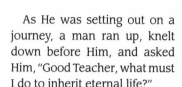

ONE THING

As He was setting out on a journey, a man ran up, knelt down before Him, and asked Him, "Good Teacher, what must I do to inherit eternal life?"

"Why do you call Me good?" Jesus asked him. "No one is good but One—God. You know the commandments: Do not murder; do not commit adultery; do not steal; do not bear false witness." . . .

He said to Him, "Teacher, I have kept all these from my youth."

Then, looking at him, Jesus loved him and said to him, "You lack one thing: Go, sell all you have and give to the poor, and you will have treasure in heaven. Then come, follow Me."

But he was stunned at this demand, and he went away grieving, because he had many possessions.

Mark 10:17–22 HCSB

What keeps us from God? How is it that we can be doing everything right, and yet be so wrong? Jesus brought those questions into focus with his interview with a young man who wanted the best of everything, including eternal life.

We may ask why Jesus made it so hard on this seeker, or why Jesus didn't just stamp his passport to heaven and move on to the next person. Like that wealthy man, most of us have quietly avoided murder, adultery, theft, and perjury. That doesn't mean, though, that we automatically make the list.

What was the "one thing" that the seeker lacked? It wasn't poverty, because Jesus clearly did not call everyone to poverty. In another passage, when Zacchaeus offered to give half his possessions to the poor, Jesus didn't scold him for hanging on to the other half. Instead, he rejoiced because "salvation has come to this house" (Luke 19:9 HCSB). No, the problem with the rich seeker was allegiance. When it came right down to it, he wanted money more than he wanted Jesus. And without Jesus we cannot have eternal life.

CATCHING MORE THAN FISH

[Jesus] sat in the boat and taught the crowds from there.

When he had finished speaking, he said to Simon, "Now go out where it is deeper, and let down your nets to catch some fish."

"Master," Simon replied, "we worked hard all last night and didn't catch a thing. But if you say so, I'll let the nets down again." And this time their nets were so full of fish they began to tear! A shout for help brought their partners in the other boat, and soon both boats were filled with fish and on the verge of sinking.

When Simon Peter realized what had happened, he fell to his knees before Jesus and said, "Oh, Lord, please leave me—I'm too much of a sinner to be around you."

Luke 5:3–8 NLT

We will never really understand who Jesus is until he shows up where we live. As long as he is merely a religious leader hiding inside a church building, he can be dismissed as irrelevant. But when he knocks on the door of your house, when he follows you to work, and when he hangs out with you, everything changes.

What would a rabbi know about fishing? You can almost hear the impatience in Peter's voice. *We know when to fish. We know how to fish. We did it right; it turned out wrong. But hey, I'll humor you.*

Each of us has a moment when we finally get it—we finally understand who Jesus really is. That was Peter's moment. As the boats strained to carry the weight of the fish, Peter understood. Jesus is not a hobby. He is life.

Peter knew he was out of his league. He was in the presence of God's Son. He couldn't scrub long enough to clean up for that. But he would soon discover that Jesus came not for the religious superstars but for all us ordinary folk.

INNER WEALTH

[Jesus said,] "I say to you who hear, love your enemies, do good to those who hate you, bless those who curse you, pray for those who mistreat you.

"Whoever hits you on the cheek, offer him the other also; and whoever takes away your coat, do not withhold your shirt from him either. . . .

"Treat others the same way you want them to treat you. . . .

"If you lend to those from whom you expect to receive, what credit is that to you? Even sinners lend to sinners in order to receive back the same amount.

"But love your enemies, and do good, and lend, expecting nothing in return; and your reward will be great, and you will be sons of the Most High; for He Himself is kind to ungrateful and evil men.

"Be merciful, just as your Father is merciful."

Luke 6:27–29, 31, 34–36 NASB

Consider the incredible power of the meek. Without being doormats, they are gracious to those who hate them. Stories are told of Christians speaking kind words even to their torturers—words that broke the tormentors' hearts and brought them into the kingdom. As the first martyr lay dying, his final words were a prayer on behalf of those who had stoned him to death. Where do men and women get this kind of power?

The best thing we can do is let ourselves be loved by God. The more deeply we experience the love of God, the less we need others to supply what God alone can give. From a place of immense inner wealth, we can begin to see things from God's perspective. Instead of pining for the approval of others and being shocked when they don't give it, we can carry God's love to those who need it most—those who have no love to share. We can have compassion on those who need to take from others in order to make up for the deficiencies they feel.

Deceived by Appearances

Turning to the woman, but speaking to Simon, [Jesus] said, "Do you see this woman? I came to your home; you provided no water for my feet, but she rained tears on my feet and dried them with her hair. You gave me no greeting, but from the time I arrived she hasn't quit kissing my feet. You provided nothing for freshening up, but she has soothed my feet with perfume. Impressive, isn't it? She was forgiven many, many sins, and so she is very, very grateful. If the forgiveness is minimal, the gratitude is minimal."

Then he spoke to her: "I forgive your sins."

That set the dinner guests talking behind his back: "Who does he think he is, forgiving sins!"

He ignored them and said to the woman, "Your faith has saved you. Go in peace."

Luke 7:44–50 MSG

The woman in this passage had a reputation. She had made all the wrong choices, and everybody in town knew it. She showed up at a dinner party uninvited and unwelcome. The host, Simon (not Simon Peter, the disciple), used this as an occasion to judge Jesus. Simon figured Jesus didn't know much if he allowed that woman to kiss his feet. If Jesus were really a man of God, Simon thought, he would tell that wayward woman to get lost.

Jesus responded by referring to the courtesies of that culture. A guest should be supplied water to wash his feet. Simon overlooked that point of etiquette, and the wayward woman far surpassed it.

Yesterday does not define today. God transforms lives. Appearances deceive. Forgiveness sets us free. As long as we make our lives with Christ a competition, we will constantly compare ourselves with others and find them to be deficient. But when we receive our lives with Christ as a gift we could never deserve, the need to compare and judge fades away. We're headed off in a different direction: love, inspired by gratitude.

THE MOMENT BEFORE THE MIRACLE

The twelve came and said to him, "Send the crowd away to go into the surrounding villages and countryside to find lodging and get provisions, for we are here in a desolate place."

But he said to them, "You give them something to eat."

They said, "We have no more than five loaves and two fish." ... For there were about five thousand men.

And he said to his disciples, "Have them sit down in groups of about fifty each." ...

And taking the five loaves and the two fish, he looked up to heaven and said a blessing over them. Then he broke the loaves and gave them to the disciples to set before the crowd. And they all ate and were satisfied. And what was left over was picked up, twelve baskets of broken pieces.

Luke 9:12–17 ESV

Pay close attention to the moment before the miracle. All Jesus had was five dinner rolls and two fish, enough for a hungry boy. The need was for a crowd of five thousand hungry men, not counting women and children. After taking a few minutes to organize the crowd so they could receive, Jesus looked not at the five thousand hungry men, not at the meager lunch, but up to heaven.

All of us will find ourselves in this place. The need is far greater than we can supply. The provision is laughable, hardly a blip on the radar. We have three choices: We can look at the need. We can look at the provision. Or we can look heavenward.

When Jesus looked up to heaven, he saw the generous heart of the Father. He saw the God who enjoys doing something new. He saw the One who takes the little we have—whether loaves and fish, five smooth stones, or whatever—and uses it to change our world.

SIMPLY BY STOPPING

As a man was going down from Jerusalem to Jericho, robbers attacked him and grabbed everything he had. They beat him up and ran off, leaving him half dead.

A priest happened to be going down the same road. But when he saw the man, he walked by on the other side. Later a temple helper . . . also went by on the other side. A man from Samaria then came traveling along that road. When he saw the man, he felt sorry for him and went over to him. He treated his wounds with olive oil and wine and bandaged them. Then he put him on his own donkey and took him to an inn, where he took care of him. The next morning he gave the innkeeper two silver coins and said, "Please take care of the man."

Luke 10:30–35 CEV

The parable of the good Samaritan may be the most famous story Jesus ever told. His hearers would have understood its meaning on many different levels—an indictment of racial prejudice, a condemnation of empty religion, a motivation for practical love. But let's focus on this perspective: the journey that we all share.

All of us are on our way "from Jerusalem to Jericho." All of us have been robbed and beaten by the Fall and left half dead. And all of us have walked by one another, crossing over to the other side. But sometimes we take a risk. Sometimes we reach out to one another, not knowing for sure if our offers to help will even be accepted. We give what we have because that's all we can give.

The amazing thing is not so much that we help but what God does with our help. There at the inn, the patient recovered. He didn't die. Simply by stopping, by caring, by doing what we know how to do, we saved a life. Our world and eternity will never be the same.

FINDING OUR WAY HOME

[Jesus said,] "You Pharisees make the outside of the cup and dish clean, but your inward part is full of greed and wickedness. Foolish ones! Did not He who made the outside make the inside also? . . .

"But woe to you Pharisees! For you tithe mint and rue and all manner of herbs, and pass by justice and the love of God. These you ought to have done, without leaving the others undone. Woe to you Pharisees! For you love the best seats in the synagogues and greetings in the marketplaces. Woe to you, scribes and Pharisees, hypocrites! For you are like graves which are not seen, and the men who walk over them are not aware of them. . . .

"You load men with burdens hard to bear, and you yourselves do not touch the burdens with one of your fingers."

Luke 11:39–40, 42–44, 46
NKJV

Why did Jesus reserve his harshest criticism for the religious leaders of his day? To answer this question, let's think about what a religious leader is supposed to do. In the original biblical language of Greek, the word for *pastor* literally means "shepherd." God was looking for someone to care for his "sheep." If the flock is in danger, the pastor protects the sheep. If a sheep is sick or injured, the shepherd cares for it. If a sheep wanders off, the shepherd searches for it and gently brings it home. By serving the flock, the pastor earns his place of leadership. Show-offs who make it hard for people to find God have no place in ministry. They are doing the enemy's work, not God's work.

Jesus' scathing rebuke of the Pharisees shows his heart toward his people. He is here to help us find our way home. He makes it clear that those who stand between us and God are not God's representatives; rather, they are God's opponents. God will do whatever he needs to do to clear the obstacles that stand between him and us.

The Back of the Line

[Jesus] told a parable to those who were invited, when He noticed how they would choose the best places for themselves: "When you are invited by someone to a wedding banquet, don't recline at the best place, because a more distinguished person than you may have been invited by your host. The one who invited both of you may come and say to you, 'Give your place to this man,' and then in humiliation, you will proceed to take the lowest place.

"But when you are invited, go and recline in the lowest place, so that when the one who invited you comes, he will say to you, 'Friend, move up higher.' You will then be honored in the presence of all the other guests. For everyone who exalts himself will be humbled, and the one who humbles himself will be exalted."

Luke 14:7–11 HCSB

Jesus had this advice for those who want to get ahead: "Start at the back of the line." Put others first. A great sales trainer saw a young boy going from door to door selling magazines. The sales trainer thought to himself, *I'm going to slam the door in his face. Then I'll call him back and teach him how to do it right.* But when the door opened, the young boy's eyes widened and his jaw dropped. "Are you so-and-so, the great sales trainer?" the boy asked, his voice full of wonder. The great sales trainer forgot all about his plan and bought a truckload of magazines.

Putting others in the limelight is a kingdom principle. We may have the best qualifications, the best theology, the best résumé, and the best experience, but none of that matters if people don't know how much we care about them. When we exalt others, we exalt ourselves. It is while we are finding the good in others that others see the good in us.

Do you want to be great? Help others to be great.

SAFE

Jesus told them this parable: "Suppose one of you has a hundred sheep and loses one of them. Does he not leave the ninety-nine in the open country and go after the lost sheep until he finds it? And when he finds it, he joyfully puts it on his shoulders and goes home. Then he calls his friends and neighbors together and says, 'Rejoice with me; I have found my lost sheep.' . . .

'Or suppose a woman has ten silver coins and loses one. Does she not light a lamp, sweep the house and search carefully until she finds it? And when she finds it, she calls her friends and neighbors together and says, 'Rejoice with me; I have found my lost coin.' In the same way, I tell you, there is rejoicing in the presence of the angels of God over one sinner who repents."

Luke 15:3–6, 8–10 NIV

If you are a parent, you have probably experienced that moment of horror when you discover that the child you thought was at your side is no longer there. She's somewhere, but you don't know where. You take a deep breath and start looking around. You call her name. You start describing your child to complete strangers, wondering if they've seen her. The rest of the family joins you in your search. As your pace quickens, you try to bar the door of your imagination to a flood of evil possibilities. Then you turn the corner, and there she is, looking up at you with innocent eyes, trying to understand why your face is so troubled. At that moment, you have to steady yourself to contain the overwhelming gratitude that you feel. Your child is safe. Everything will be okay.

God and his family are on a mission to find the children who have wandered away, to bring them back, to protect them from a flood of evil, to make them safe once again. This is priority. No one is unimportant to God.

Vindicated

[Jesus said,] "There was a judge who did not fear God and did not respect man. There was a widow in that city, and she kept coming to him, saying, 'Give me legal protection from my opponent.'

"For a while he was unwilling; but afterward he said to himself, 'Even though I do not fear God nor respect man, yet because this widow bothers me, I will give her legal protection, otherwise by continually coming she will wear me out.'"

And the Lord said, "Hear what the unrighteous judge said; now, will not God bring about justice for His elect who cry to Him day and night, and will He delay long over them? I tell you that He will bring about justice for them quickly. However, when the Son of Man comes, will He find faith on the earth?"

Luke 18:2–8 NASB

Prayer doesn't change God; it changes us. Repeating our requests day after day doesn't change God from an aloof deity to a friend. That's not how prayer works. But when we struggle through our false beliefs that God doesn't care, that he isn't here, or that he doesn't want to help, we come to a better place on the other side, where hurts and injustices don't rattle us as much as they did before. We have seen God answer prayer. But we've also seen God sometimes put our requests on hold, and we've learned to trust the purity of his motives.

Let's face it. Sometimes life doesn't make sense. Sometimes God doesn't make sense to us. But we keep going back to him because he is our Father. Even if he won't do anything we ask, we want him to hear us—and he does. As we get to know him by pouring out our hearts to him, we discover that he's never late and never wrong. In the end, we, the children of God, will be vindicated for putting our trust in him.

AT YOUR HOUSE

Jesus was going through Jericho, where a man named Zacchaeus lived. He was in charge of collecting taxes and was very rich. . . . Zacchaeus wanted to see what [Jesus] was like. But Zacchaeus was a short man and could not see over the crowd. So he ran ahead and climbed up into a sycamore tree. When Jesus got there, he looked up and said, "Zacchaeus, hurry down! I want to stay with you today." Zacchaeus hurried down and gladly welcomed Jesus.

Everyone who saw this started grumbling, "This man Zacchaeus is a sinner! And Jesus is going home to eat with him."

Later that day Zacchaeus stood up and said to the Lord, "I will give half of my property to the poor. And I will now pay back four times as much to everyone I have ever cheated."

Luke 19:1–8 CEV

It's hard not to like Zacchaeus. He was willing to make himself undignified just to get a good look at Jesus. He probably never expected that the Messiah would even give him a passing glance. But when Jesus offered to spend the day with him, he was overcome. *Jesus! My house!* That was almost too good to be true.

But this is the reality of Jesus Christ. Where does he want to be? At your house! What does he want to do? Hang out with you! Does it matter to him what other people think of that? Not at all.

What will the outcome be? What will you find yourself saying and doing as Jesus sits at your table? Will you give half your possessions to the poor? Will you pay back four times? Maybe you will, but the exact outcome cannot be prescribed or predicted because it will be the joyous expression of your heart set free. This cannot be imitated by a list of good deeds. Rather, it will flow from who you are, freshly remade by God's Spirit.

WHOLE AND LASTING LIFE

In the same way that Moses lifted the serpent in the desert so people could have something to see and then believe, it is necessary for the Son of Man to be lifted up—and everyone who looks up to him, trusting and expectant, will gain a real life, eternal life.

This is how much God loved the world: He gave his Son, his one and only Son. And this is why: so that no one need be destroyed; by believing in him, anyone can have a whole and lasting life. God didn't go to all the trouble of sending his Son merely to point an accusing finger, telling the world how bad it was. He came to help, to put the world right again. Anyone who trusts in him is acquitted.

John 3:14–18 MSG

Nowadays, the inscription *John 3:16* sometimes decorates athletes' eye black strips or bedecks signs held up by exuberant people on street corners. But what is so significant about this Bible verse that we see it publicly displayed by many in our society?

In the few sentences of the verse, the writer summed up God's loving plan for every person in every community and isolated spot on our planet. That passage declares God's amazing promise of "a whole and lasting life." It declares that a life does not end in ruins when the physical body dies.

Because of God's faithful love, he offered his only Son, Jesus, to come to earth to rescue people of every ethnicity and offer them a freeing life with a future reservation in heaven. Gratefully, God doesn't point a finger at our mistakes and misdeeds. He doesn't scold us for our bad. And he never forces faith on anyone.

Instead, God extends help and a choice. Choose to accept his gift of eternal life or choose to pass on it. Jesus came not to make just the world right again; he came also to make individual lives right again too.

THIRST QUENCHER

Jesus said to [the Samaritan woman], "Give Me a drink." . . .

The Samaritan woman said to Him, "How is it that You, being a Jew, ask me for a drink?" . . .

Jesus answered and said to her, "If you knew the gift of God, and who it is who says to you, 'Give Me a drink,' you would have asked Him, and He would have given you living water."

She said to Him, "Sir, You have nothing to draw with and the well is deep; where then do You get that living water?" . . .

Jesus answered and said to her, "Everyone who drinks of this water will thirst again; but whoever drinks of the water that I will give him shall never thirst; but the water that I will give him will become in him a well of water springing up to eternal life."

John 4:7, 9–11, 13–14 NASB

How dare Jesus talk to a Samaritan woman! In first-century Jewish culture, women were considered inferior to men and were often ignored. Add in that this particular woman was of Samaritan ethnicity, and Jesus was pushing the limits. Samaritans were people whose Israelite ancestors intermarried with Assyrians. In Jesus' day, to be a mixed-blood Samaritan was worse than simply being a woman.

Most Jews traveling near Samaria adamantly refused to set foot within that detested country, but Jesus wasn't your ordinary Jew. He purposely walked through Samaria and asked that racially outcast woman for a drink of water at the popular well of the Jewish forefather Jacob.

Surprised by Jesus' lack of ethnic prejudice, the woman with a questionable past began to question the stranger. He treated her with dignity and compassion. His talk of living water intrigued her even more. *What if this living water could parch my soul? What if this man is the Promised One who can spring up fresh waters in me and quench my thirst for life eternal?* Gratefully, that same living water is always on tap for us today, regardless of race, gender, or reputation. We're invited to drink up.

301

No More "I Can't"

One of the men lying there had been sick for thirty-eight years. When Jesus saw him . . . he asked him, "Would you like to get well?"

"I can't, sir," the sick man said, "for I have no one to put me into the pool when the water bubbles up. Someone else always gets there ahead of me."

Jesus told him, "Stand up, pick up your mat, and walk!"

Instantly, the man was healed! He rolled up his sleeping mat and began walking! But this miracle happened on the Sabbath, so the Jewish leaders objected. They said to the man who was cured, "You can't work on the Sabbath! The law doesn't allow you to carry that sleeping mat!"

But he replied, "The man who healed me told me, 'Pick up your mat and walk.'"

John 5:5–11 NLT

Jerusalem in the time of Jesus featured a public pool with five porches around which many disabled people gathered waiting for the waters to stir. Although the exact cause of those waters' bubbling is still disputed today, many people then believed an angel from God occasionally stirred the waters and that whoever dipped into the pool first would be healed.

Year after year, that afflicted man watched as the lame, blind, paralyzed, and other ill people entered the churning waters ahead of him. Yet one day, Jesus stopped by the crowded pool and spoke directly to this sick and discouraged man. Jesus' words were few but poignant: "Would you like to get well?"

Maybe after almost four decades of disability, the man had given up on healing, given up on hope. Maybe you can relate to his plight. Sometimes we are stuck in the same rut when it comes to issues of faith. Sometimes it's an overwhelming risk to trust that God can help us pick ourselves up and walk boldly with fresh hope. Jesus didn't walk away when he heard "I can't." And today he doesn't turn aside from *our* excuses for wholeness and joy.

On the Fringe

Jesus said to them, "Truly, truly, I say to you, unless you eat the flesh of the Son of Man and drink his blood, you have no life in you. Whoever feeds on my flesh and drinks my blood has eternal life." . . .

When many of his disciples heard it, they said, "This is a hard saying; who can listen to it?"

But Jesus, knowing in himself that his disciples were grumbling about this, said to them, "Do you take offense at this?" . . .

After this many of his disciples turned back and no longer walked with him. So Jesus said to the Twelve, "Do you want to go away as well?"

Simon Peter answered him, "Lord, to whom shall we go? You have the words of eternal life, and we have believed."

John 6:53–54, 60–61, 66–69
ESV

Jesus' words in this passage about eating flesh and drinking blood can be understood in the metaphorical sense of feeding on the spiritual nourishment that only he can offer.

Many times Jesus spoke in parables or illustrations that challenged people. In this passage, many of the fringe followers of Jesus decided to turn away. Their faith dedication extended only so far. It was cool to watch Jesus heal people, amazing to watch him feed the masses with just a handful of fish and bread. But stick with Jesus when his teaching required trust in him vs. trust in his miracles? That separated the casual from the committed.

It separates us too. The Bible's words are not always clear at first glance. Phenomenal truths do not always jump off the page. Instead, sometimes we're invited to ask questions and check out resources that explain Bible texts. Sometimes we're nudged to move from the fringe of faith—but always toward God and not away from him.

THE TEST OF PERFECTION

The scribes and Pharisees brought to Him a woman caught in adultery. . . . They said to Him, "Teacher, this woman was caught in adultery, in the very act." . . .

He . . . said to them, "He who is without sin among you, let him throw a stone at her first." And again He stooped down and wrote on the ground. Then those who heard it, being convicted by their conscience, went out one by one, beginning with the oldest even to the last. And Jesus was left alone, and the woman standing in the midst.

When Jesus had raised Himself up and saw no one but the woman, He said to her, "Woman, where are those accusers of yours? Has no one condemned you?"

She said, "No one, Lord."

And Jesus said to her, "Neither do I condemn you; go and sin no more."

John 8:3–4, 7–11 NKJV

The phrase "People who live in glass houses should not throw stones" fits this story in the New Testament. It's tempting to condemn the troublesome behavior of others when we ourselves could easily make the same miscue.

The Jewish religious leaders envied Jesus' popularity with the people and longed to trap Rabbi Jesus in contradicting the Hebrew law. According to centuries of Jewish rule, stoning was the punishment for anyone caught in adultery. While Jesus was teaching in the Jerusalem temple, the religious nobility interrupted him by parading an embarrassed woman in front of Jesus and his listeners.

Jesus stopped the self-righteous leaders short. He invited them to hurl stones at the woman if they were spotless in their own actions. Then he doodled in the dirt. One by one, the riled-up accusers walked away. None of them could stand the test of perfection. Neither can we stand it. Jesus extended compassionate forgiveness to that woman and to us. And he directs us all to put down our stones of condemnation and tidy up our lives by leaving behind our own moral missteps. Houses made of glass are not shatterproof.

TRUE FREEDOM

Jesus said to the Jews who believed in him, "If you continue to obey my teaching, you are truly my followers. Then you will know the truth, and the truth will make you free."

They answered, "We are Abraham's children, and we have never been anyone's slaves. So why do you say we will be free?"

Jesus answered, "I tell you the truth, everyone who lives in sin is a slave to sin. A slave does not stay with a family forever, but a son belongs to the family forever. So if the Son makes you free, you will be truly free. I know you are Abraham's children, but you want to kill me because you don't accept my teaching. I am telling you what my Father has shown me, but you do what your father has told you."

John 8:31–38 NCV

Authentic truth is liberating. But certain Jewish followers of Jesus stayed in bondage to their way of thinking and to their claims of a superior heritage. When Jesus pressed those Hebrew people to obey his teachings and live in freedom, they balked at his message. They asserted that being descendants of revered patriarch Abraham meant they were slaves of no one. Their arrogance and self-deception actually held them captive. Their complex system of religious dos and don'ts forced them behind the bars of moral slavery.

As he did in ancient Israel, Jesus still holds the keys to spiritual emancipation. His truth shines the light on falsehood, cleans up the dark places of the soul, knocks down barriers to love and acceptance, and opens the minds of the judgmental.

Admired writings and persuasive words of many esteemed individuals through the ages have led to bondage and even death. Simply consider Nero, Adolf Hitler, and Saddam Hussein, to name a few. Truth and freedom were not central in their lives. Neither was Jesus. Only Jesus imparts ultimate truth.

HE'S GOT YOUR BACK

[Jesus said,] "A thief comes only to steal and to kill and to destroy. I have come that they may have life and have it in abundance.

"I am the good shepherd. The good shepherd lays down his life for the sheep. The hired man, since he is not the shepherd and doesn't own the sheep, leaves them and runs away when he sees a wolf coming. The wolf then snatches and scatters them. [This happens] because he is a hired man and doesn't care about the sheep.

"I am the good shepherd. I know My own sheep, and they know Me, as the Father knows Me, and I know the Father. I lay down My life for the sheep. . . . No one takes it from Me, but I lay it down on My own."

John 10:10–15, 18 HCSB

Sheepherding is the first occupation mentioned in the Bible. Generation after generation of noble shepherds cared for their flocks in the pastures of Israel. The sons of Abraham, Isaac, and Jacob watched over each family's sheep, so did the Bible's Moses, Rachel, and David. Unassuming shepherds were also the first to hear of Jesus' birth.

When Jesus used the sheepherding illustration, he knew his audience would understand the skill and commitment a top-notch shepherd dedicates to the sheep under his care. Jesus called himself "the good shepherd" who knows not just each sheep's temperament but calls each sheep by name. In contrast, when a hired hand is under attack, he hightails it out of there, leaving the sheep defenseless.

As our good and faithful Shepherd, Jesus doesn't desert us when we need him most. In fact, this passage explains that he sacrificed his own life for the welfare of his sheep. He made the ultimate sacrifice for us sheep when he surrendered his life on the cross. As our ever-present Good Shepherd, we come to know his voice and trust his gentle caretaking. There's great comfort in knowing an alert and fearless Shepherd always has our backs.

A GREATER GOOD

Jesus, once more deeply moved, came to the tomb. . . . "Take away the stone," he said.

"But, Lord," said Martha, the sister of the dead man, "by this time there is a bad odor, for he has been there four days."

Then Jesus said, "Did I not tell you that if you believed, you would see the glory of God?"

So they took away the stone. Then Jesus looked up and said, "Father, I thank you that you have heard me. I knew that you always hear me, but I said this for the benefit of the people standing here, that they may believe that you sent me."

When he had said this, Jesus called in a loud voice, "Lazarus, come out!" The dead man came out, his hands and feet wrapped with strips of linen, and a cloth around his face.

John 11:38–44 NIV

One of Jesus' closest friends was a man named Lazarus from the hillside community of Bethany, southeast of Jerusalem. When Lazarus fell seriously ill, his two sisters, Mary and Martha, sent a messenger to fetch Jesus, who was with his disciples along the Jordan River. But Jesus remained by the riverside. The man who often healed strangers refused to heal one of his dearest comrades. Even Jesus' disciples questioned his lack of response, but Jesus essentially told them, "Relax. I've got a greater good in mind."

Four days after Lazarus died, Jesus finally showed up and asked for the stone sealing Lazarus's grave to be removed. Jesus then prayed that the onlooking people would truly believe that he was God sent to earth for a purpose. Miraculously, Lazarus rose from the dead. In showing his power over death, Jesus wanted his disciples, Lazarus's family and friends—and even Lazarus himself—to trust in God's timing and God's ability to overcome the worst of circumstances. We can trust God's timing and rescuing powers. No matter what we face, he has our greater good in mind.

ADORING FANS

Jesus sent two of [the disciples] on ahead. "Go into the village over there," he said. "As soon as you enter it, you will see a donkey tied there, with its colt beside it. Untie them and bring them to me." . . .

The two disciples did as Jesus commanded. They brought the donkey and the colt to him and threw their garments over the colt, and he sat on it.

Most of the crowd spread their garments on the road ahead of him, and others cut branches from the trees and spread them on the road. Jesus was in the center of the procession, and the people all around him were shouting, "Praise God for the Son of David! Blessings on the one who comes in the name of the LORD! Praise God in highest heaven!"

Matthew 21:1–2, 6–9 NLT

Jesus knew how to get a party started. As the throngs of Jewish people journeyed to Jerusalem on foot for their annual Passover festival, Jesus chose to enter the city on a donkey. What may seem like an ordinary ride to some people was actually a significant fulfillment of a prophecy by the Old Testament's Zechariah that the Promised One, the Jewish Messiah, would ride into Jerusalem on the back of a young male donkey.

Lining Jesus' path with clothing and branches was a sign of paying homage to the one they now claimed as their God-sent King. Like screaming fans watching a celebrity stroll the red carpet, the Jewish people raved over Jesus' arrival. Many considered him their long-awaited Deliverer who would rebuild Jerusalem and restore the line of King David. They hailed him as the son of David, which he was through the lineage of both Mary and Joseph.

But Jesus' glory ride would soon end in tragedy. The crowds would change their praises of him to curses. Jesus didn't come to earth for the accolades, but even today his message attracts a faithful following.

Cleaning House

They came to Jerusalem. And he entered the temple and began to drive out those who sold and those who bought in the temple, and he overturned the tables of the money changers and the seats of those who sold pigeons. And he would not allow anyone to carry anything through the temple. And he was teaching them and saying to them, "Is it not written, 'My house shall be called a house of prayer for all the nations'? But you have made it a den of robbers."

And the chief priests and the scribes heard it and were seeking a way to destroy him, for they feared him, because all the crowd was astonished at his teaching. And when evening came they went out of the city.

Mark 11:15–19 ESV

Even God is pushed to the limits at times. Jesus rightfully expressed anger at the mistreatment of Jerusalem's sacred temple. His anger was not raging and destructive the way human anger can be. Instead, Jesus' focused anger stemmed from the defilement of the center of worship for the Jewish people he loved.

Jerusalem's temple court had turned into a boisterous bazaar with raucous merchants selling birds and animals for sacrifices and other traders exchanging money into a special temple currency. But the greedy sellers gouged the worshippers with high prices and dishonest exchange rates. The religious leaders allowed this "den of robbers" and profited off the trading too.

Jesus decided to clean house on the rowdy market, which was inappropriate in a place set aside for peaceful reflection and respectful celebration of the things of God. Jesus didn't pummel the merchants; he purified the temple.

Sometimes when our lives are overrun with harmful activities or irreverent attitudes, God has to clean house. He has a long fuse, but sometimes his limit is reached. He may step in to regain order and honor. Maybe our part is to pick up a broom and offer to help him.

GIVING BACK

They sent some of the Pharisees and Herodians to Jesus to catch him in his words. They came to him and said, "Teacher, we know you are a man of integrity. You aren't swayed by men, because you pay no attention to who they are; but you teach the way of God in accordance with the truth. Is it right to pay taxes to Caesar or not? Should we pay or shouldn't we?"

But Jesus knew their hypocrisy. "Why are you trying to trap me?" he asked. "Bring me a denarius and let me look at it."

They brought the coin, and he asked them, "Whose portrait is this? And whose inscription?"

"Caesar's," they replied.

Then Jesus said to them, "Give to Caesar what is Caesar's and to God what is God's."

And they were amazed at him.

Mark 12:13–17 NIV

The Pharisees of Jesus' day were Jewish religious leaders, both priests and scribes, who guided others in applying the Hebrew Scriptures to everyday life. The Herodians were Jewish rulers appointed by the Roman government of King Herod and his successors to help oversee the region around Jerusalem. Many Pharisees and Herodians shared distaste for Jesus.

In the encounter in this passage, the naysayers attempted to trick Jesus into being disloyal to Roman dictator Caesar's government. If Jesus answered no to paying taxes, the Romans could arrest him. If he agreed to the taxes, the Jews who disdained the taxation might rise up against him. But people-pleasing did not sway Jesus.

Jesus concurred that the Jews should help support the Roman government, who provided many privileges. But Jesus didn't stop with just giving back to Caesar. He added giving "to God what is God's." Giving back to God can mean a monetary contribution, such as through a church or a faith-based ministry, but it can also mean presenting ourselves every day before him with gratitude for all his unmerited gifts. We are to give back in his honor.

A MATTER OF PRIORITIES

One of the religion scholars [asked]: "Which is most important of all the commandments?"

Jesus said, "The first in importance is, 'Listen, Israel: The Lord your God is one; so love the Lord God with all your passion and prayer and intelligence and energy.' And here is the second: 'Love others as well as you love yourself.' There is no other commandment that ranks with these."

The religion scholar said, "A wonderful answer, Teacher! So lucid and accurate—that God is one and there is no other. And loving him with all passion and intelligence and energy, and loving others as well as you love yourself. Why, that's better than all offerings and sacrifices put together!"

When Jesus realized how insightful he was, he said, "You're almost there, right on the border of God's kingdom."

Mark 12:28–34 MSG

Setting spiritual priorities as discussed in this passage is foundational to our entire lives. The Jewish scholar who approached Jesus appeared to be sincere in his question. He wasn't trying to trap Jesus or debate him, as were many other religious leaders.

Knowing that the scholar revered the written Hebrew Scriptures, Jesus relied on the books of Deuteronomy and Leviticus for his succinct response. Jesus prioritized a fervent love for God as the highest duty of humans. From this devotion to God should spring a love for others. If we get our priorities mixed up and leave God out of the picture or place people above him in our lives, we are headed for trouble. Nothing ranks up there with the first and second commandments from God in ordering our spiritual and relational lives.

Sometimes God may feel distant, and we don't have loving thoughts toward him. We can always tell him that and ask him to stoke our cooled hearts. Loving God is not some mushy feeling. It's a commitment to regard him as number one.

Staying Watchful

[Jesus said,] "Of that day and hour no one knows, not even the angels of heaven, but My Father only. But as the days of Noah were, so also will the coming of the Son of Man be. For as in the days before the flood, they were eating and drinking, marrying and giving in marriage, until the day that Noah entered the ark, and did not know until the flood came and took them all away, so also will the coming of the Son of Man be. Then two men will be in the field: one will be taken and the other left. Two women will be grinding at the mill: one will be taken and the other left.

"Watch therefore, for you do not know what hour your Lord is coming."

Matthew 24:36–42 NKJV

Making predictions is a mainstay of our culture. We tune in to weather forecasts to learn if tomorrow will be sunny or rainy. We consult financial experts to decipher the ideal investment markets. We pick our favorite film and music entertainers on annual televised awards shows. We like to predict winners, and we like to know what's coming and how we can best prepare.

Throughout the ages, plenty of individuals have tried to predict when the world would end or when Jesus would make his promised return to earth. But Jesus declared that even he and the angels do not know the time when God the Father will direct a wrap-up of earth as we know it. From these verses, we learn that this apocalyptic event will be unexpected. Some people will be prepared, and others will not.

Should we live anxiously waiting for eternity? No. Neither should we live as if that day will never come. Jesus cautioned us to be watchful and ready, not fearful or nonchalant. We need to be ready without hesitation.

The Face of Jesus

The King will say to the people on his right, "Come, my Father has given you his blessing. . . . I was hungry, and you gave me food. I was thirsty, and you gave me something to drink. I was alone and away from home, and you invited me into your house. I was without clothes, and you gave me something to wear." . . .

Then the good people will answer, "Lord, when did we see you hungry and give you food, or thirsty and give you something to drink? When did we see you alone and away from home and invite you into our house? When did we see you without clothes and give you something to wear?" . . .

The King will answer, "I tell you the truth, anything you did for even the least of my people here, you also did for me."

Matthew 25:34–38, 40 NCV

Humanitarian aid. Random acts of kindness. Altruistic service opportunities. Our world is familiar with extending tangible support, especially in times of disasters like tsunamis, earthquakes, hurricanes, fires, and tornadoes.

Individuals' coming alongside the hurting and disadvantaged is nothing new. More than two thousand years ago, Jesus called upon people to offer food, water, clothes, and hospitable caring to the needy, but particularly to those in society considered "the least." You may not know any of these lower-ranked people personally, but they live in every community in every nation across the globe. There is always someone in our lives who could use an extra hand, a smile, a compassionate act of generosity. "The least" might even be someone who possesses financial stability but is down and out in relationships or spiritually in the gutter.

Maybe the "least" in your life is the lonely widow next door or the friend's son in jail or the family burdened with medical bills. Something transforming occurs when we extend ourselves to others. Whatever we do for someone in need, we actually do for Jesus. Just think what would happen if we all looked at our world with eyes that see the face of Jesus in everyone.

MEMORABLE MEAL

When it was time, [Jesus] sat down, all the apostles with him, and said, "You've no idea how much I have looked forward to eating this Passover meal with you before I enter my time of suffering. It's the last one I'll eat until we all eat it together in the kingdom of God."

Taking the cup, he blessed it, then said, "Take this and pass it among you. As for me, I'll not drink wine again until the kingdom of God arrives."

Taking bread, he blessed it, broke it, and gave it to them, saying, "This is my body, given for you. Eat it in my memory."

He did the same with the cup after supper, saying, "This cup is the new covenant written in my blood, blood poured out for you."

Luke 22:14–20 MSG

In Bible times, the most significant and sacred feast on the Jewish religious calendar was the Passover. The Passover celebrated the occasion when God freed the Israelites from bondage in Egypt. As part of the punishment for the Egyptians' refusal to free the Jewish people, God one night killed all the firstborn Egyptian children. Those Jews who sprinkled lamb's blood on their doorposts were "passed over" by the judgment of death that fateful evening.

In anticipating his own imminent death, Jesus met with his twelve disciples for a final Passover meal, which has come to be known as the Last Supper, famously depicted by Leonardo da Vinci's mural painting. During that memorable meal, Jesus explained that the wine and bread were his blood and body that would soon be given on their behalf.

Like the Passover lamb slain by the ancient Israelites to protect their homes from death, Jesus became the sacrificial Lamb of God for all of humankind. Jesus gave his life in exchange for the death penalty exacted by God for people's wrongdoings. Jesus surrendered his life for his disciples and for everyone.

TOP DOG

They began to argue among themselves about who would be the greatest among them. Jesus told them, "In this world the kings and great men lord it over their people, yet they are called 'friends of the people.' But among you it will be different. Those who are the greatest among you should take the lowest rank, and the leader should be like a servant. Who is more important, the one who sits at the table or the one who serves? The one who sits at the table, of course. But not here! For I am among you as one who serves.

"You have stayed with me in my time of trial. And just as my Father has granted me a Kingdom, I now grant you the right to eat and drink at my table in my Kingdom."

Luke 22:24–30 NLT

Jesus' reflective last supper with his disciples was interrupted by a classic case of one-upmanship. Right in the middle of their peaceful meal, the men bickered about which of them could be considered the chief disciple. They started bragging on themselves instead of keeping the focus on Jesus and his parting words.

Graciously, Jesus commended them for being supportive during their three-year journey with him healing the sick and speaking to the masses, but he also chastised them for their egotistical attitude. Hadn't they learned about putting others first and letting go of arrogance? One certainly wonders.

It's hard to rid our desire for status and success when it's part of our spiritual DNA. Adam and Eve passed on a craving for more to their children, and the world's first murder occurred when their firstborn, Cain, felt woefully inferior to his brother, Abel. We've all inherited the tendency to look out for our own interests first and to long for recognition and a seat of honor. Yet Jesus reminds us that in his economy, being a person of true significance comes from serving.

Cheerful Humility

He poured water into the basin, and began to wash the disciples' feet and to wipe them with the towel with which He was girded.

So He came to Simon Peter. He said to Him, "Lord, do You wash my feet?"

Jesus answered and said to him, "What I do you do not realize now, but you will understand hereafter."

Peter said to Him, "Never shall You wash my feet!" Jesus answered him, "If I do not wash you, you have no part with Me."

Simon Peter said to Him, "Lord, then wash not only my feet, but also my hands and my head."

Jesus said to him, "He who has bathed needs only to wash his feet, but is completely clean."

John 13:4–10 NASB

In the early Middle East, as in many cultures of the world today, people walked around on dusty and often filthy streets and roads. In Bible times, a Hebrew hospitality custom included washing the feet of guests, which helped them feel welcomed and honored. The lowliest household servants performed this menial task.

Jesus modeled this form of servanthood and humility when he removed his outer garment and wrapped a towel around his waist just like a common servant would do. None of the disciples rushed in to help him. Perhaps they were too stunned or embarrassed to let their leader clean their smelly feet. Typically impetuous, Peter questioned Jesus' actions and refused to submit to the foot washing. Jesus kindly explained the symbolic importance of being cleansed, not just physically but spiritually. With that understanding, Peter volunteered for a whole body scrub!

With love and meekness, Jesus cleanses people's hearts and souls from the dirt and grime of the world. Without him, none of us can be truly clean.

Reservations Guaranteed

"Don't let this throw you. You trust God, don't you? Trust me. There is plenty of room for you in my Father's home. If that weren't so, would I have told you that I'm on my way to get a room ready for you? And if I'm on my way to get your room ready, I'll come back and get you so you can live where I live. And you already know the road I'm taking."

Thomas said, "Master, we have no idea where you're going. How do you expect us to know the road?"

Jesus said, "I am the Road, also the Truth, also the Life. No one gets to the Father apart from me. If you really knew me, you would know my Father as well. From now on, you do know him. You've even seen him!"

John 14:1–7 MSG

Think of the most opulent royal palaces or the finest hotels on earth—Bristol Vienna, Buckingham Palace, Bellagio Towers. The glitz and luxury of those spectacular structures pale miserably when we compare them to God's royal residence, heaven.

The Bible mentions few details about heaven, calling it a "paradise" and a dwelling of indescribable joy, beauty, and rest. In this passage, Jesus describes heaven as his eternal home. Jesus' disciples were troubled and downcast because he had just announced he would be leaving them soon. So Jesus reassured them that he would not abandon them forever but that he would journey back to heaven to prepare a room for their eventual arrival. He would guarantee their eternal reservations if they would simply follow him.

Jesus declared that he is the Road, but we, like Thomas, want to have a road map for daily life. We like to avoid potholes and sharp curves, but Jesus said we are to focus on him as the Road and trust his guiding us to our final destination. We're invited to stay on course with God and someday bask in the unsurpassed comforts of heaven.

More Fruit

I am the true grapevine, and my Father is the gardener. He cuts off every branch of mine that doesn't produce fruit, and he prunes the branches that do bear fruit so they will produce even more. You have already been pruned and purified by the message I have given you. Remain in me, and I will remain in you. For a branch cannot produce fruit if it is severed from the vine, and you cannot be fruitful unless you remain in me.

Yes, I am the vine; you are the branches. Those who remain in me, and I in them, will produce much fruit. For apart from me you can do nothing . . . But if you remain in me and my words remain in you, you may ask for anything you want, and it will be granted!

John 15:1–7 NLT

If you have a yard or garden, you understand how fast-growing weeds and overgrown branches can quickly choke out the beauty of your vegetation. Left to run wild, what was once a source of pleasure can end up being a burdensome chore to manage. Dead, unproductive fruit and flowers need occasional pruning. Even healthy stems and branches require pruning to produce even better fruit.

In Jesus' illustration, he is the grapevine, and God the Father is the master gardener. We are the branches off the main vine. Our role is to stay connected to and dependent upon Jesus. We are helpless without him, even though at times we may think we can oversee our own lives capably by ourselves.

The truth is, we get a bit scraggly when we attempt to live apart from God. Most of us dislike the process of God's trimming back areas of dead growth in our attitudes and actions. We initially cringe at giving up something that seemed just fine with us. But as we press in closer to God, we find a fresh vibrancy springing from within. And our outward lives start to "product much fruit."

Parting Is Sweet Sorrow

You will weep and lament, but the world will rejoice. You will be sorrowful, but your sorrow will turn into joy. When a woman is giving birth, she has sorrow because her hour has come, but when she has delivered the baby, she no longer remembers the anguish, for joy that a human being has been born into the world. So also you have sorrow now, but I will see you again and your hearts will rejoice, and no one will take your joy from you.

In that day you will ask nothing of me. Truly, truly, I say to you, whatever you ask of the Father in my name, he will give it to you. Until now you have asked nothing in my name. Ask, and you will receive, that your joy may be full.

John 16:20–24 ESV

Saying good-bye to loved ones moving away or leaving this earth through death is marked with searing grief and sorrow. Jesus compared his disciples' lamenting over the news of his soon return to heaven to the mixed pain and joy of childbirth. The excruciating pains of labor fade when the newborn finally arrives. Immense joy overtakes the agony once felt. In the same way, the disciples' suffering through Jesus' death and being without him would eventually turn to joy through the future promise of being with him in eternity.

Jesus' handpicked associates relied on him directly every day for strength, comfort, and direction. The disciples had little need for prayer with Jesus right beside them. So in passing along his thoughts to the men, Jesus encouraged them to stay in touch through prayer. Jesus essentially explained, "In the meantime, keep talking to me through prayer. Use my name in your prayers. Ask things of me and you'll be delightedly surprised by the responses you receive." For us too, there is relief and joy in knowing our direct line of communication with Jesus stays open 24-7. He's just a prayer away.

WHAT MATTERS MOST

All who are mine belong to you, and you have given them to me, so they bring me glory. Now I am departing from the world; they are staying in this world, but I am coming to you. . . .

I have given them your word. And the world hates them because they do not belong to the world, just as I do not belong to the world. I'm not asking you to take them out of the world, but to keep them safe from the evil one. They do not belong to this world any more than I do. Make them holy by your truth; teach them your word, which is truth. Just as you sent me into the world, I am sending them into the world. And I give myself as a holy sacrifice for them so they can be made holy by your truth.

John 17:10–11, 14–19 NLT

Jesus always looked out for his band of brothers. In the final hours before he would be apprehended and sentenced to death on a cross (a traditional form of execution in those days), Jesus shared intimate thoughts with his disciples. Jesus talked about what matters most in life.

He imparted key principles that would inspire and guide them for the rest of their years. He also turned to prayer, asking God the Father to protect not just the eleven disciples but all of his current and future followers from Satan's harm and to continue to bolster them with life-sustaining truth.

Jesus knew many in the world would not approve of the disciples' spreading Jesus' teachings after he was gone. He knew they would face opposition for standing up for their faith, yet he also understood how to undergird them with God's truth.

People who follow Jesus today sometimes face similar disapproval from the world. But faith is not about a popularity contest. Living with some resistance from the world is nothing compared to living in this world resisting him.

Whenever Acceptance

[Jesus] came out and went, as was his custom, to the Mount of Olives, and the disciples followed him. And when he came to the place, he said to them, "Pray that you may not enter into temptation." And he withdrew from them about a stone's throw, and knelt down and prayed, saying, "Father, if you are willing, remove this cup from me. Nevertheless, not my will, but yours, be done."

And there appeared to him an angel from heaven, strengthening him. And being in an agony he prayed more earnestly; and his sweat became like great drops of blood falling down to the ground. And when he rose from prayer, he came to the disciples and found them sleeping for sorrow, and he said to them, "Why are you sleeping? Rise and pray that you may not enter into temptation."

Luke 22:39–46 ESV

Whatever! edged its way into American pop slang in the 1980s as a term of indifference, reluctant agreement, or resentful compliance. Imagine if Jesus had responded to his assignment to die on the cross with a snippy "Whatever!" Imagine Jesus snubbing his nose at the Father and walking off in defiance.

Gratefully, for our sakes, this didn't happen. Jesus instead walked east of Jerusalem to the Garden of Gethsemane—one of his favorite getaway places—to reflect and pray. There he urged his disciples who tagged along to pray. He knelt to talk to the Father alone. In one of Jesus' most poignant prayers ever recorded in the Bible, he asked the Father that he be allowed, if possible, to forgo the cup of suffering to be poured out in a tortuous death on a Roman cross.

Jesus did not begrudgingly express resignation to fate, but he willingly accepted his duty to die for the higher good of humankind. He didn't shrug off his mission with a snooty "Whatever!" Instead, he calmly reacted with a "Whenever." Jesus is an example for us in how to approach God with our lives and the circumstances that try us.

ASSISTING ARREST

Judas came there with a group of soldiers and some guards from the leading priests and the Pharisees. They were carrying torches, lanterns, and weapons.

Knowing everything that would happen to him, Jesus went out and asked, "Who is it you are looking for?" They answered, "Jesus from Nazareth."

"I am he," Jesus said. . . . "So if you are looking for me, let the others go." This happened so that the words Jesus said before would come true: "I have not lost any of the ones you gave me."

Simon Peter, who had a sword, pulled it out and struck the servant of the high priest, cutting off his right ear. (The servant's name was Malchus.) Jesus said to Peter, "Put your sword back. Shouldn't I drink the cup the Father gave me?"

John 18:3–5, 8–11 NCV

Judas, one of Jesus' twelve disciples, ratted out his beloved leader to the local authorities. In a darkened garden at the foot of the Mount of Olives, Judas led a band of Romans soldiers and Jewish temple police to arrest Jesus, the Jewish rabbi who had caused a stir in the region for three years. How dare him heal people in God's name and even call himself God!

Behind the footsteps of Judas, armed officers marched into the quiet garden. They were steeled for that rebel to resist arrest, but Jesus willingly assisted the arrest. Note the words "knowing everything that would happen." Jesus, as the all-knowing God, already knew Judas would betray him, and Jesus knew the precise second that the law enforcement team would arrive.

Nothing took Jesus by surprise that night, including Peter's brashly slicing off the servant's ear. (In other Bible accounts, Jesus fully restored this maimed man's ear.) The comforting side to Jesus' capture is that he remained steadily in control. He is the same God today who knows what we will encounter each new day—both the good and the not-so-good. And he calmly steps forward to help on our behalf.

Hanging in the Shadows

While Peter was still in the courtyard, a servant girl of the high priest came up and saw Peter warming himself by the fire. She stared at him and said, "You were with Jesus from Nazareth!"

Peter replied, "That isn't true! I don't know what you're talking about. I don't have any idea what you mean." He went out to the gate, and a rooster crowed.

The servant girl saw Peter again and said to the people standing there, "This man is one of them!"

"No, I'm not!" Peter replied.

A little while later some of the people said to Peter, "You certainly are one of them. You're a Galilean!"

This time Peter began to curse and swear, "I don't even know the man you're talking about!"

Right away the rooster crowed a second time.

Mark 14:66–72 CEV

Just a few verses before this passage in Mark, Jesus warned his disciples that they would soon abandon him. The ever-impassioned Peter swore total allegiance to Jesus. Jesus calmly informed Peter that he would actually disown Jesus three times that very night.

Peter couldn't fathom walking out on Jesus after their years of solidarity and service. None of the other disciples could either. Judas led the way of defection, and then the eleven ran for their lives when Jesus was arrested. Yet Peter dared to edge into the courtyard where Jesus was detained. Peter reasoned he could just hang in the shadows out of sight and watch for Jesus from a safe distance.

Unfortunately, as in a good spy drama, Peter's cover was blown. Not just once, but three times he was recognized as "one of them." All three times Peter nervously denied that he was a Christ-follower. How easy it is for all of us when the heat is on to sidestep any association with God and a life of faith. Sometimes it feels safer just to hang in the shadows with our spiritual beliefs. But are the shadows safe?

PRISONER EXCHANGE

The crowd went up and began asking [Pilate] to do as he had been accustomed to do for them.

Pilate answered them, saying, "Do you want me to release for you the King of the Jews?"

For he was aware that the chief priests had handed Him over because of envy.

But the chief priests stirred up the crowd to ask him to release Barabbas for them instead.

Answering again, Pilate said to them, "Then what shall I do with Him whom you call the King of the Jews?"

They shouted back, "Crucify Him!"

But Pilate said to them, "Why, what evil has He done?" But they shouted all the more, "Crucify Him!"

Wishing to satisfy the crowd, Pilate released Barabbas for them, and after having Jesus scourged, he handed Him over to be crucified.

Mark 15:8–15 NASB

Each year at Passover in ancient Israel, the ruling Roman governor would release one prisoner, perhaps as a way of appeasing the Jews who were not excited to be ruled by Rome. During the Passover festival, Jesus was arrested and brought before Pilate, the fairly ruthless Roman governor.

Pilate knew Jesus was innocent of any crime, and Pilate didn't view Jesus as a political threat. The Jewish chief priests, however, envied Jesus' popularity and feared he would usurp their power. Most of the crowd didn't show particular interest in Jesus; they just wanted their revered freedom fighter Barabbas set free. The chief priests incited the people to ask for an even exchange. Murderer Barabbas would go free, and Jesus would be executed instead.

In a way, Pilate's hands were tied. Perhaps his actions proved he was more weak than cruel. Jesus' sentence was part of God's bigger plan, however. No detail of his unfair conviction escaped God's notice. No injustices in our lives escape his notice either.

SELFLESS SERVING

This all happened on Friday, the day of preparation, the day before the Sabbath. As evening approached, Joseph of Arimathea took a risk and went to Pilate and asked for Jesus' body. (Joseph was an honored member of the high council, and he was waiting for the Kingdom of God to come.) Pilate couldn't believe that Jesus was already dead, so he called for the Roman officer and asked if he had died yet. The officer confirmed that Jesus was dead, so Pilate told Joseph he could have the body.

Joseph bought a long sheet of linen cloth. Then he took Jesus' body down from the cross, wrapped it in the cloth, and laid it in a tomb that had been carved out of the rock. Then he rolled a stone in front of the entrance.

Mark 15:42–46 NLT

Not many of Jesus' loyal followers showed up to watch him die on a cross. Many feared they would be killed for associating with Jesus, but all of them must have found it gut-wrenching to watch their beloved leader die in such a cruel fashion. Jewish customs required Jesus' body to be buried before sundown. Joseph of Arimathea, a prestigious member of the Jewish ruling council and a secret follower of Jesus, secured permission from the Roman governor to bury Jesus.

That Jewish statesman risked his own reputation and social status for Jesus, an executed enemy of the state, out of love and respect for him. From other Bible accounts we learn that Joseph had just hours earlier cast a dissenting council vote in favor of Jesus' release. Joseph believed in Jesus and wanted to care for the bloodied corpse of his God. With the help of his council colleague Nicodemus, Joseph gently carried Jesus to a burial tomb that Joseph owned.

Sometimes serving behind the scenes is tiring work without any thanks or recognition. Joseph modeled both courage and selfless serving. We can all ask ourselves what we can do with less self and more serving.

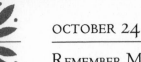

Remember Me

When they had come to the place called Calvary, there they crucified Him, and the criminals, one on the right hand and the other on the left. Then Jesus said, "Father, forgive them, for they do not know what they do." . . .

Then one of the criminals who were hanged blasphemed Him, saying, "If You are the Christ, save Yourself and us."

But the other, answering, rebuked him, saying, "Do you not even fear God, seeing you are under the same condemnation? And we indeed justly, for we receive the due reward of our deeds; but this Man has done nothing wrong." Then he said to Jesus, "Lord, remember me when You come into Your kingdom."

And Jesus said to him, "Assuredly, I say to you, today you will be with Me in Paradise."

Luke 23:33–34, 39–43 NKJV

Nailed publicly to wooden crossbeams on a site outside Jerusalem called *Calvary*, meaning "skull" in Latin, Jesus endured not just horrific physical pain, but intense verbal and emotional ridicule. Mercilessly taunted by the Roman soldiers, Jewish religious and political leaders, and everyday citizens, Jesus remained silent. Some of their words tore at his heart as the nails and crown of thorns tore into his flesh.

Finally, the battered Jesus uttered some of his most profound words ever spoken. He asked God the Father to forgive his murderers. In the bigger scheme of eternity, Jesus knew those incensed individuals didn't know they were killing God. They thought Jesus was pretending to be God.

But Jesus' forgiveness did not stop with those who participated in his execution. One criminal on the cross next to Jesus spewed slanderous words at Jesus' position as God. But the other criminal confessed his wrongdoing and guilt and asked to be remembered in heaven.

True to his merciful and compassionate character, Jesus extends forgiveness to us as well. No offense is too cruel for his pardon.

THE WEIGHT OF THE WORLD

From noon until three in the afternoon darkness came over the whole land. At about three in the afternoon Jesus cried out with a loud voice, *"Elí, Elí, lemá sabachtháni?"* that is, "My God, My God, why have You forsaken Me?" . . .

Jesus shouted again with a loud voice and gave up His spirit. Suddenly, the curtain of the sanctuary was split in two from top to bottom; the earth quaked and the rocks were split. The tombs also were opened and many bodies of the saints who had gone to their rest were raised. . . .

When the centurion and those with him, who were guarding Jesus, saw the earthquake and the things that had happened, they were terrified and said, "This man really was God's Son!"

Matthew 27:45–46, 50–54
HCSB

The ancient Romans killed their vilest criminals or the lowliest citizens by crucifixion. To the Jews, a person executed by the cross was cursed by God. Jesus didn't fit the norm of an individual sentenced to death by crucifixion. He committed no crime and was an educated Jewish rabbi. God did not condemn Jesus because he suffered on the cross, but God did condemn something else—the misdeeds of every human.

As he was dying, Jesus, sensing a devastating break in his intimate relationship with God the Father, cried out. Innocent Jesus took on the punishment for all of humanity's wrongdoing. For a while, the Father, as the righteous Judge of the universe, had to look away from the ugliness Jesus carried on behalf of every person. For a while, Jesus felt abandoned in the desolation of people's erring ways.

The Crucifixion did not rob Jesus of life. He actually surrendered his Spirit, and when he did, the earth broke loose. In all the chaos, the Roman soldiers at the foot of the cross exclaimed, "Oh, oh!" Jesus was God, after all.

ALL IN THE DETAILS

By the cross of Jesus were His mother, His mother's sister, Mary the wife of Clopas, and Mary Magdalene. When Jesus saw His mother and the disciple He loved standing there, He said to His mother, "Woman, here is your son." Then He said to the disciple, "Here is your mother." And from that hour the disciple took her into his home.

After this, when Jesus knew that everything was now accomplished that the Scripture might be fulfilled, He said, "I'm thirsty!" A jar full of sour wine was sitting there; so they fixed a sponge full of sour wine on hyssop and held it up to His mouth.

When Jesus had received the sour wine, He said, "It is finished!" Then bowing His head, He gave up His spirit.

John 19:25–30 HCSB

With Jesus' death imminent, he did not neglect to give final care instructions for his mother, nor he did he neglect to wrap up specifics on the fulfillment of several Old Testament prophecies concerning his death. In the last minutes before his final breath, Jesus was offered wine vinegar to drink, as was foretold in Psalm 69. During crucifixion, guards usually broke the criminals' legs to hasten death, but no one broke a bone of Jesus—he was already dead. Escaping the bone-breaking completed three different Old Testament passages stating Jesus would die without broken bones. To ensure Jesus was dead, a soldier pierced Jesus' side, as foreseen by the prophet Zechariah.

Jesus declared his mission accomplished, and every prediction made about his death centuries before fit perfectly in place. No single facet of the Bible is too insignificant or too humongous for God to oversee. God notices every minute detail of our lives too. He cares for the grieving. He watches over the hurting and lonely. He knows the outcomes of our labors. He understands the intentions of our hearts. He is truly a God who never forgets a single detail.

SWEET-SMELLING SPICES

Very early on the first day of the week, at dawn, the women came to the tomb, bringing the spices they had prepared. They found the stone rolled away from the entrance of the tomb, but when they went in, they did not find the body of the Lord Jesus. While they were wondering about this, two men in shining clothes suddenly stood beside them. The women were very afraid and bowed their heads to the ground.

The men said to them, "Why are you looking for a living person in this place for the dead? He is not here; he has risen from the dead. Do you remember what he told you in Galilee? He said the Son of Man must be handed over to sinful people, be crucified, and rise from the dead on the third day."

Luke 24:1–7 NCV

To beat the start of the Jewish day of rest, Joseph of Arimathea and Nicodemus quickly spread aromatic burial spices over Jesus' lifeless body as they wrapped him in clean linen strips. It is interesting to note that myrrh was used in preparing Jesus' body for burial. Myrrh was also a chief spice presented by the wise men who celebrated Jesus' birth. In this hope-filled Bible passage, myrrh actually spread its fragrance over both death and life.

Jesus' close female friends expected to add their own sweet-smelling spices to Jesus' tomb; instead, they found his grave empty. To verify those women as credible witnesses, the Bible lists them in verse 10—Mary Magdalene, Joanna, James's mother, and a few others. Soldiers had guarded Jesus' tomb all weekend, and no one had stolen his body. The angels' report to the women was true. Jesus defeated death and was back on earth to tell about it.

No other religious or political leader can make that claim. Only God can conquer physical and spiritual death. Only he can replace the things of loss and disrepair in our lives and freshen us with new life.

EYES OF EXPECTANCY

Two of Jesus' disciples were going to the village of Emmaus, which was about seven miles from Jerusalem. As they were talking and thinking about what had happened, Jesus came near and started walking along beside them. But they did not know who he was.

Jesus asked them, "What were you talking about as you walked along?"

The two of them stood there looking sad and gloomy. Then the one named Cleopas asked Jesus, "Are you the only person from Jerusalem who didn't know what was happening there these last few days?" . . .

Then Jesus asked the two disciples, "Why can't you understand? How can you be so slow to believe all that the prophets said? Didn't you know that the Messiah would have to suffer before he was given his glory?" Jesus then explained everything written about himself in the Scriptures.

Luke 24:13–18, 25–27 CEV

Jesus played dumb. He came alongside two of his followers in deep conversation about Jesus' disappearance from his burial tomb. The latest buzz around Jerusalem centered on the crucified Jewish rebel now missing from his grave. Did someone steal his body? Was he in another tomb? Or, if he was alive, where was he?

Jesus' disciples expected him to be the Promised One, the Deliverer of Israel. How could such a mighty rescuer not rescue himself from crucifixion? Now his battered body had vanished.

As Jesus conversed with Cleopas and his companion, God actually blinded them to recognizing Jesus. They were clueless to his true identity. Lest we roll our eyes at those disciples' inability to see Jesus right next to them, perhaps we should consider how we sometimes miss his presence in our lives. For some of us, he shows up in a loving embrace, a note of encouragement, a prayer answered. Sometimes he speaks through the Bible or the words of a friend. Each day we'd do well to look for him with open eyes of expectancy.

ALIVE AND WELL

[Jesus] said to them, "Peace to you!" But they were startled and terrified and thought they were seeing a ghost. "Why are you troubled?" He asked them. . . . "Look at My hands and My feet, that it is I Myself! Touch Me and see, because a ghost does not have flesh and bones as you can see I have." Having said this, He showed them His hands and feet. But while they still could not believe because of [their] joy and were amazed, He asked them, "Do you have anything here to eat?" So they gave Him a piece of a broiled fish, and He took it and ate in their presence.

Then He told them, "These are My words that I spoke to you while I was still with you—that everything written about Me . . . must be fulfilled."

Luke 24:36–44 HCSB

Once Jesus rose from the dead, he did not hover across earth with some heavenly glow. He was still God in his same human body, except now he had fresh scars on his hands, feet, and side. As God, though, he could appear and disappear in a flash—a supernatural feat without a doubt.

Even though we read comics and watch blockbuster films about superheroes that show up out of the blue, Jesus was more than some superhuman force. Jesus wanted to show the world that he was more than a mighty prophet or a kind healer. He was God. He actually defeated death and came back to life. So he showed up on several occasions in his physical body to his original eleven disciples and to hundreds of others.

He showed bewildered individuals his nail-scarred hands and feet. He ate broiled fish before their amazed eyes. And Jesus calmed people with his reassuring voice and comforting presence. Even though we cannot reach out and touch his body ourselves, we, like the early disciples, are encouraged to believe his words and hold on to faith that he is alive and well.

Follow the Leader

[Jesus] opened [the disciples'] minds so they could understand the Scriptures. He told them, "This is what is written: The Christ will suffer and rise from the dead on the third day, and repentance and forgiveness of sins will be preached in his name to all nations, beginning at Jerusalem. You are witnesses of these things. I am going to send you what my Father has promised; but stay in the city until you have been clothed with power from on high."

When he had led them out to the vicinity of Bethany, he lifted up his hands and blessed them. While he was blessing them, he left them and was taken up into heaven. Then they worshiped him and returned to Jerusalem with great joy. And they stayed continually at the temple, praising God.

Luke 24:45–53 NIV

Some religious leaders have brainwashed their followers into mass suicide with promises that they would reunite in a better place. The People's Temple chugged cyanide-tainted drinks in Jonestown, Guyana. The Heaven's Gate cult, chasing after the Hale-Bopp comet, swallowed a vodka-phenobarbital mix. The Branch Davidians died in a firestorm outside Waco, Texas.

When Jesus left this earth to return to heaven, he left his devoted followers behind. He didn't leave them with empty promises or fill their hearts with fear and mistrust. Jesus' final words comprised both encouragement and blessing. He reminded the first Christians to pass along his message of forgiveness and reassured them he would send them fresh power from on high. He prayed a special prayer of blessing over them. There were no poisonous drinks, no swindling of life's savings, no pledges to be free from earthly bodies to join a spaceship in the sky.

Jesus continued to speak the same words of truth and life he always had. Even without his physical presence, his people continued with joy and freedom. They chose the right leader to follow.

BELIEVING IS SEEING

Thomas, called the Twin, one of the twelve, was not with them when Jesus came. The other disciples therefore said to him, "We have seen the Lord."

So he said to them, "Unless I see in His hands the print of the nails, and put my finger into the print of the nails, and put my hand into His side, I will not believe."

And after eight days His disciples were again inside, and Thomas with them. Jesus came, the doors being shut, and stood in the midst, and said, "Peace to you!" Then He said to Thomas, "Reach your finger here, and look at My hands; and reach your hand here, and put it into My side. Do not be unbelieving, but believing."

And Thomas answered and said to Him, "My Lord and my God!"

John 20:24–28 NKJV

Over the years, the "doubting Thomas" label has come to describe someone who disbelieves without having sound, physical evidence. The original skeptic with this name was one of Jesus' inner-circle disciples. Thomas was not present for any of Jesus' post-Resurrection appearances, and he refused to believe the other disciples' testimony of seeing Jesus alive. Thomas brashly stated that he would not believe Jesus was walking the earth again without first seeing and touching Jesus' actual wound imprints from his death on the cross.

Like a resolute crime-scene investigator, Thomas asserted that only pure evidence would lead him to accurate facts. A week later, Jesus repeated Thomas's own words to him and challenged Thomas to touch the scars. The Bible never reveals if Thomas actually placed his hands on Jesus' healed wounds. More likely, Thomas took one look at Jesus' face and all doubts disappeared. Believing opened Thomas's eyes of faith.

Today those who believe in Jesus rely on the Bible and the witness of others through the ages as proof of Jesus' resurrection. What keeps us from a faith without hands-on evidence? What would it take for our unbelief to fade like Thomas's?

IN JESUS' NAME

Later Jesus appeared to the Eleven as they were eating. . . .

He said to them, "Go into all the world and preach the good news to all creation. Whoever believes and is baptized will be saved, but whoever does not believe will be condemned. And these signs will accompany those who believe: In my name they will drive out demons; they will speak in new tongues; they will pick up snakes with their hands; and when they drink deadly poison, it will not hurt them at all; they will place their hands on sick people, and they will get well."

After the Lord Jesus had spoken to them, he was taken up into heaven and he sat at the right hand of God. Then the disciples went out and preached everywhere, and the Lord worked with them and confirmed his word by the signs that accompanied it.

Mark 16:14–20 NIV

As Mark concluded his writings on the life and ministry of Jesus, he summed up Jesus' farewell address to his disciples. The book of Mark is the shortest of the four Gospels and moves along speedily with pithy sentences lending a sense of urgency. The final paragraphs are no exception to Mark's straightforward brevity.

Jesus essentially said, "Okay, guys, I've trained you for three years in how to teach and preach and heal. Now share with the whole world the fantastic news of my being God and offering eternal life. Go on, you can do it."

Jesus imparted the authority for the disciples to carry on his mission: "in my name." The disciples were instructed to call upon Jesus as they preached and performed miraculous signs.

Today we do not often see the specific miracles mentioned in this passage, but Jesus is still our sustaining strength. Whether we're facing tough circumstances and feeling discouraged or learning something new about the Bible and feeling on top of the world, we are reminded to stay plugged into our ultimate power source.

MULTIPLICATION

If ever there was a story of underdogs triumphing, surely it is the story of the early church. Twelve people—most of them rural, unsophisticated, and uneducated—began telling what they had seen and heard when they walked with Jesus. People listened, believed, and found in the gospel the fulfillment of all their hopes. The kingdom of God spread like wildfire. The world was never the same.

The seventh angel blew his trumpet, and there were loud voices shouting in heaven: "The world has now become the Kingdom of our Lord and of his Christ, and he will reign forever and ever." The twenty-four elders sitting on their thrones before God fell with their faces to the ground and worshiped him. And they said, "We give thanks to you, Lord God, the Almighty, the one who is and who always was, for now you have assumed your great power and have begun to reign."

Revelation 11:15–17 NLT

PROMISE OF POWER

After [Jesus] had suffered, He also presented Himself alive to them by many convincing proofs, appearing to them during 40 days and speaking about the kingdom of God.

While He was together with them, He commanded them not to leave Jerusalem, but to wait for the Father's promise. "This," [He said, "is what] you heard from Me; for John baptized with water, but you will be baptized with the Holy Spirit not many days from now." . . .

He said to them, "It is not for you to know times or periods that the Father has set by His own authority. But you will receive power when the Holy Spirit has come upon you, and you will be My witnesses in Jerusalem, in all Judea and Samaria, and to the ends of the earth."

Acts 1:3–5, 7–8 HCSB

The book of Acts, written by Luke, narrates the life of the first-century church. Nearing his last moments with his faithful team, Jesus promised to send the Holy Spirit, who is God, as an invisible ambassador who counsels and empowers people. The Father, Jesus, and the Spirit are equally one God, but each with a distinct role. God the Father pledged in the Old Testament to send his Spirit as the energizing strength for his people. Jesus also told his disciples that he would not leave them alone to carry on his teachings but that he would send the Spirit.

Soon the Spirit's power would wash over the early Christians and embolden them to take a stand for Jesus, and not just in familiar Jerusalem but also in the surrounding regions and even the whole earth. This oath of God's enlivening Spirit is a built-in feature for all who believe in Jesus. We can attempt to live each day on our own, or we can turn to the strength of God's Spirit. Acts shows us what happened when the original church let the Spirit direct their steps. He's ready and willing to direct our steps too.

CONSTANT COMPANION

When the day of Pentecost came, they were all together in one place. Suddenly a sound like the blowing of a violent wind came from heaven and filled the whole house where they were sitting. They saw what seemed to be tongues of fire that separated and came to rest on each of them. All of them were filled with the Holy Spirit and began to speak in other tongues as the Spirit enabled them.

Now there were staying in Jerusalem God-fearing Jews from every nation under heaven. When they heard this sound, a crowd came together in bewilderment, because each one heard them speaking in his own language. Utterly amazed, they asked: "Are not all these men who are speaking Galileans? Then how is it that each of us hears them in his own native language?"

Acts 2:1–8 NIV

The ancient Jews celebrated the Feast of Pentecost fifty days after the first day of Passover. The Israelites met together on Pentecost to thank God for the grain harvest and other blessings. On the day of Pentecost after Jesus had returned to heaven, the Holy Spirit made a dramatic entrance to the gathering of Jesus' followers.

The Spirit of God didn't just show up for the first time at this get-together in Jerusalem. At Creation, the Spirit of God "was hovering over the waters" (Gen. 1:2 NIV). Throughout the Old Testament, the Holy Spirit worked in many people's lives both spectacularly and silently. But on this Pentecost Day, the Spirit was commissioned to empower every individual believer in Jesus—young and old and of every language. The Spirit had made guest appearances on earth before, and now he was free to stay put. The tongues of fire and people speaking in different tongues were outward signs of an inward change.

God's Spirit is forever present with those who trust in Jesus. The Bible explains that the Spirit resides in the heart and the soul. God's Spirit is our constant companion and never-ending energizer.

CONNECTED ON PURPOSE

Those who had received his word were baptized; and that day there were added about three thousand souls. They were continually devoting themselves to the apostles' teaching and to fellowship, to the breaking of bread and to prayer.

Everyone kept feeling a sense of awe; and many wonders and signs were taking place through the apostles. And all those who had believed were together and had all things in common; and they began selling their property and possessions and were sharing them with all, as anyone might have need.

Day by day continuing with one mind in the temple, and breaking bread from house to house, they were taking their meals together with gladness and sincerity of heart, praising God and having favor with all the people. And the Lord was adding to their number day by day.

Acts 2:41–47 NASB

Almost overnight, the church in the first century exploded in its numbers. On the day of Pentecost alone, three thousand people heard God's words of truth, and through baptism, publicly expressed their newfound faith. This family of Christ-followers dedicated themselves to gathering for teaching and prayer and eating meals together.

But they didn't stop with a weekly church-type meeting. They met daily. Not only did they joyfully interact with each other, but also they dug deep and shared their personal finances with anyone in need. That style of intimacy with close comrades is not exactly modeled in our culture today. Our society tends to praise the individualistic nature of people and pounce on those who willingly interconnect with others. The world tells us to "be the captain of your own destiny," but God says, "I'll guide you as you belong to a trusting community of my people." Our culture breeds selfishness; God encourages selflessness.

Members of the early church intertwined their lives together, not perfectly but purposely. They depended on one another in times of prosperity and times of pain—Christianity at its finest.

TRUE FREEDOM

There was a man crippled from birth being carried up. Every day he was set down at the Temple gate, the one named Beautiful, to beg from those going into the Temple. When he saw Peter and John about to enter the Temple, he asked for a handout. Peter, with John at his side, looked him straight in the eye and said, "Look here." . . .

Peter said, "I don't have a nickel to my name, but what I do have, I give you: In the name of Jesus Christ of Nazareth, walk!" He grabbed him by the right hand and pulled him up. In an instant his feet and ankles became firm. He jumped to his feet and walked.

The man went into the Temple with them, walking back and forth, dancing and praising God.

Acts 3:2–4, 6–8 MSG

In the original days of Jewish people, begging was not typically a part of their customs. The Jewish laws urged relief for the poor, and monies were set aside in a general charity fund to help the less fortunate. By New Testament times, beggars were commonplace along the pathways Jewish pilgrims traveled for festivals and at the gate of Jerusalem's magnificent temple.

At that very gate, Jesus' disciples Peter and John met a man handicapped from birth. Day after day, the impoverished man depended on the generosity of others. Many people probably never even looked in this man's direction. They just shuffled past him. Others tossed a few coins his way. Peter and John actually stopped and looked the pauper in the eyes.

With the authority that Jesus granted them, Peter boldly ordered the man to walk "in the name of Jesus Christ." In contrast to years with lifeless legs, this man exuberantly danced. That's what happens when God heals and restores. Many things can keep us from dancing in life—unbelief, worry, fear, anger. Maybe it's time to call upon the name of Jesus and be set free.

FREE SPEECH

They ordered Peter and John out of the council chamber and conferred among themselves.

"What should we do with these men?" they asked each other. "We can't deny that they have performed a miraculous sign, and everybody in Jerusalem knows about it. But to keep them from spreading their propaganda any further, we must warn them not to speak to anyone in Jesus' name again." So they called the apostles back in and commanded them never again to speak or teach in the name of Jesus.

But Peter and John replied, "Do you think God wants us to obey you rather than him? We cannot stop telling about everything we have seen and heard."

The council then threatened them further, but they finally let them go because they didn't know how to punish them without starting a riot.

Acts 4:15–21 NLT

Peter and John spent a night in jail for preaching in Jerusalem. They didn't just call out on a street corner. They addressed people in the holy Jewish temple. On top of that, they proclaimed the resurrection of Jesus from the dead—to some of the very Jews who had helped expedite Jesus' murder. No wonder the temple authorities were riled up; no wonder they jailed the two.

The next day, the highest level of Jewish leaders debated how to deal with Peter and John. The best they could concoct was to warn Peter and John never to speak or teach in Jesus' name again. Peter and John quickly replied that nothing could keep them from sharing their life-transforming experience in knowing Jesus.

Just a few weeks earlier, Peter had cowered and denied his association with Jesus. But a restorative encounter with the resurrected Jesus and the filling of God's Spirit emboldened Peter to preach fearlessly on Jesus' behalf. The God of second chances turned the timid into the triumphant. Nothing can stifle the good news of Jesus. Free speech rules when it comes to "telling about everything" God does for us.

PURITY VS. PRETENSE

There was a certain man named Ananias who, with his wife, Sapphira, sold some property. He brought part of the money to the apostles, claiming it was the full amount. With his wife's consent, he kept the rest.

Then Peter said, "Ananias, why have you let Satan fill your heart? You lied to the Holy Spirit, and you kept some of the money for yourself. The property was yours to sell or not sell, as you wished. And after selling it, the money was also yours to give away. How could you do a thing like this? You weren't lying to us but to God!"

As soon as Ananias heard these words, he fell to the floor and died. Everyone who heard about it was terrified. Then some young men got up, wrapped him in a sheet, and took him out and buried him.

Acts 5:1–6 NLT

Deception is as old as the first husband and wife in the Garden of Eden. Centuries later in this account of a husband and wife in the budding Christian church, Satan was still up to his conniving stunts. The central issue in Ananias and Sapphira's story wasn't the money but their misdeed of lying.

No one demanded that the couple sell their property and give the proceeds to their church family. Many of the new Christ-followers were freely selling possessions to help those in need. Giving was a private matter, and Ananias and Sapphira could be commended for selling property for the benefit of others. But their deliberate dishonesty cost both of them their lives.

Is that harsh judgment for holding back some promised money? Not in God's eyes. God detests when our lips say one thing and our actions say another. He does not advocate hypocrisy. God ushered instantaneous and intense punishment in this case to prevent blatant deception from invading the newborn church. In the end, the church grew even stronger as people realized God desires purity of heart and not pretense.

STOPPING AT NOTHING

A Pharisee in the council named Gamaliel . . . said to them, "Men of Israel, take care what you are about to do with these men. For before these days Theudas rose up, claiming to be somebody, and a number of men, about four hundred, joined him. He was killed, and all who followed him were dispersed and came to nothing. After him Judas the Galilean rose up in the days of the census and drew away some of the people after him. He too perished, and all who followed him were scattered. So in the present case I tell you, keep away from these men and let them alone, for if this plan or this undertaking is of man, it will fail; but if it is of God, you will not be able to overthrow them."

Acts 5:34–39 ESV

Gamaliel was a well-respected teacher of the Jewish law. As a top Pharisee, he helped people apply the Hebrew Scriptures to everyday life. The apostle Paul studied under Rabbi Gamaliel, and Gamaliel most likely learned from Hillel, one of the greatest Jewish rabbis of all times. When Gamaliel spoke, people listened.

In this passage, the honored councilman shared his sage advice about Peter and the other enthusiastic followers of Jesus, who caused enough of a stir. The incensed Jewish authorities were threatening to kill Peter and his fellow Christian leaders when Gamaliel interrupted with a few choice words. Gamaliel reminded the council of several other religious groups that banded together over the years but eventually faded away. Surely, those Christian fanatics would end up disillusioned and dispersed in time too.

Gamaliel's counsel stood the test of time: if God is behind something, nothing can stop him. God's purposes cannot be thwarted no matter how charismatic the person or how colossal the plan. After more than two thousand years, Christianity is still flourishing. God is still at work in the world to draw people to himself. Gamaliel spoke the truth.

WHO ARE YOU?

When the council members heard Stephen's speech, they were angry and furious. But Stephen was filled with the Holy Spirit. He looked toward heaven, where he saw our glorious God and Jesus standing at his right side. Then Stephen said, "I see heaven open and the Son of Man standing at the right side of God!" The council members shouted and covered their ears. At once they all attacked Stephen and dragged him out of the city. Then they started throwing stones at him.

The men who had brought charges against him put their coats at the feet of a young man named Saul. As Stephen was being stoned to death, he called out, "Lord Jesus, please welcome me!" He knelt down and shouted, "Lord, don't blame them for what they have done." Then he died.

Acts 7:54–60 CEV

Sometimes our words can tick people off. Sometimes enraged people band together and impulsively act out with a "mob mentality" or "herd behavior." We see this crazed response in the account of Stephen. In the early church, Stephen was appointed to help oversee the distribution of food to the needy. He modeled a stellar reputation and was filled with God's Spirit and wisdom.

Empowered by God, Stephen presented the longest speech in defense of Jesus recorded in Acts. His words, though, fell on intolerant ears. For an instant, God allowed Stephen a glimpse of heaven with Jesus standing right next to God the Father. Sharing what he saw, Stephen essentially asserted that Jesus was who he said he was—God. Stephen's declaration ignited the Jewish mob. They didn't wait for a trial or jailing. Instead, they stoned Stephen into silence. In his final words, Stephen expressed almost the exact words of forgiveness Jesus extended on the cross.

Being a Christ-follower does not insulate us from harm. Thousands have died for staying true to their faith. Yet no matter the pressure to disown Jesus, forgiveness will always set us apart from the crowd.

WORDS OF FORGIVENESS

In Jerusalem Saul was still threatening the followers of the Lord by saying he would kill them. So he went to the high priest and asked him to write letters to the synagogues in the city of Damascus. Then if Saul found any followers of Christ's Way, men or women, he would arrest them and bring them back to Jerusalem.

So Saul headed toward Damascus. As he came near the city, a bright light from heaven suddenly flashed around him.

Saul fell to the ground and heard a voice saying to him, "Saul, Saul! Why are you persecuting me?"

Saul said, "Who are you, Lord?"

The voice answered, "I am Jesus, whom you are persecuting. Get up now and go into the city. Someone there will tell you what you must do."

Acts 9:1–6 NCV

We first read of Jewish rabble-rouser Saul in the report on Stephen's stoning. Saul stood watch over the coats of the Jews who murdered Stephen. After Stephen's death, a mass persecution of Christians swept across the regions around Jerusalem. Young Saul found himself enlivened by the rampage. He frequently dragged Christ-followers to prison and spewed murderous threats against individuals who identified themselves with the crucified and resurrected leader.

So on his journey to Damascus to menace more people loyal to Jesus, Saul was stopped cold in his tracks. A loathsome critic of anything associated with Jesus, Saul suddenly saw the light. God called out Saul's name twice. God had his man, and God meant business.

Saul had to face up to his own beliefs about the Promised One. He could no longer condemn the faith of others. Saul uttered the four words we all need to ask at some point in our lives: "Who are you, Lord?" When we ask this, God will make himself known to us. God longs for us to know him. As Saul came to realize, faith is about a one-to-one relationship with God. Faith isn't about a religion.

GIVING SOMEONE A BREAK

Saul increased all the more in strength, and confounded the Jews who dwelt in Damascus, proving that this Jesus is the Christ.

Now after many days were past, the Jews plotted to kill him. But their plot became known to Saul. And they watched the gates day and night, to kill him. Then the disciples took him by night and let him down through the wall in a large basket.

And when Saul had come to Jerusalem, he tried to join the disciples; but they were all afraid of him, and did not believe that he was a disciple. But Barnabas took him and brought him to the apostles. And he declared to them how he had seen the Lord on the road, and that He had spoken to him, and how he had preached boldly.

Acts 9:22–27 NKJV

The dazzling light on his way to Damascus blinded Saul. But he faced a more serious ailment—spiritual blindness. For three days, Saul sat in darkness in a house in Damascus. Saul did some soul-searching. God sent a Christian named Ananias to proclaim Saul's physical and spiritual healing. With restored eyesight and a renewed soul, Saul listened to the teachings of Jesus from other disciples.

Before long, Saul visited Jewish places of worship and talked about his newfound faith in Jesus. The Jews considered Saul a traitor. How could a devout Jew who deplored anything connected to Jesus suddenly be praising Jesus' name? The offended Jews planned to kill Saul.

Saul escaped to Jerusalem only to find that the people who were loyal to Jesus were frightened. They didn't trust the former Christian-persecutor. But respected Barnabas risked his reputation to stick up for Saul. Barnabas personally took Saul to meet the key church leaders and affirmed Saul's reformed character.

People can change, even those with incredulous histories. Changed people also need a break to prove their trustworthy integrity. Barnabas extended this break to Saul. Maybe we need to extend a similar break to someone today.

WHEN GOD ROCKS OUR WORLD

Peter went up to pray on the housetop at about noon. Then he became hungry and wanted to eat, but while they were preparing something he went into a visionary state. He saw heaven opened and an object coming down that resembled a large sheet being lowered to the earth by its four corners. In it were all the four-footed animals and reptiles of the earth, and the birds of the sky. Then a voice said to him, "Get up, Peter; kill and eat!"

"No, Lord!" Peter said. "For I have never eaten anything common and unclean!"

Again, a second time, a voice said to him, "What God has made clean, you must not call common." This happened three times, and then the object was taken up into heaven.

Acts 10:9–16 HCSB

Just when you think you have it all figured out, God comes along and rocks your world. Peter was a good Christian. He was doing his best to carry out what he understood to be God's instructions. Long ago, God gave Moses a list of forbidden foods. Peter never touched any of them.

Now things were changing. The need for the list was gone, because God was letting people know that goodness and holiness happen in your heart, not in your stomach. More important, God was opening the door for people from every nation to come to him. In the past, the people of God avoided their non-Jewish neighbors because they didn't want to be corrupted by pagan religions. Non-Jews were considered "unclean." Things were turned around. The good news of Jesus Christ was so powerful that it could purify anyone, no matter how "unclean" that person might be.

At some point in our lives, God will call us to see things from a new perspective. This needs to happen for us to grow. When it does, a new world will be opened up to us.

Bigger Plans

Some men came down from Judea and began teaching the brethren, "Unless you are circumcised according to the custom of Moses, you cannot be saved."

And when Paul and Barnabas had great dissension and debate with them, the brethren determined that Paul and Barnabas and some others of them should go up to Jerusalem to the apostles and elders concerning this issue. . . .

After there had been much debate, Peter stood up and said to them, "Brethren, you know that in the early days God made a choice among you, that by my mouth the Gentiles would hear the word of the gospel and believe.

"And God, who knows the heart, testified to them giving them the Holy Spirit, just as He also did to us; and He made no distinction between us and them, cleansing their hearts by faith."

Acts 15:1–2, 7–9 NASB

No matter how big your plans are, God has bigger plans. Small-minded people try to limit the purposes of God, but God cannot be boxed in. In the case in this passage, there were some new players on the field, and the home team was saying, "Unless you play by our rules, you can't play."

Nonsense! The game was bigger than that, and God was taking all his people out of the minors into the big leagues. What gets us into the family of God isn't surgery on the body but surgery on the heart. Now that the door to God's house was wide open for people from every nation, many Jewish customs no longer applied. God was the same, but there were new rules.

Growing as individuals requires us to learn new ways of doing things. In the same way, growing as a church—a worldwide family of believers—requires us to make room for the new things that God is doing. Christians rightly emphasize preserving what is good. But we must also be ready to adapt and change when God is on the move.

WHEN GOOD PEOPLE DIFFER

Paul and Barnabas remained in Antioch, teaching and preaching the word of the Lord, with many others also.

And after some days Paul said to Barnabas, "Let us return and visit the brothers in every city where we proclaimed the word of the Lord, and see how they are." Now Barnabas wanted to take with them John called Mark. But Paul thought best not to take with them one who had withdrawn from them in Pamphylia and had not gone with them to the work. And there arose a sharp disagreement, so that they separated from each other. Barnabas took Mark with him and sailed away to Cyprus, but Paul chose Silas and departed, having been commended by the brothers to the grace of the Lord. And he went through Syria and Cilicia, strengthening the churches.

Acts 15:35–41 ESV

Good people differ. Though we all might be filled with the same Holy Spirit, we see things through different eyes. Part of this is because we are different people, and part of this is because we grow in different ways.

In this passage, Paul, a visionary apostle, was interested in maximum mileage with minimum distraction. But Barnabas, a builder of people, saw great potential in Mark and didn't want him left on the side of the road as wreckage. Who was right? They both were. Barnabas dropped out of the story and out of the limelight. But he continued to do what he knew he should do—build up other people. Paul moved on to plant churches and open new regions for the gospel. At the end of his life, Paul looked back with gratitude for the work Barnabas did with Mark. In 2 Timothy 4:11 we learn that Mark was one of the few people Paul could count on after almost everyone else had deserted him.

Next time you find yourself disagreeing with another Christian, consider a new possibility: you both might be right.

The Power of the Gospel

Suddenly, there was a massive earthquake, and the prison was shaken to its foundations. All the doors immediately flew open, and the chains of every prisoner fell off! The jailer woke up to see the prison doors wide open. He assumed the prisoners had escaped, so he drew his sword to kill himself. But Paul shouted to him, "Stop! Don't kill yourself! We are all here!"

The jailer called for lights and ran to the dungeon and fell down trembling before Paul and Silas. Then he brought them out and asked, "Sirs, what must I do to be saved?"

They replied, "Believe in the Lord Jesus and you will be saved, along with everyone in your household." And they shared the word of the Lord with him and with all who lived in his household.

Acts 16:26–32 NLT

This passage shows the power of the gospel. The apostle Paul and his companion Silas were severely beaten and thrown into the basement of a smelly, rat-infested prison where they were chained to the wall. From that place of pain and isolation, they lifted their voices to sing praise to God, who can make everything right. The jailer and the prisoners were a captive audience. *What kind of person rejoices when the worst happens to him?*

There was only one way to test the impact of the gospel on those hardened criminals. Loose the chains and open the doors! The prisoners sat right where they were, no longer prisoners of Rome, but awestruck by the joy of Jesus Christ.

As soon as the jailer realized that he wouldn't be executed for allowing prisoners to escape, the full weight of what had just happened came crashing down on him. He wanted in. He believed, and that same life that filled Paul and Silas with joy was his.

HELPING PEOPLE SEE

Paul stood up in front of the council and said: People of Athens, I see that you are very religious. As I was going through your city and looking at the things you worship, I found an altar with the words, "To an Unknown God." You worship this God, but you don't really know him. So I want to tell you about him. This God made the world and everything in it. He is Lord of heaven and earth, and he doesn't live in temples built by human hands. He doesn't need help from anyone. He gives life, breath, and everything else to all people. . . . He isn't far from any of us, and he gives us the power to live, to move, and to be who we are. "We are his children," just as some of your poets have said.

Acts 17:22–25, 27–28 CEV

Jesus matters. In this passage, Paul struck up a conversation with people who thought differently than he did. They valued different things than Paul did. But that didn't slow Paul down at all. He immediately started building bridges.

Paul looked to see what kinds of questions the people were asking. He wanted to know what they felt they needed. Part of our role as Christians is what today we call marketing. That doesn't mean we lie, exaggerate, and push people into making decisions they don't want to make. Instead, it means that we reposition Jesus Christ in the minds of the people around us. We help people see Jesus for who he really is.

In doing this, we affirm people, listen to them, and encourage them. We help them see things they never saw before. All of us can learn these skills, and we need them to reach the people God wants us to reach.

LEARNING FROM OPPOSITION

About that time there arose a great commotion about the Way. For a certain man named Demetrius, a silversmith, who made silver shrines of Diana, brought no small profit to the craftsmen. He called them together with the workers of similar occupation, and said: "Men, you know that we have our prosperity by this trade. Moreover you see and hear that not only at Ephesus, but throughout almost all Asia, this Paul has persuaded and turned away many people, saying that they are not gods which are made with hands." . . .

Now when they heard this, they were full of wrath and cried out, saying, "Great is Diana of the Ephesians!" So the whole city was filled with confusion, and rushed into the theater with one accord, having seized Gaius and Aristarchus, Macedonians, Paul's travel companions.

Acts 19:23–26, 28–29 NKJV

Expect opposition. You are here to change your world, and not everybody is going to like that. In this passage, those who profited from pagan idolatry saw that the message of Jesus Christ was going to make their business obsolete. For them, this was a dollars-and-cents decision. Stirring up a mob isn't hard if you know what you're doing. So, in a matter of minutes, it was everyone in town vs. a couple of Christians.

Opposition is often just an indication that you're doing something right. Take the opposition back to God and ask him what he wants you to learn from it. In some cases, criticism, even when based almost wholly on lies, contains a nugget of truth that can help us become better people. In some cases, opposition will show us better strategies for getting the job done.

Don't be afraid of opposition. God won't allow anything into your life that won't make you a better, stronger person. Learn from him. He will show you when and how to stand, and when and how to overcome.

Two Paths

No flesh will be justified in His sight by the works of the law, for through the law [comes] the knowledge of sin. But now, apart from the law, God's righteousness has been revealed—attested by the Law and the Prophets—that is, God's righteousness through faith in Jesus Christ, to all who believe, since there is no distinction. For all have sinned and fall short of the glory of God. They are justified freely by His grace through the redemption that is in Christ Jesus. God presented Him as a propitiation through faith in His blood, to demonstrate His righteousness, because in His restraint God passed over the sins previously committed. He presented Him to demonstrate His righteousness at the present time, so that He would be righteous and declare righteous the one who has faith in Jesus.

Romans 3:20–26 HCSB

There are two paths. On one hand, we can try to make the grade by ourselves. We can try to be good enough to please God. We can find the list of his laws and observe all of them every day of every week from birth to death, and never make a single slipup, not even in our thoughts. That would be something like a person using a walker trying to win the 100-meter race at the Olympics. It wouldn't happen.

On the other hand, we can find Jesus, the One who already pleased God, and walk through the door he created. We can understand that by his death, Jesus took our place. We can know that God no longer needs to condemn us for our wrongdoings because Jesus did everything for us. While some people will reject him and insult the God who gave his only Son, we may embrace him and his plan for us. Faith receives the gift freely offered by God.

WHAT JESUS OFFERS

By faith we have been made acceptable to God. And now, because of our Lord Jesus Christ, we live at peace with God. . . . Christ died for us at a time when we were helpless and sinful. No one is really willing to die for an honest person, though someone might be willing to die for a truly good person. But God showed how much he loved us by having Christ die for us, even though we were sinful.

But there is more! Now that God has accepted us because Christ sacrificed his life's blood, we will also be kept safe from God's anger. Even when we were God's enemies, he made peace with us, because his Son died for us. Yet something even greater than friendship is ours. Now that we are at peace with God, we will be saved by his Son's life.

Romans 5:1, 6–10 CEV

Consider where we started and where we are now. At the outset, God looked down from heaven and found us as we were—hostile, indifferent, guilty, condemned. He could have abandoned us. He could have terrified us with justifiable fury over how we messed up the perfect world he created. He could have wiped the slate clean and started over.

God did none of those things. He made himself small, weak, and fragile in the person of his Son, Jesus. There was only one way to settle beyond doubt that God loves us. Jesus chose that one way. He embraced the pain of a Roman execution as a demonstration of his love for us.

Jesus offered to God and to us his death as a way of making peace between us. He offered us eternal life. Death has no power over us. We enter eternity as God's friends.

HORRIBLY WRONG

I know that nothing good dwells in me, that is, in my flesh. For I have the desire to do what is right, but not the ability to carry it out. For I do not do the good I want, but the evil I do not want is what I keep on doing. Now if I do what I do not want, it is no longer I who do it, but sin that dwells within me. . . .

For I delight in the law of God, in my inner being, but I see in my members another law waging war against the law of my mind and making me captive to the law of sin that dwells in my members. Wretched man that I am! Who will deliver me from this body of death?

Romans 7:18–20, 22–24 ESV

Something is horribly wrong. We are not functioning as we were designed to function. Like an out-of-control washing machine frothing suds all over, we pollute our lives and our world with sin. Like a computer with a virus, we've forgotten our original programming, and we find ourselves carrying out destructive commands. We have moments gone haywire.

What's the cure? How do we escape our anxieties and addictions, our life-controlling issues, our secret sins?

The first step is to get real. We can't even move forward until we come out of denial, get honest with ourselves and with God, and admit complete helplessness. Most of us are stuck right there. We want to pretend we are good enough, that we aren't quite as bad as that heroin addict we read about or that sex offender who was on TV. We want to convince God that if he would give us enough time, we could pull through on our own without any help from anyone.

But we can't do it on our own. We need Jesus.

FREEDOM

There is no condemnation for those who belong to Christ Jesus. And because you belong to him, the power of the life-giving Spirit has freed you from the power of sin that leads to death. The law of Moses was unable to save us because of the weakness of our sinful nature. So God did what the law could not do. He sent his own Son in a body like the bodies we sinners have. And in that body God declared an end to sin's control over us by giving his Son as a sacrifice for our sins. He did this so that the just requirement of the law would be fully satisfied for us, who no longer follow our sinful nature but instead follow the Spirit.

Romans 8:1–4 NLT

Imagine what it must have been like for slaves at the end of the American Civil War to receive the news that they were not—nor could they ever again become—someone else's property. They were free. They could walk off the plantation. They could rejoin their families. They could go where they wanted and do what they wanted.

Jesus offers us an even deeper kind of freedom. While the law was a constant reminder that we messed up, Jesus broke the chains that tethered us to the law and to our sinful inclinations. He restructured the inside of our hearts. He restored the signature of God that was ours at Creation. With God's Spirit taking the lead, we are free to explore the many ways to please God as his sons and daughters. We are free to live our lives under the smile of God.

MORE THAN WORTH IT

I consider that our present sufferings are not worth comparing with the glory that will be revealed in us. The creation waits in eager expectation for the sons of God to be revealed. For the creation was subjected to frustration, not by its own choice, but by the will of the one who subjected it, in hope that the creation itself will be liberated from its bondage to decay and brought into the glorious freedom of the children of God.

We know that the whole creation has been groaning as in the pains of childbirth right up to the present time. Not only so, but we ourselves, who have the firstfruits of the Spirit, groan inwardly as we wait eagerly for our adoption as sons, the redemption of our bodies.

Romans 8:18–23 NIV

At first glance, it appears that these verses are saying that everything we suffer will be nothing compared to all the good stuff we are going to get in heaven. That's true, no doubt. But the focus in this passage is on something else: "the glory that will be revealed *in* us."

Heaven isn't heaven because of real estate. If we were suddenly transported to heaven, it would be wonderful, of course. But after a while we would run into difficulty. There would be squabbles, discontent, depression, and all sorts of problems. In fact, if left unchecked, there would be crime, violence, and every kind of evil because we must be transformed on the inside before the outside of heaven will bring eternal joy. Something needs to change deep inside of us to cause us always to choose love, to delight in putting others ahead of ourselves, and to be energized by righteousness.

That "something" has already begun. All creation is lined up to see the show: Suffering will be over. Our true, God-stamped selves will be revealed. It is more than worth it.

ETERNAL PURPOSES

God is always at work for the good of everyone who loves him. They are the ones God has chosen for his purpose, and he has always known who his chosen ones would be. . . . God then accepted the people he had already decided to choose, and he has shared his glory with them.

What can we say about all this? If God is on our side, can anyone be against us? God did not keep back his own Son, but he gave him for us. If God did this, won't he freely give us everything else? If God says his chosen ones are acceptable to him, can anyone bring charges against them? Or can anyone condemn them? No indeed! Christ died and was raised to life, and now he is at God's right side, speaking to him for us.

Romans 8:28–34 CEV

A positive thinker can take a bad experience and put a positive spin on it. But a Christian looks at reality. Who is God? What is he doing? How does he feel about us? What is he willing to do for us?

God is the One who takes every bad experience that comes into our lives and turns it into an opportunity for good. Since he demonstrated his love for us by allowing Roman soldiers to pound nails into the hands and feet of his Son, is there anything he wouldn't be willing to do for us? Guilt is swallowed up by forgiveness. Shame is transformed by the truth that we are radiant in him. No one can successfully prosecute us for our crimes against God.

Apart from Christ, a positive thinker must create reality. A Christian lives *in* reality. We are part of something far bigger than we are. We are part of the eternal purposes of God.

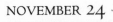

A Measure of Faith

I appeal to you therefore, brothers, by the mercies of God, to present your bodies as a living sacrifice, holy and acceptable to God, which is your spiritual worship. Do not be conformed to this world, but be transformed by the renewal of your mind, that by testing you may discern what is the will of God, what is good and acceptable and perfect.

For by the grace given to me I say to everyone among you not to think of himself more highly than he ought to think, but to think with sober judgment, each according to the measure of faith that God has assigned. For as in one body we have many members, and the members do not all have the same function, so we, though many, are one body in Christ, and individually members one of another.

Romans 12:1–5 ESV

What happens when we give to God? A small boy gave his lunch to Jesus, and with that lunch more than five thousand people were fed (see Matt. 14:13–21). In the same way, when we give our lives to Jesus, something supernatural happens. God supernaturally empowers us to see the world and ourselves from his perspective. When we understand how loved we are and how important we are to God, we no longer need to steal the show from someone else in order to find our significance. We can rejoice in the role God has given us. This frees us to love and serve one another with the gifts we have been given.

Be encouraged. God has given you a measure of faith that won't run out. With it, you will go out and enrich the lives of others.

Hidden from the Arrogant

Remember, dear brothers and sisters, that few of you were wise in the world's eyes or powerful or wealthy when God called you. Instead, God chose things the world considers foolish in order to shame those who think they are wise. And he chose things that are powerless to shame those who are powerful. God chose things despised by the world, things counted as nothing at all, and used them to bring to nothing what the world considers important. As a result, no one can ever boast in the presence of God.

God has united you with Christ Jesus. . . . Christ made us right with God; he made us pure and holy, and he freed us from sin. Therefore, as the Scriptures say, "If you want to boast, boast only about the LORD."

1 Corinthians 1:26–31 NLT

Here is the beauty of the gospel. It is so simple that a child can embrace it, but so profound that a world-class intellectual cannot wrap his mind around it. Why would God hide the gospel from the arrogant? Why would he instead make it clear to the powerless? God specializes in the overlooked, the forgotten, and the marginalized. There are no second-class citizens in his kingdom. The caste system takes many forms on earth, but none in heaven. God makes his home with the humble.

None of us are perfectly smart or incredibly powerful. But that's okay, because Jesus came to fill up everything that is lacking in us. We realize that it isn't our great intelligence or our willpower or anything else about us that brings about the beautiful work of God. Rather, God himself, working in us, transforms us into something more than we can be on our own.

THE CURE FOR EVERYTHING

Love is patient, love is kind. It does not envy, it does not boast, it is not proud. It is not rude, it is not self-seeking, it is not easily angered, it keeps no record of wrongs. Love does not delight in evil but rejoices with the truth. It always protects, always trusts, always hopes, always perseveres.

Love never fails. But where there are prophecies, they will cease; where there are tongues, they will be stilled; where there is knowledge, it will pass away. For we know in part and we prophesy in part, but when perfection comes, the imperfect disappears. . . . Now we see but a poor reflection as in a mirror; then we shall see face to face. . . .

And now these three remain: faith, hope and love. But the greatest of these is love.

1 Corinthians 13:4–10, 12–13
NIV

We know that God is good when we look at the kind of family that he is building. Imagine a family where no one gets annoyed and no one gets provoked. Each one respects the other and looks for ways to honor the other. Each one rejoices when the other is exalted, and each one believes and focuses on the best in the other.

This collection of choices is called love, and love makes heaven what it is. Love makes eternity worth pursuing. Eternal life is defined by a quality of community, by a deep sense of belonging.

It's easy to get distracted by myriad things that sound important—gifts, supernatural experiences, learning, missions, and so on. But those things don't endure. They are just the trappings of a Christian life. If you want to find the heart of God, look no further than the verses in this passage. For everything that has gone wrong, you find God's cure—kindness, patience, courtesy, humility, faith, celebration, and love.

OUR ETERNAL IDENTITY

Behold, I tell you a mystery: We shall not all sleep, but we shall all be changed—in a moment, in the twinkling of an eye, at the last trumpet. For the trumpet will sound, and the dead will be raised incorruptible, and we shall be changed. For this corruptible must put on incorruption, and this mortal must put on immortality. So when this corruptible has put on incorruption, and this mortal has put on immortality, then shall be brought to pass the saying that is written: "Death is swallowed up in victory."

"O Death, where is your sting? O Hades, where is your victory?"

The sting of death is sin, and the strength of sin is the law. But thanks be to God, who gives us the victory through our Lord Jesus Christ.

1 Corinthians 15:51–57 NKJV

In one instant, two huge changes will take place in every Christian believer. First, the choke chain of death will be taken from our necks. Everything we fear will be removed. No longer will we grow old. No longer will we get sick. No longer will anything or anyone harm us. No accident or incident will suddenly snuff out our lives. We will be indestructible. Second, our struggle with sin will end. Nothing can tempt us. No one will be able to corrupt us. No one can back us into a corner and force us to do wrong. Every desire to do evil will be replaced with delight in doing good.

Everything moves us closer to that moment of total transformation. The march of time is a march toward our final freedom.

Meanwhile, keep in mind just who you are. The real you faces life unafraid. The real you laughs at temptation because you know it offers nothing. The real you cannot be corrupted. This is your eternal identity. This is the understanding that will empower you to live your life on a different level.

The Power to Persevere

We now have this light shining in our hearts, but we ourselves are like fragile clay jars containing this great treasure. This makes it clear that our great power is from God, not from ourselves.

We are pressed on every side by troubles, but we are not crushed. We are perplexed, but not driven to despair. We are hunted down, but never abandoned by God. We get knocked down, but we are not destroyed. . . .

That is why we never give up. Though our bodies are dying, our spirits are being renewed every day. For our present troubles are small and won't last very long. Yet they produce for us a glory that vastly outweighs them and will last forever! So we don't look at the troubles we can see now; rather, we fix our gaze on things that cannot be seen.

2 Corinthians 4:7–9, 16–18
NLT

One of the things that make our troubles challenging is the lies we believe deep inside. Take, for example, that someone has taken our parking spot and we find ourselves boiling over with anger. Certainly, the anger isn't about a lost parking place. Rather, it's about some twisted life lesson we learned early on, some lesson like "I don't belong," or "I'm not important because other people can take things I thought were mine." We may not consciously summon those messages to mind, but they lurk in the background, adding insult to injury whenever we face one of life's injustices.

Like the writer of this passage, we may have troubles on every side, but they don't crush us. They don't drive us to despair. We are neither abandoned nor destroyed. Truth gives us the power to persevere. Transformation gives us the power to see clearly.

We are carrying around inside us the priceless treasure of the Spirit of Christ. Because of that, we can never be overcome.

THE "MAGIC" OF GIVING

Remember: A stingy planter gets a stingy crop; a lavish planter gets a lavish crop. I want each of you to take plenty of time to think it over, and make up your own mind what you will give. That will protect you against sob stories and arm-twisting. God loves it when the giver delights in the giving.

God can pour on the blessings in astonishing ways so that you're ready for anything and everything, more than just ready to do what needs to be done. As one psalmist puts it, He throws caution to the winds, giving to the needy in reckless abandon. His right-living, right-giving ways never run out, never wear out.

This most generous God who gives seed to the farmer that becomes bread for your meals is more than extravagant with you.

2 Corinthians 9:6–10 MSG

There is "magic" in giving that defies reason and mathematics. Almost anyone who has given faithfully, sacrificially, and cheerfully has his own stories to tell: money mysteriously appearing in mailboxes, bills somehow getting paid, expenses evaporating, provision being found.

That, of course, is not the reason we give. We give because we are smart investors. We know that earthly stocks and bonds rise and fall, but the value of heavenly investments always appreciates. We give because we care. We give because we want to make a difference. A tetracycline injection costing a couple of dollars can save the life of a child. In many countries, ten dollars will feed a family for a week. We have tremendous power to make a difference. And we give because Jesus himself receives every dollar we give as a gift to him.

We don't give out of guilt because God wants us to enjoy his perspective. He gives to us because it is pure fun to be extravagantly generous.

Fool's Gold

I am shocked that you are turning away so soon from God, who called you to himself through the loving mercy of Christ. You are following a different way that pretends to be the Good News but is not the Good News at all. You are being fooled by those who deliberately twist the truth concerning Christ.

Let God's curse fall on anyone, including us or even an angel from heaven, who preaches a different kind of Good News than the one we preached to you. I say again what we have said before: If anyone preaches any other Good News than the one you welcomed, let that person be cursed.

Obviously, I'm not trying to win the approval of people, but of God. If pleasing people were my goal, I would not be Christ's servant.

Galatians 1:6–10 NLT

The good news (or gospel) brings us back to God. That's why the gospel must be defended from impostors who try to peddle cheap imitations. Their snake oil doesn't bring us back to God at all. Instead, it sends us on a wild-goose chase of religion that ends in frustration and failure.

We can protect ourselves from false teachers by getting to know the gospel and the God behind it. The more we enjoy the presence of God, the more we recognize a false god when we encounter one. The more we soak in the truth of God's Word, the more we'll recognize lies sticking out like a sore thumb. The more we study the history of the church, the more we understand that today's wayward trends are simply reruns of yesterday's errors. The more we are around good people who love God, the less we're tempted by cult leaders who prey on those who are searching for a place to belong.

A Russian proverb says, "All is not gold that glitters." Soak up the real thing, and you won't be led astray by a peddler of fool's gold.

PERFORMANCE VS. FAITH

O foolish Galatians! Who has bewitched you that you should not obey the truth, before whose eyes Jesus Christ was clearly portrayed among you as crucified?

This only I want to learn from you: Did you receive the Spirit by the works of the law, or by the hearing of faith? Are you so foolish? Having begun in the Spirit, are you now being made perfect by the flesh? Have you suffered so many things in vain—if indeed it was in vain?

Therefore He who supplies the Spirit to you and works miracles among you, does He do it by the works of the law, or by the hearing of faith?—just as Abraham "believed God, and it was accounted to him for righteousness." Therefore know that only those who are of faith are sons of Abraham.

Galatians 3:1–7 NKJV

This is simple. As soon as we start dressing up for God, we will lose our moorings. We can't get good enough by ourselves. We can't outperform God.

Jesus died on the cross because there was no other way. If we could be made good enough by our own performance, God would not have sacrificed his only Son. We aren't good enough. Nor can we be. So God stepped in on our behalf.

The early believers were still closely connected to Jewish life and culture. It was a big temptation to jettison what they had learned from Paul and return to their religious regulations. But, in so doing, Paul recognized they would cut themselves off from the power of God in their lives.

We get the power to live a life that pleases God directly from him. No codebook is required. All we have to do is ask and believe.

BACKED INTO A CORNER

Why then the law? It was added because of transgressions, until the offspring should come to whom the promise had been made. . . . Is the law then contrary to the promises of God? Certainly not! For if a law had been given that could give life, then righteousness would indeed be by the law. But the Scripture imprisoned everything under sin, so that the promise by faith in Jesus Christ might be given to those who believe.

Now before faith came, we were held captive under the law, imprisoned until the coming faith would be revealed. So then, the law was our guardian until Christ came, in order that we might be justified by faith. But now that faith has come, we are no longer under a guardian, for in Christ Jesus you are all sons of God, through faith.

Galatians 3:19, 21–26 ESV

There is a progression in the plan of God. As centuries of history go by, we learn more about God's plan for us. In this passage, we discover what God was getting across during the centuries when his law was the centerpiece of his revelation to humanity.

The purpose of the law was to show how wonderful God is and how wonderful we are not. As people kept bumping up against God's righteous requirements and falling short, the lesson was drilled into his people's heads. As one innocent lamb after another bled and died at the altar for our shortcomings, the message became clear: sin costs something.

The law backed us into a corner with only one way out: Jesus. Not only is Jesus "the Lamb of God who takes away the sin of the world" (John 1:29 NKJV), but he is also the One who lived the perfect life we never could. Hidden in him, we are made right. God is no longer our Judge but our Father.

COMPETING OR EMBRACING?

We have freedom now, because Christ made us free. So stand strong. Do not change and go back into the slavery of the law. Listen, I Paul tell you that if you go back to the law by being circumcised, Christ does you no good. Again, I warn every man: If you allow yourselves to be circumcised, you must follow all the law. If you try to be made right with God through the law, your life with Christ is over—you have left God's grace. But we have the true hope that comes from being made right with God, and by the Spirit we wait eagerly for this hope. When we are in Christ Jesus, it is not important if we are circumcised or not. The important thing is faith—the kind of faith that works through love.

Galatians 5:1–6 NCV

If we want God as Judge, we must understand that the standard is perfection. God cares too much about his family to allow anything less than perfection into his heaven. That's really bad news for those who want to compete with Jesus Christ. This is a reality check—compete with Jesus, and you lose.

This is wonderful news for those who embrace Jesus. We're on the winning team. We're part of the family of God. The focus is no longer on our performance. The focus is on our faith. Faith is living in God-revealed reality. Jesus offered us the payment for our sins through his death on the cross. When we receive that gift from him, we are responding in faith. Jesus knocks at the door, and we respond by opening the door. Our faith in Jesus creates a conduit through which God's love flows into our lives and out to bring good into the lives of many people.

THE SECRET OF FRUIT

I say, walk by the Spirit, and you will not carry out the desire of the flesh.

For the flesh sets its desire against the Spirit, and the Spirit against the flesh; for these are in opposition to one another, so that you may not do the things that you please. But if you are led by the Spirit, you are not under the Law.

Now the deeds of the flesh are evident, which are: immorality, impurity, sensuality, idolatry, sorcery, enmities, strife, jealousy, outbursts of anger, disputes, dissensions, factions, envying, drunkenness, carousing, and things like these, of which I forewarn you . . . those who practice such things will not inherit the kingdom of God.

But the fruit of the Spirit is love, joy, peace, patience, kindness, goodness, faithfulness, gentleness, self-control; against such things there is no law.

Galatians 5:16–23 NASB

Notice two words in this passage: *deeds* and *fruit*. Operating from the part of us not connected to Christ, we do deeds. Our deeds may be religious, but in the end, they will stink. Fruit, however, arrives a different way. You can't "do" fruit; you can only grow fruit. For fruit to grow, it must be connected to the tree. Without roots, there is no fruit.

Many frustrated people will go around trying to do *deeds* of love, joy, peace, patience, and so on. But this is not how fruit is grown. Fruit is grown by our connection to the Spirit of Christ.

We walk by the Spirit when we invite him in. And whenever something gets in the way, we need to keep inviting the Spirit in. When we lack love, joy, peace, or patience, we need the Spirit. The Spirit will transform our lives.

Two Foundational Questions

Ever since I first heard of your strong faith in the Lord Jesus and your love for God's people everywhere, I have not stopped thanking God for you. I pray for you constantly, asking God, the glorious Father of our Lord Jesus Christ, to give you spiritual wisdom and insight so that you might grow in your knowledge of God. I pray that your hearts will be flooded with light so that you can understand the confident hope he has given to those he called—his holy people who are his rich and glorious inheritance.

I also pray that you will understand the incredible greatness of God's power for us who believe him. This is the same mighty power that raised Christ from the dead and seated him in the place of honor at God's right hand in the heavenly realms.

Ephesians 1:15–20 NLT

Paul understood that the real battle is inside our minds. And the two most important questions that must be settled deep inside are these: Who is God? Who are we? Every evil, from the Holocaust to human trafficking, can ultimately be traced back to a profound deception and corruption of our hearts in those two areas.

If God is absent, aloof, capricious, uncaring, arbitrary, or irrelevant, then it is no wonder that people defy him. If we are nothing more than a chemical reaction, a cosmic mistake, or a karmic rerun, we will act out of this tragic identity.

In this passage, Paul constantly asked God to help his people understand the truth that God cares and that they can have hope. This fallen world is not forever, and God is building something better. The world's bullies are no match for God. They will be swept aside by the power of God's presence, until even death itself will not remain standing.

We can start this understanding by learning from God the truth on every level so that we not only know it with our minds but we also feel it deep inside.

God's Good Work

You He made alive, who were dead in trespasses and sins. . . .

But God, who is rich in mercy, because of His great love with which He loved us, even when we were dead in trespasses, made us alive together with Christ (by grace you have been saved), and raised us up together, and made us sit together in the heavenly places in Christ Jesus, that in the ages to come He might show the exceeding riches of His grace in His kindness toward us in Christ Jesus. For by grace you have been saved through faith, and that not of yourselves; it is the gift of God, not of works, lest anyone should boast. For we are His workmanship, created in Christ Jesus for good works, which God prepared beforehand that we should walk in them.

Ephesians 2:1, 4–10 NKJV

God is at work doing all the things we could never do ourselves. We could never save ourselves. We were dead! We could never act so good in God's sight that we would be able to brag in his presence. Even our faith is a gift from him. We receive the gift of faith, open it, exercise it, and find ourselves connected to Jesus, placed in a position of honor that we didn't earn, deserve, or build on our own.

This is different from the treadmill of false religion that demands an unrealistic level of performance in exchange for an uncertain and unreliable promise. Instead, we are set free to do good because we have been redesigned by God to delight in loving and serving other people.

We can't brag, because all we have is a gift from God. We are God's workmanship, not our own. As we look around at the gifts we have been given, our only response is to look up with wonder and gratitude.

NO LONGER ENEMIES

Now in Christ Jesus you who once were far off have been brought near by the blood of Christ. For he himself is our peace, who has made us both one and has broken down in his flesh the dividing wall of hostility by abolishing the law of commandments expressed in ordinances, that he might create in himself one new man in place of the two, so making peace, and might reconcile us both to God in one body through the cross, thereby killing the hostility. And he came and preached peace to you who were far off and peace to those who were near. . . . So then you are no longer strangers and aliens, but you are fellow citizens with the saints and members of the household of God.

Ephesians 2:13–19 ESV

In William Golding's famous novel *Lord of the Flies*, a group of boys marooned on an island try to cope with the reality that they might not be rescued for a long, long time. At the beginning, one of the leaders says, "We'll have rules! Lots of rules!" By the time the story is over, that same leader has started a war that leaves two dead and nearly burns down the island.

The law taught us much about the beautiful character of God. But it did nothing to change our character. Nor did it accomplish what was always in God's heart, reaching out to every people group and inviting each person into a relationship with God.

Just as it took the arrival of a British naval officer on the island to end the insanity on that fictional island in *Lord of the Flies*, so also it took the arrival of God-in-the-flesh, Jesus Christ, to end the war that raged between us and inside us. Now the door is open. We walk inside and sit down at the table with our God. We are no longer enemies. We are family.

YOUR NEW IDENTITY

My response is to get down on my knees before the Father, this magnificent Father who parcels out all heaven and earth. I ask him to strengthen you by his Spirit—not a brute strength but a glorious inner strength—that Christ will live in you as you open the door and invite him in. And I ask him that with both feet planted firmly on love, you'll be able to take in with all Christians the extravagant dimensions of Christ's love. Reach out and experience the breadth! Test its length! Plumb the depths! Rise to the heights! Live full lives, full in the fullness of God.

God can do anything, you know—far more than you could ever imagine or guess or request in your wildest dreams!

Ephesians 3:14–20 MSG

Do you want to dream? Dream big. Do you want to ask God for something? Ask big. Doing the "impossible" through ordinary folk is all part of a working day for God. And the faith to expect the "impossible" from God comes from bathing our hearts in his love.

Understand what this means. It does not mean going out and trying to drum up some kind of love for God or love for other people. Love doesn't work that way. Rather, it means receiving what we cannot manufacture on our own. As we go back to God day after day to receive from him his love for us, we make some amazing discoveries about ourselves. We are not the failing, self-sufficient, inadequate, independent, double-minded people we thought we were. Rather, we are royal sons and daughters of God. What our family doesn't already own, our family can create. What our family hasn't already done, our family can do.

Discover your new identity. Let yourself be loved by God.

THE REAL ENEMY

Our fight is not against people on earth but against . . . the powers of this world's darkness, against the spiritual powers of evil in the heavenly world. That is why you need to put on God's full armor. Then on the day of evil you will be able to stand strong. And when you have finished the whole fight, you will still be standing. So stand strong, with the belt of truth tied around your waist and the protection of right living on your chest. On your feet wear the Good News of peace to help you stand strong. And also use the shield of faith with which you can stop all the burning arrows of the Evil One. Accept God's salvation as your helmet, and take the sword of the Spirit, which is the word of God.

Ephesians 6:12–17 NCV

It helps to understand who our real enemy is.

The evil emperor in the *Star Wars* series was a master at getting people to fight one another when they should have been fighting him. Every battle furthered his agenda and helped establish him in a place of power. In the same way, our enemy will paint targets on the people around us to keep us from resisting him.

But we can take a stand against the unseen personalities that extend their influence over humanity. God has given us armor. Our armor disables the enemy's attacks. Truth and faith expose deception for what it is. The good news that God has set us free and the right living that comes from that freedom make the enemy's temptations look like what they are—garbage. The salvation we share in Christ protects us from all the enemy's threats, and the word of God sends him scrambling.

We don't need to look for this fight. The enemy's attacks will come. But we, dressed in God's armor, will stand, unmoved and victorious.

OUR ANCHOR

I give thanks to my God for every remembrance of you, always praying with joy for all of you in my every prayer, because of your partnership in the gospel from the first day until now. I am sure of this, that He who started a good work in you will carry it on to completion until the day of Christ Jesus. . . .

For God is my witness, how I deeply miss all of you with the affection of Christ Jesus. And I pray this: that your love will keep on growing in knowledge and every kind of discernment, so that you can determine what really matters and can be pure and blameless in the day of Christ, filled with the fruit of righteousness that [comes] through Jesus Christ, to the glory and praise of God.

Philippians 1:3–6, 8–11 HCSB

This is our anchor: God is at work in us. When we stumble, when we fail, when we get discouraged, when we get apathetic, and when we just don't care anymore, God is at work in us. The old Sunday school chorus "Jesus Loves Me" tells us the profound truth: "They [we] are weak, but he [Jesus] is strong." Nobody promised that we would make it on our own. That isn't how life works. Our own resources are quickly drained, but God's are not. When we can't go on, he can. We fail, but God's work in us never fails.

We go through times when even as Christians all we have to offer God is our brokenness and our inadequacies. But it's okay. God is at work in us.

God's work in us will be brought to completion. We can plant the flag of victory.

An Opportunity to Make a Difference

I know that through your prayers and the help given by the Spirit of Jesus Christ, what has happened to me will turn out for my deliverance. I eagerly expect and hope that I will in no way be ashamed, but will have sufficient courage so that now as always Christ will be exalted in my body, whether by life or by death. For to me, to live is Christ and to die is gain. . . . I am torn between the two: I desire to depart and be with Christ, which is better by far; but it is more necessary for you that I remain in the body. Convinced of this, I know that I will remain, and I will continue with all of you for your progress and joy in the faith.

Philippians 1:19–21, 23–25
NIV

Tradition has it that while Paul was penning these words, an executioner in a nearby room was sharpening his ax. That may or may not be true, but we do learn that Paul was released from prison after writing this. He continued his ministry until he was rearrested years later and died a martyr's death under the emperor Nero.

Only Jesus has the power to free us from our fear of death. Jesus stands alone in all of human history. Only Jesus voluntarily laid down his life and three days later took it up again. Only Jesus holds the keys to death and Hades (see Rev. 1:18).

Free from fear, Paul and we are empowered to weigh the options. For us, death is a step up, but life is an opportunity to bring good into the lives of those around us.

A Russian proverb says, "Death takes not the old but the ripe." One day, God will say to each of us that our lives on earth have completed their purpose. When that day comes, we will be welcomed into his arms forever. Meanwhile, every day is an opportunity to make a difference.

THE GATEWAY TO GREATNESS

Do nothing from selfishness or empty conceit, but with humility of mind regard one another as more important than yourselves; do not merely look out for your own personal interests, but also for the interests of others.

Have this attitude in yourselves which was also in Christ Jesus, who, although He existed in the form of God, did not regard equality with God a thing to be grasped, but emptied Himself, taking the form of a bond-servant, and being made in the likeness of men.

Being found in appearance as a man, He humbled Himself by becoming obedient to the point of death, even death on a cross.

For this reason also, God highly exalted Him, and bestowed on Him the name which is above every name, so that at the name of Jesus every knee will bow.

Philippians 2:3–10 NASB

Theologians have pointed to this passage as one of the most profound in all of Scripture. And yet, it was written in an offhand way, as an illustration of humility and love.

In Christ, God in all his great power stooped down, like an adult kneeling before a child, in order to find us where we are. He not only took on the form of a man, but he also took on the form of a despised and rejected man. From this, the lowest of positions, Christ comes to us so that we can look into God's heart. There we see his unfailing love.

As our knees drop to the ground before Jesus Christ, we realize that we got it wrong. The lowest place is not a thing to fear at all. Rather, it is the gateway to greatness. From that place, we change our world by inviting others into the grace we find. All the barriers except pride have been removed.

KNOWING CHRIST

The very credentials these people are waving around as something special, I'm tearing up and throwing out with the trash—along with everything else I used to take credit for. And why? Because of Christ. Yes, all the things I once thought were so important are gone from my life. Compared to the high privilege of knowing Christ Jesus as my Master, firsthand, everything I once thought I had going for me is insignificant—dog dung. I've dumped it all in the trash so that I could embrace Christ and be embraced by him. I didn't want some petty, inferior brand of righteousness that comes from keeping a list of rules when I could get the robust kind that comes from trusting Christ—*God's* righteousness.

I gave up all that inferior stuff so I could know Christ personally.

Philippians 3:7–10 MSG

The popular reality television show *Extreme Makeover Home Edition* always includes an interesting feature about twenty minutes into the episode—demolition. Without getting the old house out of the way, the team simply cannot make room for the new house, the dream home.

The same is true in our lives. If we want the best, we need to let go of the clutter that keeps us from the best. Often the biggest enemy to our growth in Christ is our own self-righteousness. Sure, we prayed, went to church, gave our money, did good deeds, helped the poor, learned the Bible, shared the gospel, and . . . But does it matter?

What matters is that we know Christ. For Martha scurrying around in the kitchen, that meant to be still and listen (see Luke 10:38–42). In the same way, when we stop focusing on our list of good deeds and instead focus on Jesus, the unimportant things fade away and the thing that really matters remains. When knowing Christ becomes more important than knowing anything else, our priorities are clear.

The Presence of Peace

Let everyone see that you are considerate in all you do. Remember, the Lord is coming soon.

Don't worry about anything; instead, pray about everything. Tell God what you need, and thank him for all he has done. Then you will experience God's peace, which exceeds anything we can understand. His peace will guard your hearts and minds as you live in Christ Jesus.

And now, dear brothers and sisters, one final thing. Fix your thoughts on what is true, and honorable, and right, and pure, and lovely, and admirable. Think about things that are excellent and worthy of praise. Keep putting into practice all you learned and received from me—everything you heard from me and saw me doing. Then the God of peace will be with you.

Philippians 4:5–9 NLT

God's presence in our lives always bears fruit. He returns us to peace—a peace that the world cannot understand. Our troubles don't always go away, but our anxiety does. From this position of strength inside the storm, we can reach out to show courtesy and kindness to those around us, even to grumpy people.

We access this peace when we share our requests with God. He wants to know what we want. Ask him for it. This is different from whining or complaining. This is exercising our rights and privileges as royal sons and daughters of God. Along the way, we give thanks because we're on the winning team. No matter how God answers our requests, we win. God is for us.

We can keep this focus by remembering to dwell on the things that are true, honorable, right, pure, lovely, and admirable. All those things come from God, and they serve to remind us how God feels about us and what he has in store for us.

THE NAME OF JESUS

Put on then, as God's chosen ones, holy and beloved, compassion, kindness, humility, meekness, and patience, bearing with one another and, if one has a complaint against another, forgiving each other; as the Lord has forgiven you, so you also must forgive. And above all these put on love, which binds everything together in perfect harmony. And let the peace of Christ rule in your hearts, to which indeed you were called in one body. And be thankful. Let the word of Christ dwell in you richly, teaching and admonishing one another in all wisdom, singing psalms and hymns and spiritual songs, with thankfulness in your hearts to God.

And whatever you do, in word or deed, do everything in the name of the Lord Jesus, giving thanks to God the Father through him.

Colossians 3:12–17 ESV

Suppose we could substitute Jesus for each of the seven billion people alive on planet Earth. Imagine what the world would look like—no more crime, oppression, corruption, or abuse. Day or night, a five-year-old child alone would be perfectly safe in the most dangerous neighborhood in the world. Prisons would be empty because there would be no need for them. Homes would be filled with laughter and peace. There would no longer be hunger.

Just as the gospel rebuilds lives, so also it rebuilds families, communities, and entire nations. In this passage, Paul explained what it meant to do everything in the "name of the Lord Jesus." This was more than an incantation to tack onto the end of prayers. This was an invitation to bring Jesus into everything so that families, churches, and communities would be transformed.

The more we are filled with the Spirit, the more we are an expression of Jesus in our world. As this happens, the world takes notice, and lives are changed.

THE SECRET OF CONTENTMENT

Godliness with contentment is great gain. For we brought nothing into this world, and it is certain we can carry nothing out. And having food and clothing, with these we shall be content. But those who desire to be rich fall into temptation and a snare, and into many foolish and harmful lusts which drown men in destruction and perdition. For the love of money is a root of all kinds of evil, for which some have strayed from the faith in their greediness, and pierced themselves through with many sorrows.

But you, O man of God, flee these things and pursue righteousness, godliness, faith, love, patience, gentleness. Fight the good fight of faith, lay hold on eternal life, to which you were also called and have confessed the good confession in the presence of many witnesses.

1 Timothy 6:6–12 NKJV

We all need a certain amount of money. If one billion Christians had zero money, we would be a liability on this earth and not an asset. Paul was not setting up a hate relationship with money. Rather, he was helping God's people understand that there are certain things money cannot do. If we need money to feel good about ourselves, we are giving money a place in our lives that it shouldn't have. If we value God's gifts more than we value him, we've missed the point.

Greed and contentment are the barometers, not wealth and poverty. What is the secret to contentment? Richard Wurmbrand, who wrote *Tortured for Christ*, spoke of leaping for joy in prison. He got to that point because he found Jesus in the place where he didn't want to go.

We find contentment most often when the things we want are taken away from us. The deeper we get into situations we don't like, the more we discover that Jesus is already there. Life is defined not by our circumstances but by our Savior.

PAYING YOUR DUES

Be strong in the grace we have in Christ Jesus. You should teach people whom you can trust the things you and many others have heard me say. Then they will be able to teach others. Share in the troubles we have like a good soldier of Christ Jesus. A soldier wants to please the enlisting officer, so no one serving in the army wastes time with everyday matters. Also an athlete who takes part in a contest must obey all the rules in order to win. The farmer who works hard should be the first person to get some of the food that was grown. . . .

So I patiently accept all these troubles so that those whom God has chosen can have the salvation that is in Christ Jesus. With that salvation comes glory that never ends.

2 Timothy 2:1–6, 10 NCV

Do you want to make a difference? There is a price to pay and a process to go through. This is universal in life. Everyone pays dues. A successful entrepreneur, for example, often needs to work days, weeks, months, or longer without any pay whatsoever, sustained by the belief that what he is doing will pay off in the end. The apostle Paul suffered much in order to make a difference in many lives. He was jailed, chained, beaten, harassed, humiliated, betrayed, stoned, and shipwrecked.

But Paul found strength in Jesus Christ. Paul knew who he was in Christ, and he knew where he was going. He put up with sleepless nights and harrowing days because he understood the value of what he was doing.

Paul had a message that was worth suffering for. It was a message that he could communicate and others could pass on. In the same way, God will define for you how he wants his message expressed through your life, and you will be able to impart it to others for them to pass on to succeeding generations.

LESSONS FROM THE AIRPLANE

Proclaim the message; persist in it whether convenient or not; rebuke, correct, and encourage with great patience and teaching. For the time will come when they will not tolerate sound doctrine, but according to their own desires, will accumulate teachers for themselves because they have an itch to hear something new. They will turn away from hearing the truth and will turn aside to myths. But as for you, keep a clear head about everything, endure hardship, do the work of an evangelist, fulfill your ministry. . . .

I have fought the good fight, I have finished the race, I have kept the faith. In the future, there is reserved for me the crown of righteousness, which the Lord, the righteous Judge, will give me on that day, and not only to me, but to all those who have loved His appearing.

2 Timothy 4:2–5, 7–8 HCSB

In order to learn how to fly, you need to find your way to the runway. In order to land correctly, you must start making decisions miles away from where you touch down, when the airport looks like a tiny postage stamp far away. In this passage, Paul was nearly there. His landing gear was locked, and he would soon touch down on the runway of eternity. But before he landed, he sent this last message to Timothy, the young man he had been mentoring.

Just as an airplane relies on instruments so that it can fly through clouds, fog, and darkness without veering off course, so also we Christians need truth as revealed by God to keep us from veering off course and missing our final destination. Pilots who ignore their instruments can become distracted and disoriented, fly into storms, and crash far from the safety of the airport.

Some people may try to convince you that the gospel has gone out of style. Paul reaches forward through the centuries to assure you that truth never goes out of style. God remains the same. The truth will get us home.

THE POWER WE HAVE BEEN GIVEN

Although in Christ I could be bold and order you to do what you ought to do, yet I appeal to you on the basis of love. I then, as Paul . . . appeal to you for my son Onesimus, who became my son while I was in chains. Formerly he was useless to you, but now he has become useful both to you and to me.

I am sending him—who is my very heart—back to you. . . .

But I did not want to do anything without your consent, so that any favor you do will be spontaneous and not forced. Perhaps the reason he was separated from you for a little while was that you might have him back for good—no longer as a slave, but better than a slave, as a dear brother.

Philemon 8–12, 14–16 NIV

The short book of Philemon is a personal letter from Paul to Philemon on behalf of a runaway slave, Onesimus. In the times in which Paul lived, slavery was common. People of all races were slaves. Some Christians owned slaves. Philemon was one of those Christians. The penalty for a slave running away was death or any other punishment the slave master wanted to impose. But after running away, Onesimus met Paul and came to faith in Christ.

Paul interceded for Onesimus, asking Philemon not only to withhold punishment but also to receive his former slave as a brother in Christ and, possibly, to free him and return him to Paul so that he could assist Paul in the ministry. Confident that Philemon was a good man, Paul was sure that he would do all that Paul asked and more.

While many have pointed to Onesimus as a metaphor for Christians freed from the slavery of sin, there is another important message in the book—what will we do with the power we have? Will we use it to empower others and to set them free?

What God Sees

Let us be diligent to enter that rest, so that no one will fall. . . .

For the word of God is living and active and sharper than any two-edged sword, and piercing as far as the division of soul and spirit, of both joints and marrow, and able to judge the thoughts and intentions of the heart. . . .

Therefore, since we have a great high priest who has passed through the heavens, Jesus the Son of God, let us hold fast our confession.

For we do not have a high priest who cannot sympathize with our weaknesses, but One who has been tempted in all things as we are, yet without sin.

Therefore let us draw near with confidence to the throne of grace, so that we may receive mercy and find grace to help in time of need.

Hebrews 4:11–16 NASB

Why do we hide? Ever since humanity's fall in the Garden, we have been hiding from God, afraid to come out into the open where God can see who we are and what we've done.

This passage frees us from those fears. God does see. He sees every hidden nuance of corruption and shame that we carefully conceal from those around us and, sometimes, even from ourselves. He knows it all. In addition, God does feel. Jesus knows what it's like to be tempted because he experienced temptation without succumbing to sin. He can and does empathize with us in our inner struggles. God does not take this knowledge and use it against us, however. Rather, he invites us into the light where he can shower a greater reality on us, the reality that Jesus can wash us clean.

God invites those who have not experienced forgiveness to receive it. He invites those who do not feel forgiven to experience the truth about forgiveness.

The Door to Heaven Opened

When Christ appeared as a high priest of the good things that have come, then through the greater and more perfect tent (not made with hands, that is, not of this creation) he entered once for all into the holy places, not by means of the blood of goats and calves but by means of his own blood, thus securing an eternal redemption. For if the blood of goats and bulls, and the sprinkling of defiled persons with the ashes of a heifer, sanctify for the purification of the flesh, how much more will the blood of Christ, who through the eternal Spirit offered himself without blemish to God, purify our conscience from dead works to serve the living God.

Therefore he is the mediator of a new covenant, so that those who are called may receive the promised eternal inheritance.

Hebrews 9:11–15 ESV

The original readers of this letter were intimately familiar with the ancient Jewish sacrificial system. Each year, on the Day of Atonement (Yom Kippur), the high priest went into the Most Holy Place to sprinkle the blood of an innocent animal over the sacred chest, or ark, of God's promise (covenant), which contained the stone tablets inscribed with the Ten Commandments. It was clearly understood that the blood symbolized the need for payment for the many ways people violated the Ten Commandments.

In this passage, God assured his people that the sacrificial system had come to completion. The blood of Jesus was recognized in heaven as the final, total, and complete payment for the sins of humanity. The door to heaven opened. Jesus fundamentally changed God's transaction with the human race.

We are no longer trapped in the endless cycle of sin, atonement, sin, atonement. Now we are free. With this freedom, the same Spirit that inspired the Ten Commandments now inspires us to love God and carry out his purposes here on earth.

THE SECRET OF FAITH

Faith is the assurance of things hoped for, the conviction of things not seen. For by it the people of old received their commendation. By faith we understand that the universe was created by the word of God, so that what is seen was not made out of things that are visible.

By faith Abel offered to God a more acceptable sacrifice than Cain, through which he was commended as righteous. . . . By faith Enoch was taken up so that he should not see death, and he was not found, because God had taken him.

Now before he was taken he was commended as having pleased God. And without faith it is impossible to please him, for whoever would draw near to God must believe that he exists and that he rewards those who seek him.

Hebrews 11:1–6 ESV

Do you want to please God? This passage tells us how. The key is faith. Faith isn't some kind of mystical, hard-to-understand charm. Faith, in this context, is simply your practical answer to who God is.

For example, there are few theological atheists but many practical atheists, who live as if God is absent.

God is responsive. He is present. He gives good gifts. He rewards those who seek him. He wants a relationship with us. We can sign a piece of paper that says he does these things, or we can live as if he really does. Faith is living in this actuality. It is walking with God just as Enoch did. Faith requires that every action consider God and his character. Faith is the pursuit of God. Faith is learning, loving, enjoying, and expecting God to be who he is.

STRENGTH TO ENDURE

Since we are surrounded by so great a cloud of witnesses, let us also lay aside every weight, and sin which clings so closely, and let us run with endurance the race that is set before us, looking to Jesus, the founder and perfecter of our faith, who for the joy that was set before him endured the cross, despising the shame, and is seated at the right hand of the throne of God.

Consider him who endured from sinners such hostility against himself, so that you may not grow weary or faint-hearted. . . .

It is for discipline that you have to endure. God is treating you as sons. For what son is there whom his father does not discipline? If you are left without discipline, in which all have participated, then you are illegitimate children and not sons.

Hebrews 12:1–3, 7–8 ESV

We get the strength to endure from our heavenly family. Jesus looked straight into eternity and found a joy that could not be measured. He set his course unswervingly for that joy, even though it took him through all the brutality that humanity could throw at him. From the other side, he calls us forward. Our brothers and sisters who have gone ahead also beckon to us with their lives, showing us that the price they paid was well worth it.

God the Father assures us that we also are his sons and daughters and will be found on the other side.

It doesn't feel good to be going through the troubles of today, and it sometimes feels as if we are victims of senseless misery. But none of this has escaped the Father's notice. He will make sure that every trial serves a purpose. Not a single tear that falls will be wasted.

EVIDENCE

What does it profit, my brethren, if someone says he has faith but does not have works? Can faith save him? If a brother or sister is naked and destitute of daily food, and one of you says to them, "Depart in peace, be warmed and filled," but you do not give them the things which are needed for the body, what does it profit? Thus also faith by itself, if it does not have works, is dead.

But someone will say, "You have faith, and I have works."

Show me your faith without your works, and I will show you my faith by my works. You believe that there is one God. You do well. Even the demons believe—and tremble! But do you want to know, O foolish man, that faith without works is dead?

James 2:14–20 NKJV

Christianity is unique. We don't work to earn points with God. We don't earn our way into his favor. He did the work for us. By faith, we receive as a gift all that Christ did for us. But where does that leave us? Are we just salvation ticket holders on the train to heaven? Has God's work for us reduced Christianity to a spectator sport where God is on the field and we are in the stands?

James argued no. The same faith that saves also inspires a difference. Faith brought us into God's family with a family identity and a family mission. We are active. Trying to separate faith from works is like taking the batteries out of the flashlight. Just as the light is evidence that the batteries are good, so also are our works evidence that our faith is good.

Works don't save us. Instead, works are an outflow of gratitude, the evidence of a life set free.

GOOD WORDS

If anyone does not stumble in what he says, he is a mature man who is also able to control his whole body.

Now when we put bits into the mouths of horses to make them obey us, we also guide the whole animal. And consider ships: though very large and driven by fierce winds, they are guided by a very small rudder wherever the will of the pilot directs. So too, though the tongue is a small part [of the body], it boasts great things. Consider how large a forest a small fire ignites. And the tongue is a fire. The tongue, a world of unrighteousness, is placed among the parts of our [bodies]; it pollutes the whole body, sets the course of life on fire, and is set on fire by hell.

James 3:2–6 HCSB

At some point or another, all of us have been hurt by the words of others. And all of us have hurt others with our words. Usually we don't mean it, but sometimes we do. In any case, our words have tremendous power for good and evil. They can heal, and they can hurt. Our words can tear apart long-standing friendships and start conflicts that lead to full-scale wars.

Jesus said, "Out of the overflow of the heart the mouth speaks" (Matt. 12:34 NIV). What brims over in our hearts? Are we replaying mental messages of hurt that haunt us from the past? Are we searching for solutions that don't satisfy?

The comforting, calming presence of Christ tames our words. As he comes in and heals our hurts, we no longer feel the need to lash out when we feel hurt by someone else. As he shows us our place in his family, we begin using our words to build others up rather than tear them down. The more Jesus fills us, the more our hearts overflow with good words.

No Halfway

You adulterous people, don't you know that friendship with the world is hatred toward God? Anyone who chooses to be a friend of the world becomes an enemy of God. Or do you think Scripture says without reason that the spirit he caused to live in us envies intensely? But he gives us more grace. That is why Scripture says: "God opposes the proud but gives grace to the humble."

Submit yourselves, then, to God. Resist the devil, and he will flee from you. Come near to God and he will come near to you. Wash your hands, you sinners, and purify your hearts, you double-minded. Grieve, mourn and wail. Change your laughter to mourning and your joy to gloom. Humble yourselves before the Lord, and he will lift you up.

James 4:4–10 NIV

There comes a time when each of us needs to make a decision. Are we in or are we out? There's no halfway.

At the marriage altar, we make vows. Part of the promise is to "forsake all others." A husband and a wife count on each other to be faithful. They need each other to be fully in the marriage and not playing the field.

In the same way, God wants us in, not halfway, but all the way. If we're playing around with the things that take us away from God, it's better to cry tears of repentance now than to cry tears of regret later. God takes this seriously, just as a married person takes his or her spouse's faithfulness seriously.

If we are ready to say no to evil, God is there, ready to push the enemy away. We get the power to triumph over evil when we make room for God in our lives.

JUST LIKE HIM

Yes, my dear children, live in him so that when Christ comes back, we can be without fear and not be ashamed in his presence. Since you know that Christ is righteous, you know that all who do right are God's children.

The Father has loved us so much that we are called children of God. And we really are his children. The reason the people in the world do not know us is that they have not known him. Dear friends, now we are children of God, and we have not yet been shown what we will be in the future. But we know that when Christ comes again, we will be like him, because we will see him as he really is. Christ is pure, and all who have this hope in Christ keep themselves pure like Christ.

1 John 2:28–3:3 NCV

Studies have demonstrated that when teachers believe students are highly intelligent, the students' performance soars. The teachers communicate an expectation, or identity, to those children, and the children live up to that identity. That's why wealthy entrepreneurs can lose millions or even billions of dollars and yet in a few years be wealthy again. They live their learned identity.

Our identity is that we are part of the eternal family of God. We are pure. We have hope. We may not be understood by the world, but we are loved by God. The more we absorb that identity, the more we live it. We can verify our identity by examining our lives. The evidence of God's parenting will be written in our actions.

All this is a work in progress, but the day is coming when the work will be complete. Jesus himself will set foot on the earth, and we, the members of his family, will be revealed to be like him.

LOVE—A WAY OF LIFE

Dear friends, let us love one another, because love is from God, and everyone who loves has been born of God and knows God. The one who does not love does not know God, because God is love. God's love was revealed among us in this way: God sent His One and Only Son into the world so that we might live through Him. . . .

There is no fear in love; instead, perfect love drives out fear, because fear involves punishment. So the one who fears has not reached perfection in love. We love because He first loved us.

If anyone says, "I love God," yet hates his brother, he is a liar. For the person who does not love his brother whom he has seen cannot love God whom he has not seen.

1 John 4:7–9, 18–20 HCSB

There's an old story about heaven and hell. In hell, everyone sat around starving and dejected because strapped to each person's hand was a fork with a handle too long to allow the person to get the food back into his mouth. In heaven, everyone was happy and laughing. Yet, each person had the same long-handled fork strapped to his hands. What was the difference? In heaven, each person was using the fork to feed the person across from him.

Though this is not an accurate depiction of heaven and hell, it does illustrate a point. Love transforms families, churches, and nations.

We love because God first loved us. His love changes us. His love lifts our eyes from our petty concerns and enables us to see others. We discover that we care about someone else and want the best for that person. We will give that person our time, our money, and, if needed, our very lives. Soon, the love we have for one other person is multiplied to others until love becomes a way of life.

FULLY ALIVE AND IN CHARGE

I, John, with you all the way in the trial and the Kingdom and the passion of patience in Jesus, was on the island called Patmos because of God's Word, the witness of Jesus. It was Sunday and I was in the Spirit, praying. I heard a loud voice behind me, trumpet-clear and piercing: "Write what you see into a book. Send it to the seven churches: to Ephesus, Smyrna, Pergamum, Thyatira, Sardis, Philadelphia, Laodicea. . . .

"Don't fear: I am First, I am Last, I'm Alive. I died, but I came to life, and my life is now forever. See these keys in my hand? They open and lock Death's doors, they open and lock Hell's gates. Now write down everything you see: things that are, things about to be."

Revelation 1:9–11, 17–19 MSG

With those words, the apostle John, then an old man living in exile because of his faith, introduced one of the most remarkable books in the Bible, the book of Revelation. The centerpiece is Jesus, fully alive. He never grew old or tired. Though his servant and friend John was in exile, Jesus remained fully in command of everything, including death and hell itself.

God's people were on Jesus' mind as he showed up to speak to John. He was concerned about the people in the churches of that day and this. He had a message for us, and he wanted to make sure it was written down to preserve it for all of us to read today.

His message was simply this: Even though our lives may be turned upside down and things may go awry, God hasn't forgotten us. He has things under control. No one gets away with evil forever. We his children will be rewarded. God himself will take charge of our wayward planet, and he will bring his powerful presence to rest right here on earth. Things will be set straight.

EVERYTHING NEW

I saw a new heaven and a new earth; for the first heaven and the first earth passed away, and there is no longer any sea.

And I saw the holy city, new Jerusalem, coming down out of heaven from God, made ready as a bride adorned for her husband.

And I heard a loud voice from the throne, saying, "Behold, the tabernacle of God is among men, and He will dwell among them, and they shall be His people, and God Himself will be among them, and He will wipe away every tear from their eyes; and there will no longer be any death; there will no longer be any mourning, or crying, or pain; the first things have passed away."

And He who sits on the throne said, "Behold, I am making all things new."

Revelation 21:1–5 NASB

Do you dream? Are there things you would like to do or have or experience? Most of us dream of what we'd like to do. We may want to travel the world, get married, adopt a child, or learn to fly.

In this passage, we see God's dream. This is what he longs for. This is what he is planning. This is what he is working toward. And then the time will come. God will remove everything stained with corruption, oppression, and evil. With his hands, he will make the entire universe new for his children.

He will do this so we can be together as a family, enjoying him and enjoying one another forever. The time for pain will be gone. The time for joy will have come.

In the leisurely pace of eternity, God will begin unpacking the gifts he has stored up for his children. We will hear words of affirmation from him. Our inner beauty will be revealed as we have fun doing things that we never had time to do in this life. Most of all, God will be sharing eternal life with us.

YOUR INVITATION

The Spirit and the bride say, "Come." Let anyone who hears this say, "Come." Let anyone who is thirsty come. Let anyone who desires drink freely from the water of life. And I solemnly declare to everyone who hears the words of prophecy written in this book: If anyone adds anything to what is written here, God will add to that person the plagues described in this book. And if anyone removes any of the words from this book of prophecy, God will remove that person's share in the tree of life and in the holy city that are described in this book.

He who is the faithful witness to all these things says, "Yes, I am coming soon!"

Amen! Come, Lord Jesus!

May the grace of the Lord Jesus be with God's holy people.

Revelation 22:17–21 NLT

The invitation will be open, and God will hold the door to heaven open for us. We will experience and enjoy every good thing he has for us. Most of all, we will be with him. We will have a place in his heart that no one can replace, and we will experience eternal life with him.

But God won't force us. The choice is ours. We can say yes or no.

The entire Bible is important in guiding each of us as we make this momentous choice. God will not tolerate anyone who tampers with his Word, who obscures his invitation, or who makes it difficult for those he loves to say yes.

God welcomes all of us who say yes, no matter where we are in our spiritual journey. And the grace of Jesus will be with us.

If you have knowledge,
let others light their candles by it.

—Thomas Fuller

I want you woven into a tapestry of love, in touch with everything there is to know of God.

—Colossians 2:2 MSG

The best evidence of the Bible's being the word of God is to be found between its covers. It proves itself.

—Charles Hodge

Heaven and earth will pass away,
but My words will by no means pass away.

—Matthew 24:35 NKJV

I praise the LORD because he
advises me. Even at night, I
feel his leading. I keep the LORD
before me always. Because
he is close by my side,
I will not be hurt.

—Psalm 16:7–8 NCV